Ageing with Smartphones in Uganda

Ageing with Smartphones in Uganda

Togetherness in the dotcom age

Charlotte Hawkins

First published in 2023 by
UCL Press
University College London
Gower Street
London WC1E 6BT

Available to download free: www.uclpress.co.uk

Text © Author, 2023
Images © Author and copyright holders named in captions, 2023

The author has asserted her rights under the Copyright, Designs and Patents Act 1988 to be identified as the author of this work.

A CIP catalogue record for this book is available from The British Library.

Any third-party material in this book is published under the book's Creative Commons licence unless indicated otherwise in the credit line to the material. If you would like to reuse any third-party material not covered by the book's Creative Commons licence, you will need to obtain permission directly from the copyright holder.

This book is published under a Creative Commons Attribution Non-commercial Non-derivative 4.0 International licence (CC BY-NC-ND 4.0). This licence allows you to share, copy, distribute and transmit the work for personal and non-commercial use providing author and publisher attribution is clearly stated. Attribution should include the following information:

Hawkins, C. 2023. *Ageing with Smartphones in Uganda: Togetherness in the dotcom age.* London: UCL Press. https://doi.org/10.14324/111.9781800085138

Further details about Creative Commons licences are available at http://creative commons.org/licenses/

ISBN: 978-1-80008-515-2 (Hbk)
ISBN: 978-1-80008-514-5 (Pbk)
ISBN: 978-1-80008-513-8 (PDF)
ISBN: 978-1-80008-516-9 (epub)
DOI: https://doi.org/10.14324/111.9781800085138

This monograph is dedicated to all the grandmothers who made it possible, especially those we sadly lost last year. Hopefully one day we can all be as wise, witty and generous as you!

Contents

List of figures	ix
Series foreword	xi
Abbreviations	xiii
Preface	xv
Acknowledgements	xvii
1 Our book	1
2 Elders in the city	33
3 Age and work	55
4 Togetherness is strength	81
5 The dotcom wave	109
6 Health and care: who is responsible?	135
7 Co-operative morality	163
8 Conclusion: permanent questions	179
Bibliography	195
Index	211

List of figures

1.1a and 1.1b	Photos taken in Lusozi by Charlotte Hawkins.	8
1.2	Signs in a primary school in Lusozi reading 'Always be God Fearing', 'The fear of the Lord is the beginning of Wisdom'. Photo by Charlotte Hawkins.	10
1.3	Map of Uganda, 'Sub-regions of Uganda as of 12 May 2020'. Uganda Bureau of Statistics (UBOS).	13
1.4	A research participant's family elders showing land boundaries to the younger men. Kitgum District, Uganda. Photo by Charlotte Hawkins.	15
1.5	Housing in Lusozi. Photo by Charlotte Hawkins.	17
1.6	Lusozi mosque with demolished housing in the foreground. Photo by Charlotte Hawkins.	18
2.1	A still from the film 'We as elders have a duty'. https://bit.ly/44P9rHt.	45
2.2	Ladit's dance group practising outside his former home in Lusozi. Photo by Charlotte Hawkins.	47
3.1.	A still from the film about 'Mobile money'. https://bit.ly/46ZquIS.	64
3.2	A still from the film 'Everyday life'. https://bit.ly/3OmXqni.	68
3.3	A still from the film *Boda boda*. https://bit.ly/3XXKAPw.	69
4.1	TIS members at a Sunday meeting in the bar. Photo by Charlotte Hawkins.	86
4.2	TIS members using a sports app. Photo by Charlotte Hawkins.	90

4.3	Group members enjoying the Sunday party. The week's beneficiary and two honorary members are in the foreground of the photo, where they face the other women dancing throughout the evening. Photo by Charlotte Hawkins.	93
4.4	A member taking photographs of the *mugoole* and her honorary members. Photo by Charlotte Hawkins.	95
4.5	A still from the film 'Who should enrich you?' https://bit.ly/3NWU1dn.	97
4.6	Women in an exercise class at Place of Peace. Photo by Charlotte Hawkins.	99
4.7	An English lesson at Place of Peace. Photo by Charlotte Hawkins.	101
5.1	Making a phone call. Photo by Charlotte Hawkins.	111
5.2	Nakito with her son and grandson in their salon. Photo by Charlotte Hawkins.	114
5.3	A research participant helping his daughter with her homework, using the torch on his mobile phone. Photo by Charlotte Hawkins.	116
6.1	Health workers preparing to administer vaccinations in Lusozi Hospital. Photo by Charlotte Hawkins.	140

Series foreword

This book series is based on a project called ASSA – the Anthropology of Smartphones and Smart Ageing. It was primarily funded by the European Research Council (ERC) and located at the Department of Anthropology, UCL. The project had three main goals. The first was to study ageing. Our premise was that most studies of ageing focus on those defined by age, that is youth and the elderly. This project would focus upon people who did not regard themselves as either young or elderly. We anticipated that their sense of ageing would also be impacted by the recent spread of smartphone use. Smartphones were thereby transformed from a youth technology to a device used by anyone. This also meant that, for the first time, we could make a general assessment of the use and consequences of smartphones as a global technology, beyond those connotations of youth. The third goal was more practical. We wanted to consider how the smartphone has impacted upon the health of people in this age group and whether we could contribute to this field. More specifically, this would be the arena of mHealth, that is, smartphone apps designed for health purposes.

The project consists of 11 researchers working in 10 fieldsites across nine countries, as follows: Al-Quds (East Jerusalem) studied by Laila Abed Rabho and Maya de Vries; Bento, in São Paulo, Brazil studied by Marília Duque; Cuan in Ireland studied by Daniel Miller; Lusozi in Kampala, Uganda studied by Charlotte Hawkins; Kochi and Kyoto in Japan studied by Laura Haapio-Kirk; NoLo in Milan, Italy studied by Shireen Walton; Santiago in Chile studied by Alfonso Otaegui; Shanghai in China studied by Xinyuan Wang; Thornhill in Ireland studied by Pauline Garvey; and Yaoundé in Cameroon studied by Patrick Awondo. Several of the fieldsite names are pseudonyms.

Most of the researchers are funded by the European Research Council. The exceptions are Alfonso Otaegui, who is funded by the Pontificia Universidad Católica de Chile, and Marília Duque, Laila Abed Rabho and Maya de Vries, who are mainly self-funded. Pauline Garvey is based at Maynooth University. The research was simultaneous except for the research in Al-Quds, which has been extended since the researchers are also working as they research.

The project has published a comparative book about the use and consequences of smartphones called *The Global Smartphone*. In addition, we intend to publish an edited collection presenting our work in the area of mHealth. There will also be nine monographs representing our ethnographic research, the two fieldsites in Ireland being combined in a single volume. These ethnographic monographs will mostly have the same chapter headings. This will enable readers to consider our work comparatively. The project has been highly collaborative and comparative from the beginning. We have been blogging since its inception at https://blogs.ucl.ac.uk/assa/. Further information about the project may be found on our project's main website, at https://www.ucl.ac.uk/anthropology/assa/. The core of this website is translated into the languages of our fieldsites and we hope that the comparative book and the monographs will also appear in translation. As far as possible, all our work is available without cost, under a creative commons licence.

Abbreviations

ART	Antiretroviral Medication
BBC	British Broadcasting Corporation
CBHI	Community Based Health Insurance
DRC	Democratic Republic of Congo
GDP	Gross Domestic Product
GEM	Global Entrepreneurship Monitor
GSMA	Global System for Mobile Communications
HIV/AIDS	Human Immunodeficiency Virus / Acquired Immunodeficiency Syndrome
HSM	Holy Spirit Movement
IDP	Internally Displaced People
ICTs	Information Communication Technologies
ID	Identification
KCCA	Kampala City Council Authority
LC	Local Councillor
LRA	Lord's Resistance Army
MC	Master of Ceremonies
MPPS	Micro Public Private Services
MTN	Mobile Telephone Network (South African cellular service provider)
NCDs	Non-Communicable Diseases
NGO	Non-Governmental Organisation
NITA-U	The National Information Technology Authority Uganda
NLFS	National Labour Force Survey
NMS	Ugandan National Medical Stores
NSSF	National Social Security Fund
NTVUganda	National Television Uganda
NRM	National Resistance Movement (the governing political party in Uganda since 1986)
OTT	Over the Top Tax
P1–P7	Primary school levels 1–7
SACCOS	Savings and Cooperative Credit Organisations
SAGE	Social Assistance Grants for Empowerment
SAP	Structural Adjustment Policies
TAFU	The Aged Family Uganda
UBOS	Uganda Bureau of Statistics
UCC	Uganda Communications Commission
UGX	Ugandan shilling
UN	United Nations
UPDF	Uganda People's Defence Force

UPE	Universal Primary Education
USE	Universal Secondary Education
UNHS	Uganda National Household Survey
URAA	Uganda Reach the Aged Association
VHT	Village Health Team
VPN	Virtual Private Network
WHO	World Health Organization

Preface

In taking the lens of the smartphone to understand experiences of ageing in a diverse neighbourhood in Kampala, Uganda, this monograph presents the articulation and practice of 'togetherness in the dotcom age'. Taking a 'convivial' approach, which celebrates multiple ways of knowing about social life, the monograph draws from these expressions about co-operative morality and modernity to consider the everyday mitigation of profound social change. 'Dotcom' is understood to encompass everything from the influence of ICTs to urban migration and lifestyles in the city to shifts in ways of knowing and relating. At the same time dotcom tools, such as mobile phones and smartphones, facilitate elder care despite distances, for example through regular mobile money remittances.

This monograph is concerned with how dotcom manifests in relation to older people's health, care norms, social standing, values of respect and relatedness and their intergenerational relationships – both political and personal. It re-frames the youth-centricity of research on the city and work, new media and technology, politics and service provision in Uganda. Through ethnographic consideration of everyday life and self-formation in this context, the monograph seeks to contribute to an ever-incomplete understanding of how we relate to each other and to the world around us.

Acknowledgements

Thanks to all of the people in Kampala and Kitgum who took care of me, offered me their time and helped me to learn. Kilongeni, Adul, Amor, Smiley, Chol, Jaja and the babies for taking me in – I will never forget it. Hope for your welcome. Ladit for your wisdom. *Laphonya* for your patient teaching and community spirit. *Apwuyo matek*. Madame M for your stories. Henry and family for showing me around and welcoming me at home. Mr and Mrs O for your friendship. All of the members of participating savings and women's groups, especially 'Togetherness is Strength', 'Place of Peace' and 'Who should enrich you?' for allowing me to join your meetings and take part. Isaac, Emmanuel, Zizuke and Josh for your film-making skills. The hospital staff, especially the physiotherapy team, for hosting me. The TMCG team for the collaboration. Danny for your encouragement, friendship and inspiring optimism. Sara for your insight. The whole ASSA team for four years of wonderful, mind-opening conversation. All of the PhD students at UCL anthropology for reminding me how to 'imagine alternatives'. My family and friends for always being there, despite distances.

This book is affiliated with the 'Ageing in a Time of Mobility' Research Group at the Max Planck Institute for the Study of Religious and Ethnic Diversity where author Charlotte Hawkins is a writing fellow.

1
Our book

Introduction

'Our book': this is how Amor, my friend and colleague, refers to this monograph. It is something created collaboratively, alongside many other people in the neighbourhood she grew up in and our project team working around the world. This research is part of a global comparative study of ageing, health and smartphones called the 'Anthropology of Smartphones and Smart Ageing' (ASSA). As we introduced the project to our many research participants in their forties, fifties, sixties and above, we would explain that its primary purpose is to educate others about their experiences of ageing, initially through an open-access monograph, as well as comparative books and articles, workshops, blog posts, partnerships with health workers and short films. When we introduced the project to Achola, a 60-year-old grandmother, she said she had no questions because she felt *'the book could help my grandchildren'*, as she would not always be there to teach them. We asked what she most hoped they would learn, to which she replied she wants them to *'read it and know how to help each other'*. Like many other people encountered during this research, Achola sees this as the main role of older people – to teach the younger generation how to work together. *'Even if you're not from the same place you stay together.'*

This book outlines experiences present up to the time of the research and explores the ways they have been expressed by the people we worked with. Often this is framed by a shared ideal of ageing that is contemporary, collaborative and in motion, adapted to the city and its diversity. In response to reading drafts of this book, some participants have written further contributions and even described a few Acholi songs and dances. As one older man observed, song is:

> Our book, our way of recording an event … Instead of going to write down, you just sing about it, it remains in your head.

How much is lost in translation, or in the fixture of a song or story on a page? To Acholi poet and social anthropologist Okot p'Bitek culture exists only as it is lived and celebrated in the here and now, so distinguishing the meanings attributed to social life and the world renders them meaningless.[1] This is a process that has done much harm in Uganda and Africa more broadly, externally 'defined and confined' in the 'single stories' of harmful Western narratives and scholarship.[2] This has obscured the reality of complex social processes, such as shared histories within diverse multi-ethnic urban communities like the one in which this research took place.

As stated by anthropologist Professor Francis Nyamnjoh, whose writing frames the analysis underpinning this book, 'social truth is negotiable and requires humility'.[3] In this vein, and in line with the 'convivial scholarship' Nyamnjoh proposes, it is important to begin by emphasising that this monograph is an account co-produced through dialogue, which does not aspire to represent a singular social reality or objective position.[4] It draws from patterns in stories, idioms, shared concerns and aspirations, everyday work and routines, home and family lives to build a contemporary picture of ageing in relation to the Kampala context, introduced later in this chapter. I hope it can contribute to an imaginative awareness of lived experiences as they fit into a wider shared context in the 'dotcom era', and of the potential for a 'convivial' anthropology committed to openness, flexibility and friendship.

Elders of the dotcom generation

This study re-frames the youth-centricity of research on the city and work, new media and technology, politics and service provision in Uganda. It is based on a 16-month ethnography in a neighbourhood in Kampala, the capital city, here named 'Lusozi', meaning 'hill' in Luganda. The neighbourhood is diverse; the people who live there originate from all over the country and regions beyond. Many people said they do not consider it to be a 'real home', and instead aspire to move back to their rural homes of origin as they grow older, once they no longer need to work in the city to pay for their children's school fees. In the meantime they maintain regular contact with their relatives at home through phone calls and mobile money remittances.

About half of Lusozi's residents – and participants in this research – are Acholi people from northern Uganda, many of whom were displaced during the 20-year civil war in the region which continued until 2006. In the urban Kampala context, Acholi histories are retold and 'home' reconfigured.[5] Given the significance of 'home' in everyday experiences of ageing and aspirations for later life, this research is also informed by time spent in participants' home villages in rural northern Uganda, in Kitgum District, also introduced later in this chapter.

As noted, this study is part of the larger comparative 'ASSA' project, which was funded by the European Research Council (ERC) and included 11 researchers working in 10 fieldsites across nine countries: Laila Abed Rabho and Maya de Vries in Al-Quds, East Jerusalem; Marília Duque in São Paulo, Brazil; Daniel Miller in Cuan, Ireland; Charlotte Hawkins in Kampala, Uganda; Laura Haapio-Kirk in Kochi and Kyoto, Japan; Shireen Walton in Milan, Italy; Alfonso Otaegui in Santiago, Chile; Xinyuan Wang in Shanghai, China; Pauline Garvey in Thornhill, Ireland; Patrick Awondo in Yaoundé, Cameroon. We were interested in understanding people's experiences of ageing and health in light of the growing ubiquity of smartphone access. We designed the research approach and questions collaboratively, while retaining adequate breadth, holism and flexibility to accommodate the diversity of our research settings and the people we worked with. During our research we wrote monthly 5,000-word reports on particular themes, such as health practices and family relationships, ensuring consistent integration and support across the team. Our research therefore benefited from this collaborative and cross-cultural perspective, and at times throughout the monograph I will reference insights from my colleagues' research.

Each of us has produced monographs under the shared 'Ageing with Smartphones' title and with the same chapter structure. In line with project commitments of providing accessible outputs and education, these books are intended for non-academic audiences, as well as the comparative volumes, articles, regular blog posts and free online courses that have been produced. More detailed engagement with relevant academic literature is included in end notes throughout this monograph. To support the open-access dissemination aims of the project, we also took photographs and made nine short films, some of which are included in the monograph. All images and films were reviewed with the people represented to ensure they were happy with the outputs.

The project also included an applied aim of contributing ethnographic insights to a digital health initiative, so that our research participants may also benefit more directly from the project. For this I have worked with a leading digital health organisation in Uganda called 'the Medical Concierge Group' or TMCG, contributing towards formative considerations, collaborative papers[6] and successful applications for a pilot digital mental health programme in Kampala.[7]

The ASSA project initially proposed an interest in experiences of 'mid-life' or 'middle age', between 40 and 75, neither young nor elderly, and therefore often overlooked in research and service provision. In Uganda, this age group is a minority; the 2019/2020 Uganda National Survey found that 54 per cent of the population are under the age of 18.[8] Only 3.7 per cent of the population are over the age of 65, up from 3.2 per cent in 2016/17, with 4 per cent in rural areas and 3 per cent in urban.[9] This compares with 21 per cent over the age of 65 in Europe and 13 per cent worldwide.[10] However, with a 3.6 per cent annual population growth,[11] in contrast with 0.6 per cent globally,[12] the actual numbers of older people are growing fast, posing an additional strain to support networks largely based on family. Family support systems for older people are already challenged by complex economic shifts and also by the HIV/AIDs epidemic, to which many of the older generation lost their adult children.[13] Many people in the 'middle generation' therefore have caring responsibilities for their parents, their children and grandchildren, and for themselves. This means that while Uganda has one of the youngest populations in the world, age remains a significant demographic and socio-political characteristic, with older people a growing and marginalised minority.

In line with the World Health Organization (WHO), some researchers of ageing in Uganda and in East Africa set the boundary for 'old' at 50 and above.[14] The UN also defines older persons as those over the age of 60 years old.[15] However, this research in Kampala found that categories of age, 'elderly' and 'middle aged', for example, are in fact fluid and socially determined, rather than 'natural'.[16] For example, people can be considered an elder at 40, depending on their social position and experience. Among those concerned with ageing in Uganda, including researchers, NGOs, health workers and older participants themselves, 'oldness' is also defined by environment. Harsh living due to work and poverty are thought to make someone 'old', while maintaining health through good nutrition, exercise, physical work, a positive outlook and abstinence can keep someone young. Everyday routines and ways of maintaining health are described in Chapter 3.

Ideally, with age comes respect. Respect means being acknowledged and approached with humility by younger people in the family and community. Many people said they feel gratified when addressed as an elder, or when younger people would seek their advice. Similarly, in a study among HIV patients over the age of 50 at a health centre in Kampala, participants said they felt respected by health workers who called them '*muzee*' or 'elderly'.[17] Acholi society in particular is 'gerontocratic', with elders occupying positions of authority within their family, clan and community.[18] Older people, particularly older men, tend to make decisions on behalf of their younger relatives and neighbours, enacting roles of everyday governance through ideals of elder respect, which can produce both harmony and hierarchy.[19] This is also evident in national socio-political dynamics and narratives, which draw on an idiom of family, age and power. However, the declining social value, isolation and loneliness of older people in Uganda is also an increasing concern among various researchers of ageing in Uganda,[20] as well as age-based NGOs, health workers and older participants themselves. These concerns are also reflected in various studies of ageing elsewhere in Africa,[21] sometimes related to the widespread movement away from an agricultural to a cash economy, and from villages to urban centres.[22]

In Lusozi, younger people can sometimes be referred to by older people as 'the dotcom generation', increasingly exposed to global information via school education and new media. This 'dotcom wave' represents wider social and political changes, and an erosion of long-standing social ideals based on respect for elders and 'togetherness'. The concept of 'togetherness' has been discussed throughout this research, with many older participants saying that it is their role to encourage people in their families and communities to 'work together'. This is the explicit objective stated by the community groups described in Chapter 4, as they seek to foster mutual support, belonging and friendship, and to help people manage the stresses of work and family responsibility. As shown in this chapter, Acholi participants pointed out that a concept of 'working together' may relate to a farming practice called *pur aleya* or work parties called *awak*,[23] in which people 'pool their labour to work on each member's farm in succession', followed by a celebration.[24] This depicts a pragmatic idea of togetherness, through which individual interests are enabled by the collective. The ways that togetherness is defined, discussed and enacted highlights how people forge continuities in social life, despite drastic shifts in the wider world.[25] This includes multiple processes of adaptation to urbanisation and displacement, health and economic crises, technological change and a rapidly growing population.

Dotcom, specifically in the form of smartphones and mobile phones, can also facilitate respect and togetherness, as will be explored further in Chapter 5. Despite stereotypes, older people actively partake in the use of these technologies, appropriating them for their needs, values, relationships and preferences. If knowledge of phones is thought to belong to the younger dotcom generation, along with the potential to undermine reverence for older people's knowledge, younger people sharing 'dotcom' knowledge and connections with them can also show respect.[26] And just as many older people said that they feel respected and cared for by their children and grandchildren, the majority continue to care and respect for their own elders – even 'at a distance'[27] – for example through mobile money remittances.[28] This may not represent the ideal of ageing at home surrounded by family, but offers an imperfect replacement.[29] This is one of the primary findings of this research about ageing with smartphones in Uganda: that the same dotcom technologies associated with declining respect for elders and their experiences also accommodate their care across shifting terrains.

As shown in these examples, processes of adapting to social change are particularly apparent in consideration of ageing and care, and how family expectations for elder care are re-configured across distances and generations. This is the focus of Chapter 6, which seeks to highlight the connection between intimate care practices with the wider world – particularly as those connections are illuminated by participants themselves, including health workers, hospital administrators, older people and their relatives. For example, family expectations can be redefined against a 'social imagination' of institutionalised elder care in other contexts around the world, like care homes in the UK where I am from.[30] Or health problems such as hypertension or 'pressure' can be equated with global economic 'pressures' and related care burdens.

Overall, this monograph considers the ways everyday 'togetherness' is discussed and practised with reference to the broader social and political context. This is specific to the urban neighbourhood of Lusozi, a place of population density and diversity. As Nyamnjoh puts it, this 'reflect[s] the reality of cities and places and spaces of incompleteness, requiring trust, interdependence, solidarity and mutual support to get by'.[31] There people 'dynamically adapt to the challenging contemporary context of Western-inspired modernity'; interdependencies are not just 'pushed aside', but are 'continually promoted through conviviality amidst diverse world-views'.[32] This study of ageing with smartphones informs considerations about co-operative morality, how people discuss and define 'goodness' in terms of social expectations, money and disposition, which is the focus of Chapter 7. The latter is perhaps particularly apparent to me as a visiting researcher, shown hospitality throughout my 16 months in Kampala. In the following sections I outline a picture of the research setting and the city, which is 'mixed in every sense'.[33] Nyamnjoh's concept of 'conviviality' and its relevance in Lusozi is then outlined, along with the implications this has had for my own research ethics, methodology and analysis.

Lusozi: 'The United States of Kampala'

Kampala sits on seven hills. As with the rest of the capital city, Lusozi hill has starkly contrasting socio-economic areas; wealthier gated housing is often found at the top of the hills with the poorer housing areas, 'slums', at the bottom. According to national figures, Lusozi is estimated to have 2,080 households of 10,400 people, with an average of five people per household.[34] But the local leadership who participated in this research estimated the population to be more than 15,000, and the initial household survey in this research of 50 respondents found an average of seven people per household. Household composition is diverse. It includes, for example, multi-generational families, polygynous and monogamous marriages, female-headed households, older people living alone, young men living and working together, co-habiting couples or siblings, single grandmothers and their grandchildren. This likely explains why my own household survey shows more average residents in Lusozi than the national statistics, due to the ways that households are narrowly defined in demographic data.[35]

Morning and evening, Lusozi is busy with activity (Figs 1.1a and 1.1b). As well as the central market with about 20 stalls, households often have small shops outside their front door, selling essential food like tomatoes, eggs, groundnuts, onions, sugar, maize flour or *posho* and cooking oil. Others are mobile vendors, selling mobile money, airtime and repair services. At 5 a.m. many of the market vendors go to the district market nearby, buying in bulk and reselling their wares for a small profit. The *boda boda* (motorbike taxi) drivers start taking their deliveries to hotels and restaurants, taking customers to work and school. Further down the hill, people navigate their way to work through the narrow corridors, sometimes greeting neighbours as they pass. Men push bicycles laden with deliveries – sacks of flour or *matooke* (savoury banana). Women make samosas, frying them to sell to the kids on their way to school. Trucks piled with charcoal arrive, offloaded for the various vendors to sort and sell. Men carry them quickly over the shoulder, heads bent. Young girls fetch and carry 20-litre jerry cans of water, lining them up at home for drinking, showering and washing. Swift hands wash clothes and hang them out to dry, peel cassava, mingle *posho* over

Figures 1.1 a and 1.1b   Photos taken in Lusozi by Charlotte Hawkins.

burning charcoal or take tea. Young children play. Women walk slowly, carrying heavy loads on their heads, baskets of mangoes for selling in town, wood for burning. Barrows full of fresh fruit, peeled and quartered, are wheeled in to sell watermelon, pineapple, jackfruit, mango. G-nuts are ground into paste. People pass dressed for prayers. Young men congregate to play games, big boards or smartphone screens for ludo… An older man known as *Salongo* (father of twins) would often patrol the area in a high-vis jacket, demanding the residents clean up their rubbish for collection day. *Boda* drivers relax together, lining up their motorbikes at their stage, waiting for their next customer. Hawkers carry clothes, *kitenge* (fabric) and woven mats for sale, occasionally stopping to negotiate. Music of various genres – especially gospel, Acholi music, afrobeat, reggae, 'Lingala' or rumba – plays from big sound systems outside shops selling flash discs. At around 1 p.m. children come home for their lunch. By then, the chapatis are rolled out for frying with eggs to make 'rollex'. Market vendors take it in turns to come home for a break in the afternoon, to wash and rest for an hour before returning to their stalls. In the evening maize, goat's meat and offal are barbecued. Rush hour traffic brings people home. Babies sitting in basins cry as the soap is rubbed out of their eyes. People come back for dinner while uniformed security guards are picked up for their night shift. The headlights of the *boda bodas* turn on, as their journeys continue into the night.

Ethnographies of Kampala social life have long identified the 'extreme heterogeneity' of the city, as well as the historic tendency to diversity, mobility, compromise and openness in Uganda.[36] Lusozi is representative of this diverse social context in terms of language, religion and ethnicity. English is the official language in Uganda and is particularly widely spoken in Kampala. However, not all participants are fluent in English and mother tongues in the area are diverse. Languages spoken include: Luganda, the language of the Baganda people from the central Buganda region, the largest ethnic group in Uganda; Luo, the language spoken by the Alur and Acholi people in northern Uganda,[37] as well as people in neighbouring Kenya and Sudan; Kiswahili, a Bantu language spoken widely throughout East Africa, and in Lusozi particularly among police officers who have travelled across the region; Nubian, a Sudanic language spoken by Nubian people, who are often the longest-standing residents in Lusozi and regard it as their village, the place in which they will grow old. Approximately 40 per cent of the interviews in this book were translated by Amor, who grew up in the area and therefore speaks all these languages fluently. **Quotations from these translated interviews are given in italics to differentiate them throughout the monograph.**

At the time of the research in Lusozi, there was one mosque, one Catholic church, one Anglican church and seven Pentecostal churches, including the one of the first Full Gospel Churches established in Kampala. Religion here is 'an integral part of culture', regarded as a source of strength and comfort, and acceptance of adversity as God's will (Fig. 1.2).[38] In the 2014 census[39] only 0.2 per cent of the population claimed to have no religion. 14 per cent of the population in Uganda are Muslim and 84 per cent are Christian. Of the latter, 11 per cent are Pentecostal or *Murokole*, contrasting with just 5 per cent in 2002, reflecting the rapid growth of Pentecostalism. Likely the proportion will have shifted again since 2014, with many participants in this research saying they have become Born Again within the last five years. However,

Figure 1.2 Signs in a primary school in Lusozi reading 'Always be God Fearing', 'The fear of the Lord is the beginning of Wisdom'. Photo by Charlotte Hawkins.

statistics on religion in the region need to be taken with caution, as recognised by theologian Mbiti:

> Many millions of Africans are followers of more than one religion, even if they may register or be counted in census as adherents of only one.[40]

British colonisation in Uganda began in 1894, after the arrival of Arab traders in the seventeenth century, the European explorers and Christian missionaries during the late eighteenth century and the devastation of the nineteenth-century slave trade.[41] British imperial efforts were initially focused in the central region of Uganda, particularly among the populous and hierarchically centralised Baganda people.[42] Kampala became 'the centre of political, commercial and religious life' in the country.[43] Between 1894 and 1919, legislative, economic, educational, medical and governmental services were formed, and the diverse country was divided into a national system of districts, counties and villages.[44] Borders were drawn, fixing previously fluid boundaries and identities;[45] Uganda was industrialised and raw materials extracted with forced labour;[46] market requirements moved people from rural to urban areas, enforcing a 'fragmentation' between the two;[47] the English language was imposed, and histories re-written in texts to suit the colonial narrative;[48] customs were 'instrumentalised' to cement power and 'annulled' as civil authorities saw morally fit;[49] privileges and oppressions were distributed based on binary European notions of race, gender and sexuality;[50] and spirituality and education were 'monopolised' by Christian missionaries.[51] The legacies of imperial violence and racism remain resilient up to today.[52]

Independence was gained in 1962, to be followed by years of political and economic insecurity, including civil war under Idi Amin.[53] The subsequent conditions of international trade policy, development and structural adjustment programmes (SAPs) imposed by the World Bank and International Monetary Fund in the 1980s continue to suffocate industry and public spending, contributing to severe cuts in social services such as healthcare.[54] Uganda is now categorised as a low-income country by the World Bank,[55] and while poverty rates in Uganda have decreased from 56 per cent in 1992/3 to 20 per cent in 2019/20,[56] inequality continues to rise.[57] The National Labour Force Survey (NLFS) 2016/17[58] found that 41 per cent of the population work in subsistence agriculture; of those who do not, 85 per cent work in what is known as the 'informal economy',[59] which generates over half of national GDP. This contributes to Uganda being ranked the third highest nation in the Global Entrepreneurship Monitor (GEM) in 2014, with 28 per cent of adults owning their own businesses,[60] including many of the older people who participated in this research.

People who live in Lusozi come from all over the country and the region beyond. Local leadership and residents often call Lusozi 'the United States of Kampala', demonstrating the celebrated multiplicity of residents' ethnic, geographic, linguistic and cultural origins, known as tribes,[61] of which there are said to be 39 in Uganda. Roughly half of the people living in Lusozi today originate from northern Uganda. They either migrated to seek employment in the city or were more recently displaced during the 20-year civil war in the region. This includes Amor, whose parents fled to Kampala soon after she was born. Northern Ugandan, specifically Acholi culture, has therefore been particularly influential in this research. While some Acholi people like Amor have been raised in Lusozi, with the conveniences of the city, it is often not considered a 'real home'; instead it is seen as a place of work. As an Acholi elder explains in Chapter 3, a 'real home' is a place where you have *'extended families and cultural practices around you'*, unlike in Lusozi which *'can never be seen as a home'*. From the perspective of the city, 'home' is therefore significant to participants' everyday lives and aspirations, their experiences of ageing. They often discussed plans to move back home as soon as possible – once school fees have been paid, money saved and house and land have been prepared. In the meantime, many people maintain regular phone contact with relatives living at home, sending them remittances via mobile money. We therefore spent a month in Kitgum District in northern Uganda during the course of the research, staying in the home of Amor's Jaja (grandmother). Insights from these visits also inform the monograph, particularly based on conversations with Amor's family elders.

Acholi sub-region

Based on the Ugandan administrative structure, the Acholi sub-region, also known as Acholiland, is comprised of eight districts: Agago, Amuru, Gulu, Kitgum, Lamwo, Nwoya, Pader and Omoro (see Fig. 1.3 below). In the 2019/20 household survey census, the population of the Acholi sub-region represents 4.3 per cent of the Ugandan population. Amor's family home is in Palabek, Kitgum, a 12-hour journey from Kampala, by bus, car and *boda boda* (motorbike taxi) and close to South Sudan and the refugee camp at the border. Amor's paternal family have lived there for 10 generations, over 300 years. The village has 84 households, each with at least five residents and many children, so they estimate that over 400 people live there. Kitgum District has a population of 204,048, of which 10 per cent are aged between 40 and 59 and 5 per cent are aged over 60.[62] Farming is the main source of livelihood for 80 per cent[63] of the 39,697 households.[64] Crops include millet, sesame, groundnuts, peas, sorghum and vegetables, and many people keep livestock. Most houses are a circular structure made with bricks of dried earth and a grass thatched roof with a high peak. They are often neatly arranged in groups of five or more, surrounded by the family land. Several such hamlets, with a population of around 150 people, make up a village.

During Uganda's colonial period, fixed geographical boundaries were outlined between regions. As Okot p'Bitek puts it:

> [t]he term Acholi which originally referred to a linguistic group later became a geographical term when the colonial administration divided up the territory of Uganda into districts.[65]

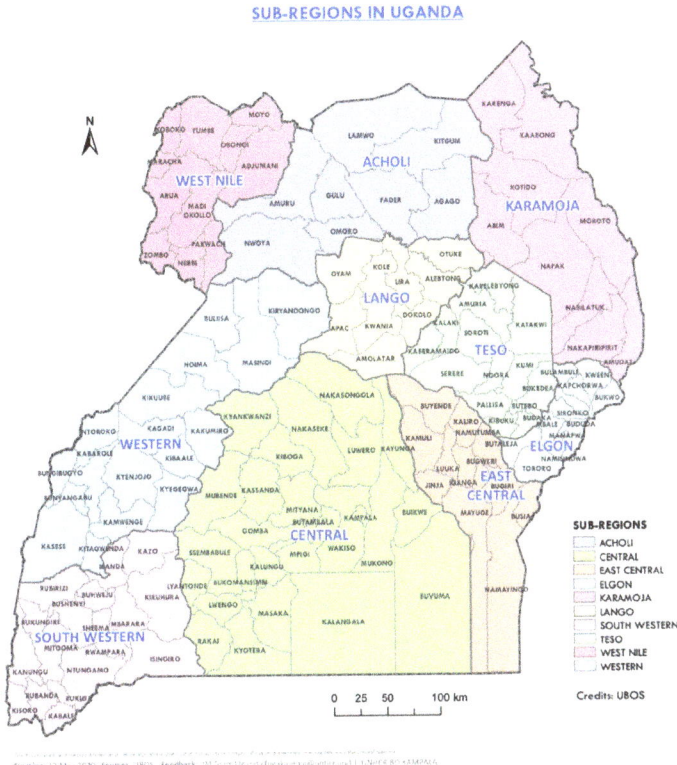

Figure 1.3 Map of Uganda, 'Sub-regions of Uganda as of 12 May 2020'. Uganda Bureau of Statistics (UBOS).[66]

Crops and industries were also distributed geographically, and while cash crops and legislative roles were introduced in the south, people in the north were generally employed for staple crop farming, manual work and the military.[67] This has had a lasting effect in terms of regional socio-economic inequities. The Acholi sub-region has been found to be the poorest in the country,[68] also reflected in access to technology, healthcare and education.

The recent civil war in northern Uganda is considered to be 'rooted' in the inequities fostered during the colonial period, with the political marginalisation of the region attributed to the rise of Joseph Kony's 'Lord's Resistance Army' (LRA) and their rebellion against Museveni's oppression of the north.[69] In 1987 Kony and his rebels began recruiting young men into their army by force,[70] and an estimated 30,000 children were abducted and forced to work as child-soldiers.[71]

During the years that followed, according to research participants, the rebel and government troops travelled through the region, looking for their opponents and food to sustain their armies, leaving devastation in their wake. Meanwhile people would sleep in the bush, hiding out of harm's way, returning to their homes only to cook and eat.

After failed peace talks in 1994, the arbitrary violence of Kony's army intensified. Some people managed to dodge roadblocks and escape to find relatives in Kampala, as is the story of many of the Acholi people encountered in Lusozi. There, however, they could face further violence and discrimination. Those left behind were eventually detained in camps or 'protected villages' for Internally Displaced People (IDP), where people continued to be regularly attacked.[72] Being displaced from their land, people were reliant on food aid from the World Food Programme and the camps are now known for conditions of overcrowding, disease and malnutrition; the World Health Organization (WHO) has estimated that 1,000 excess lives were lost each week from January to July 2005.[73] From 2006 onwards people were permitted to return to their homes via 'satellite camps' – but, according to many people today, peace remains fragile, largely due to the land conflicts that pervade the region.[74]

'This Land is Not for Sale'

As much as 80 per cent of land in Uganda is owned through customary tenure,[75] which varies regionally and is mostly found in northern and eastern Uganda.[76] In the Acholi sub-region, as across northern Uganda, customary land is predominantly held within extended families or clans; it is typically inherited along patrilineal lines, fathers to sons or maritally, husbands to wives. Customary land is a significant component of elder authority,[77] with older men in particular allocating land access among family and called upon to determine land boundaries.[78]

Land is said to be the most valuable thing in Acholi culture, representing home and wealth for former, current and future generations; as Amor's uncle explained, the value of land is 'the only thing which does not depreciate'. Where historically land could be gifted by the clan to outsiders such as in-laws and friends, with increasing shortages of land, these 'guests' and their successors' claims to land may now be contested.[79] The formalisation of customary ownership is said to have been 'co-created' by colonial authorities and local leaders,[80] as part of the wider imposition of individualised freehold ownership[81] and the bid for 'indirect rule' over rural populations.[82] Today, without documentation, customary land lacks official legal recognition and state protection in contrast with freehold tenure, leaving it vulnerable to increased privatisation and 'landlordism'.[83] In this way, colonisation effected relations to land, increasing inequities and the threats of eviction,[84] shaping contemporary land holding and disputes.

Customary tenure has also been disrupted by long-term displacement during the LRA war and the death of many clan elders with knowledge of land boundaries – as well as increasing national and global regulations, population growth and large-scale investments or 'land grabbing'. This has resulted in confusion around land claims and disputes are common (Fig. 1.4), often on generational or gendered bases.[85] For example, younger people are expected to wait patiently for allocated land, respectfully deferring to their elder's knowledge; disparaging stories of younger men selling family land to buy a *boda* or move to town are common.[86] The sale of customary land is generally prohibited, with the moralised implications of pursuing short-term self-interest over long-term collective gain.[87]

Land ownership is therefore considered a determinant of older people's social value, as they can decide when it is inherited by younger people, ensuring they are respected and cared for.[88] For Acholi people it is also necessary to be buried at home; men in the land of their father's

Figure 1.4 A research participant's family elders showing land boundaries to the younger men. Kitgum District, Uganda. Photo by Charlotte Hawkins.

clan and formally married women (those whose husbands have paid bridewealth) in their husband's family land, connecting the land across former and future generations. Gendered and generational ideals related to land inheritance and bridewealth payments, and therefore patrilineal and patrilocal access to 'home', have also been disrupted by displacement and economic difficulties.[89]

Bridewealth, for example, has become increasingly unaffordable, with families often arranging for 'gradual instalments' instead, leaving couples 'in a state of marital limbo'.[90] The resulting marital instability is thought to leave Acholi women in a particularly tenuous position,[91] with many left as the sole carers of their children.[92] Women's claims to land are particularly challenged;[93] some families, such as Amor's, may make provision for this and share the land equally between sons and daughters.[94] However, some of the older women we met in Lusozi had been chased from their land by their brothers, in-laws or co-wives, themselves and their future sons considered a threat to shared resources. Instead, as in social anthropologist Christine Obbo's earlier study in two Kampala suburbs on 'African women and their struggle for economic independence',[95] they have employed 'mobility' and 'hard work' to attain financial autonomy and provide for their children.

From the perspective of the capital city, land insecurity also represents a significant threat. Many people regularly returned home to protect their land boundaries, as is often expected of older family members.[96] Some, such as Kevin, had husbands or wives who remain in the village to protect their land:

> When we all stay here [in Kampala], people are very funny, you will just get information that they have taken your land. You have to look after that land.

Land ownership and tenancy within Lusozi is also under threat. In an initial household survey, 50 participants had lived in the neighbourhood for an average of 22 years, some for less than a year, others for their whole lifetime. For some people, such as Joe, whose family had lived there for three generations, 'it is my village'. Joe's grandfather, like many older participants in Kampala, would have lived through the latter years of British protectorate rule, as well as the subsequent civil wars. He grew up in the house that his grandfather built 'when Lusozi was all bush'. Joe's house (Fig. 1.5), where he had lived since 2007, consisted of a small room with two beds that he shared with his wife and six daughters then aged between three and 13. The image shows the expensive housing looming

Figure 1.5 Housing in Lusozi. Photo by Charlotte Hawkins.

alongside, its luxurious foliage spilling over the wall. This is indicative of a burgeoning housing crisis in Kampala, particularly in central locations like this. The government and private developers are in the process of demolishing many of the central slum areas and replacing them with housing too expensive for its previous residents. Lusozi is no exception; as shown below (Fig. 1.6), you can see piles of bricks which only recently were homes.

With the development of buildings in the area, many fear impending displacement, as in the outskirts of the area where houses are already being demolished with little warning in place of high-rise blocks of flats. A few houses in these areas have defiantly painted 'Not For Sale' on the walls, a sign that is also visible throughout the city and beyond.

> Where will we go? In three years' time you won't find us here. Now that construction has started, who will accept to see these kinds of houses here.

We often heard the expression 'Lusozi any time', as in at any time the land could be sold at the will of more powerful and wealthy people. This was also a key concern of local politicians, including the District Mayor at the time, whose speeches in the neighbourhood promised the

Figure 1.6 Lusozi mosque with demolished housing in the foreground. Photo by Charlotte Hawkins.

community that he is taking care of the land, protecting the many titles from 'land grabbers'.

Development

Having lived in Lusozi for many years, Achola had seen how things have changed in Kampala. *'In those days it wasn't this way,'* she explains, *'there's been a lot of development.'* By 'development', she meant that there are more buildings, as well as more people studying in schools and travelling overseas. The English word 'development' would often be used by the people we worked with to refer to these diverse semantics of social change, informed by these visible processes of urban development, as well as prominent media, government and NGO discourses. At this broader scale, 'development' can be understood as an institutional legacy of colonialism, informed by assumptions that there is a linear historical process which defines Africa as 'under-developed'.[97] As an everyday idiom for characterising social life, 'development' sometimes represents nostalgia for the past, ambivalence towards the present or aspirations for the future. As one shopkeeper wondered, business used to be more than this … I don't know if it's development or poverty bringing this now.

Like Achola, some people understood 'development' as a process of improvement, hoping that their own life chances could also 'develop' with the gradual influx of middle-class people and housing development in the Lusozi area. A 60-year-old local councillor compared the 'growth' of Lusozi to the growth of a child, or to their progress through school:

> The child grows slowly, slowly, starts walking and starts talking. So, the same thing with Lusozi … they have injected money, doing this and that… You aim for the better one. Like now you go to school from nursery, to Primary 1 you aim better, better, better, until the top, like University, like now you.

As in this analogy of a child's linear progress through school, development is also closely related to school education. With these established connotations of 'development',[98] school education can confer a particular identity, offering the potential for social mobility and closing the gap between what is sought and what is possible.[99] Beyond its practical necessity today, education evokes 'collective and individual hopes and dreams about the future'.[100]

If education is potentially enabling, mobilising, liberating, then what is the cost of its inaccessibility?[101] Studies have shown how the increasing privatisation of public goods has undermined the state's capacity to provide education and social security.[102] Despite efforts to universalise access to education, with the introduction of Universal Primary Education (UPE) in 1997 and Universal Secondary Education (USE) in 2006, people still face considerable barriers in seeking education and subsequent employment opportunities. There are increasing costs in attending both government and private schools. This becomes apparent throughout this monograph in various conversations about the challenges of paying school fees. Higher education is particularly elitist, being increasingly commercialised and therefore reserved for those 'from the higher echelons of society'.[103]

With school offering both essential skills for employment and a certain 'modern' identity, what Bourdieu defines as 'cultural capital', barriers to accessing education can therefore reproduce inequalities and sustain them across generations.[104] As Godfrey, aged 60, put it, 'this development, if a person is not educated, they will suffer the costs'. As relevant to this monograph, 'cultural capital' can also be conferred through access to digital tools such as smartphones and their capacities, thus acquiring 'digital capital' – which is in turn convertible to other forms of capital such as health and education itself.[105]

Various studies have found the formal curriculum in East African contexts to be inadequate, or irrelevant, to lived experiences and immediate needs, particularly in rural areas.[106] This is underlined by the fact that it is a legal requirement for classes across rural and urban schools to be taught in English, reflecting and reinforcing the hegemony of the language in Uganda.[107] As shown in Chapter 4, this is evident in the education of some of the older woman in Lusozi, which is primarily focused on English; some joked that they had been in Primary 1 for 10 years as a result. To Kenyan language scholar and novelist Ngũgĩ wa Thiong'o, English being 'the main determinant of a child's progress up the ladder of formal education'[108] alienates school children from their culture, oral traditions, memory and history.[109] Nyamnjoh agrees, finding that while Euro-American languages and knowledge systems are championed, colonial knowledge hierarchies and social divisions are enhanced.[110] Older participants express this tension in terms of the shifting emphasis they have witnessed in their lifetimes, from the knowledge of elders to knowledge gained at school or through 'dotcom' media, and the impact that this has on their intergenerational relationships. As far as possible, by adopting a 'convivial' framework outlined below, I seek to acknowledge and address these hierarchies in ways of knowing, which underlie academic research and the history of anthropology itself.

Convivial scholarship

Generosity was continually extended to me throughout my time working in Lusozi. Many people were extremely hospitable to me and the research, in particular Amor, my colleague and translator who grew up in Lusozi, and her whole family: her dad Kilongeni, her mum Adul, her brothers and sisters and her late Jaja (grandmother). Hope, at the time the Women's Councillor of the Lusozi division (Local Councillor 3 or LC3), permitted me to spend 16 months working there and supported the project in various ways, for example by inviting me regularly to attend her women's group meetings. The speaker of this group, Winston, became my *laphonya* (teacher) of Acholi language and many other things. Most of the local councillors in the area, known as Local Councillor 1 (LC1) at village level and Local Councillor 2 (LC2) at parish level, were also supportive of the project, and were generous with their time. The local hospital, especially the physiotherapy department, allowed me to conduct research there, observing consultations and interviewing health workers. I was widely hosted by many other people, given food, stories, time and protection. Beyond that I was accepted within families, as a daughter and sister.

Finnström, a Swedish anthropologist who worked in the Acholi sub-region in northern Uganda during the civil war, with similar family ties extended to him over his long-term research, argues that being a visitor does not necessarily infer methodological inferiority.[111] And Katrien Pype, who works with older people in Kinshasha, found her identity as a young white woman from Europe to be an advantage in accessing 'the lifeworlds of the elderly', in part due to initial expectations of financial or bureaucratic assistance.[112] It is true that my ethnography also benefited from participants' openness to visitors. But there was also an imbalance in the fact of my presence as a white European visitor in Africa. The ongoing history in which our ancestors colonised the continent, stole its knowledge, resources and people, thwarted customs, religions, borders, languages and re-wrote histories; violence of incomprehensible depth and breadth. Yet it is the same shared history that allowed me to take what is still so often a one-way journey, a white British researcher in encounter with a black Ugandan experience. In most day-to-day social interactions in Lusozi, these imbalances were not foregrounded, but it is important to highlight that there are no neutral visitors in this inherited context.

This context, and my position within it, therefore has significant implications for conducting research, which should be considered and explicit throughout, from methodology to analysis to dissemination here. As Nyamnjoh cautions in 'divining the future of anthropology in Africa', it is not 'as if anything is knowable to anyone who comes knocking with questions'.[113] His 'divination' includes the following critical approaches. First, as has been introduced here, in recognising the ways I am socially and historically linked to the place where I have been doing research. These complex historical ties will also become evident in participants' cited depictions of colonialism, 'Westernisation', education and 'development'. Second, to acknowledge that producing observations and interpretations of social realities through interactions and dialogue means that they are actually *co-produced*.[114] This can involve mutual 'blindness',[115] as well as inevitable assumptions about identity such as race, class, sexuality, gender, income and education level, which can inform the way in which experiences are expressed.[116] For instance, being in dialogue with me may have encouraged a particular reflection on how values of ageing may differ from the monopolising values of where I come from – a 'social imagination'[117] that manifests in the everyday characterisation and experience of ageing and social life. Third, by considering stories from many perspectives through critical description. Finally, by prioritising the everyday, banal, 'taken-for-granted' stuff, relationships and the (extra)ordinary. The picture I present is built from the ground up, based on observable patterns in the stories, idioms, shared concerns and aspirations, work and routines, home and family lives, as encountered during the research.

It is also important to note that this is a study about ageing conducted by a young woman, 27 to 28 at the time of the research, accompanied by my age-mate Amor. We therefore approached this research as young people seeking to learn from older people with more life experience, as informed by Amor's respectful approach to her elders, seeking their knowledge and advice in line with the intergenerational expectations outlined in Chapter 2. As young women, it was generally more appropriate for us to spend time with older women, which is why the ethnography in general focuses on women's perspectives and experiences.[118] Many of the older women we worked with are heads of households with sole responsibility for finances and care, meaning that their perspectives are politically significant and can inform more equitable social policy and practice.[119]

By here foregrounding context, dialogue and 'unknowability', I am also paying respect to what Nyamnjoh has termed 'convivial scholarship'.[120] Conviviality prioritises interconnections with other people and the (super)natural, through interdependence, dialogue and compassion; arguably aligning closely with the ideal of 'togetherness' often discussed with participants in Lusozi. Convivial scholarship in such diverse urban settings should therefore be, in Nyamnjoh's words, a 'quest for knowledge in its complexity and nuance', with open-ended methodology and analysis:

> With convivial scholarship, there are no final answers, only permanent questions.[121]

As in much ethnographic research,[122] my methodology was founded on attempting to respond as flexibly as possible to the setting and the people I have been working with, 'allowing different truths and voices to emerge'.[123] Fortunately for me, this meant my research was most often a convivial experience of seeking mutual connection through conversation, humour, dancing, learning and friendship. Ethnographic priorities of building relationships, sustained presence among the people you work with and an explicit acknowledgement of my own limited capacity to know, were well suited and openly accommodated in this research setting. This monograph expresses my encounter, the stories I was fortunate to hear and observe.

Methodology

Following the idea of 'convivial scholarship', the ethnographic method is here defined by its 'incompleteness', flexibility, open-endedness and sustained dialogue. Ethnography allows for research questions and methodological choices to follow contextual realities, the preferences of participants and the subject at hand. This means that I have drawn from a variety of methods to accommodate the breadth of research interests, as well as the preferences of participants, both as collaborators and potential readers.

Primarily, the research was based on in-depth qualitative methods, including interviews and participant observation. Overall we conducted over 250 interviews, with many key participants taking part in multiple interviews over the course of the research. Participants include 85 older women (average age 53); 60 older men (average age 54); 21 younger people (below 40), including 8 men and 13 women; 31 health workers, including doctors, nurses and administrators at the government hospital, as well as private clinicians and traditional healers; 17 political and religious leaders, including local councillors (LCs), imams and pastors; 18 mobile phone service providers; 17 older relatives of participants in Kampala who live in rural northern Uganda; 7 age-related NGO representatives. Health workers, service providers, politicians and religious leaders are broadly exposed to issues across their institution and community, so interviews with them are particularly helpful in understanding ageing in context.

Like other researchers working with older people in Uganda,[124] interviews in the community were in-depth, face to face conversations in people's homes, often over the course of about an hour. In the home setting interviews were generally informal and conversational in tone, with open-ended questions allowing for participants' interpretations. The discussions were dictated as much as possible by the participant and their interests; their business or family concerns, for example, and the 'taken-for-granted stuff of everyday life'.[125] As shown in a study of support systems for older adults in Uganda by Golaz, Rutaremwa and Wandera,[126] visiting one area in Kampala over a long period of time enhances an in-depth interview focus on familial relations. The everyday focus of conversations was also informed by the breadth of wider study objectives: to understand experiences of ageing and health in relation to smartphone and mobile phone access. This is not to mention the likely influence of my own interests and experiences and those of Amor, for example in relation to family responsibility and co-operation, single motherhood and care work, conviviality and humour and the political economy of health.

Interviews are also contextualised within general participant observation based on close proximity over 16 months. Participant observation implies taking part in different social settings while acknowledging the ethnographer's role as researcher and observer. To some extent this is continuous throughout casual encounter and conversation, particularly in public spaces, such as in the market and the central bar in Lusozi. As is discussed in more detail in Chapter 4 on social relations, I also participated actively in different community groups, primarily in three groups well attended by older people. I participated in the weekly meetings of 'Place of Peace', a group formed by an international, faith-based NGO to support single mothers. This is considered by local leadership and others in the community as the only NGO effectively supporting people in Lusozi. Many of the older women who participated in the research are also part of this group. As outlined in Chapter 4, the discussions during the meetings, and with members during individual interviews, offered opportunities for extensive learning about expectations of social relations, especially family, friendship, community and the role of women.

The other two community groups were "Togetherness is Strength' (TIS) and 'Who should enrich you?' (WSEY); these are primarily savings groups or Savings and Cooperative Credit Organisations (SACCOs), of which there are many in Lusozi and around the world. In savings groups people save money collectively as a way of rotating or accumulating and growing funds, providing a financial safety net for members. WSEY is mostly a women's group, and every Sunday the beneficiary of the savings exchange is celebrated with a ceremony of gift-giving and dancing, which we often attended. The members of TIS are primarily men; they generously agreed to share their constitution with me and allow me to join as a saving member for a year. This offered an opportunity to participate in a group started by older Acholi men to encourage unity and togetherness in the Lusozi community.

For the purpose of collecting more systematic data, we also conducted questionnaires with 250 respondents on household information and phone use. Quantitative data outlined throughout the monograph will be derived from the following five surveys:

1) An initial household survey with 50 participants. This sought basic household information during the primary stage of the research, such as the age and gender of residents, ownership of phones and preferred health services.
2) A questionnaire on phone use with 50 participants who have access to a mobile phone or smartphone. This questionnaire included questions about: the ownership and sharing of mobile phones and smartphones across the household, by age and gender; the number of calls and text messages sent and received in the past week; topping up airtime and data; social media use; details of prior three calls and remittances; sending and receiving airtime; and 'beeps' (dropped or cancelled calls).
3) A survey on mobile money use with 200 participants. Amor asked consenting mobile money customers at a particular stand in Lusozi about the purpose of their transfer, the amount and their relationship to the recipient or sender.
4) App interviews with 30 participants. We asked participants to discuss each of their apps and to describe their use of them.
5) A final survey of 150 participants for comparative data across the ASSA project, and for additional household and financial data. This consolidated findings and reiterated questions on phone use from questionnaire 2.

These survey data are useful to corroborate qualitative observations, as well as providing new insights. Furthermore, survey data is also helpful in communicating findings across different disciplines; collaborating digital health practitioners, for example, particularly valued quantifiable and systematic data on phone habits. Surveys on phone use in particular aimed to take advantage of the opportunity to gain insight into phone practices based on information accessible within them, which may otherwise be forgotten or overlooked in conversational interviews. For example, tracing phone calls and remittances within the family, to and from the home village, offers a networked understanding of social relations and intergenerational care.[127]

Understanding phone use required diverse methodological approaches. More open-ended methods such as interviews or a 'story-based approach'[128] contributed to an understanding of how people conceptualise, aspire towards, reject or negotiate access to smartphone capacities, with stories about smartphones often drawing out wider discussions about family and social expectations. These insights were supported with information about more 'mundane' day to day use,[129] often found looking at recent phone usage based on data within the phone such as call lists and sought through structured questionnaires. For these 'phone surveys' we looked for participants whom we already knew and who might be comfortable in sharing this personal data.

All research was approved by relevant institutions including Lusozi Hospital, the University College London (UCL) ethics board, Makerere School of Social Sciences Research Ethics Committee (MAKSS REC) and the Ugandan National Council of Science and Technology (UNCST). In line with community requirements for conducting ethical research, we also began by seeking permissions from relevant local leadership to work in the area, including LC3s and LC1s for the area. All participation was based on fully informed consent. In particular, we took care to emphasise the ongoing nature of consent and the option for people to withdraw their participation at any point. We have also reviewed research outputs with interested key participants for their feedback, which has been integrated as appropriate. All names used here are pseudonyms to protect people's identities.

From these methodological choices through to analysis and dissemination, this project champions open-endedness, inquisitiveness and collaboration as productive ways of knowing. When applying this to practical recommendations and projects related to policy, education or health services, the aim is often to accommodate people's everyday lived realities, and to alleviate the inequalities which can be seen to perpetually reproduce themselves and constrain people's life chances. These aims and underlying biases are reflected throughout the monograph. The reader is also asked to keep in mind throughout that knowledge about a particular social reality is always going to be incomplete, particularly from someone who 'comes knocking with questions'.[130] As in Nyamnjoh's vision of a 'convivial scholarship', an awareness of these limits encourages social knowledge 'in its complexity and nuance', through 'permanent questions and questioning', without any final answers.[131]

Notes

1. p'Bitek 1986, 23.
2. Mamdani 2012; Mamdani 1996; p'Bitek 1986.
3. Nyamnjoh 2012b, 65.
4. Nyamnjoh 2017; Haraway 1988.

5. Gupta and Ferguson 1997, 3; Sigona et al. 2015, xix.
   Stories of 'the past in the present' (Allen 1988, 48; Jackson 1998, 2) have historically been employed as a methodology for understanding Luo and Acholi origins (Crazzolara 1950; Ogot 1967; Onyango-Ku-Odongo and Webster 1976; Atkinson 1994), which has been critiqued as speculative and 'futile' (Allen 2019; Allen 1991a; Campbell 2006; p'Bitek 1971) for obscuring the instability of the past and for failing to recognise that 'oral traditions are concerned … with the foundation and maintenance of existing institutions' (p'Bitek 1970, 3), and '[l]egends whose proper function was to make the world intelligible have been read for history, the events related taken as if they actually took place' (p'Bitek 1970, 11). As well as Acholi qualities 'emerging out of dialogue' with colonial administrators and missionaries, as highlighted in the earlier work of anthropologists Girling (Girling 2019 [1960], 200) and p'Bitek (1970), English-language scholarship has also recursively informed oral histories themselves. These histories often rely not only on the narrow views of elite men such as clan elders, but also on an assumed boundedness of clans, generations and the Luo as a whole (Campbell 2006, 81), according oral testimonies as 'facts' rather than 'situated knowledge reflecting contemporary processes' (Campbell 2006, 82). Overall, Allen argues that this work has obscured the instability of the past, such as chaos in the region during the slave trade era, and that this has contributed to the characterisation of pre-colonial and colonial times as 'a lost era of tranquillity', with a tendency to 'claims about how social life today should be enhanced with reference to cultural heritage and customary forms of dispute resolution' (Allen 2019, 17). He shows how reified notions of Acholi-ness and Acholi history have been particularly harmful during recent attempts by international agencies to enact traditional forms of conflict resolution after the war (Allen 2007), as discussed further in Chapter 2.
6. Hawkins et al. 2020; Bwanika et al. 2022.
7. Hawkins and Bwanika, forthcoming 2023.
8. UBOS 2020. 'Uganda national survey report 2019/2020'. Accessed 15 June 2022. https://www.ubos.org/wp-content/uploads/publications/09_2021Uganda-National-Survey-Report-2019-2020.pdf, 14.
9. UBOS 2020. 'Uganda national survey report 2019/2020'. Accessed 15 June 2022. https://www.ubos.org/wp-content/uploads/publications/09_2021Uganda-National-Survey-Report-2019-2020.pdf, 12.
10. World Bank 2019. 'Population ages 65 and above (% of total population)'. Accessed 8 June 2021. https://data.worldbank.org/indicator/SP.POP.65UP.TO.ZS?name_desc=false. See also: UN 2015. 'World population ageing'. Accessed 22 October 2019. https://www.un.org/en/development/desa/population/publications/pdf/ageing/WPA2015_Highlights.pdf.
11. World Bank 2019. 'Population growth (annual %): Uganda'. Accessed 8 June 2021. https://data.worldbank.org/indicator/SP.POP.GROW?locations=UG.
12. World Population Review 2021. 'Uganda Population 2021'. Accessed 8 June 2021. https://worldpopulationreview.com/countries/uganda-population. World Bank 2019, 'Population growth (annual %): Uganda'. Accessed 8 June 2021. https://data.worldbank.org/indicator/SP.POP.GROW?locations=UG.
13. de Klerk and Moyer 2017; Golaz, Wandera and Rutaremwa 2017; Kuteesa et al. 2012; Nankwanga, Neema and Phillips 2013; Ssengonzi 2007.
14. de Klerk and Moyer 2017; Kuteesa et al. 2012; Velkoff and Kowal 2007.
15. UN 2019. 'New measures of population ageing'. Accessed 23 May 2022. https://www.un.org/en/development/desa/population/events/pdf/expert/29/session1/EGM_25Feb2019_S1_SergeiScherbov.pdf, 6.
16. Honwana 2012, 11.
17. Kuteesa et al. 2012, 203.
18. Finnström 2001; Whyte and Acio 2017.
19. The Centre for Public Authority and International Development (CPAID) Report 2021. Accessed 7 November 2022. https://issuu.com/leslfca/docs/centre_for_public_authority_and_international_deve.
20. Golaz, Wandera and Rutaremwa 2017; Nankwanga and Neema 2020; Nzabona, Ntozi and Rutaremwa 2016; Whyte and Acio 2017; Wandera et al. 2017.
21. Aboderin 2004; Maharaj 2020; Maniragaba et al. 2019; Oppong 2006; van der Geest 1997a, 1997b.
22. Van der Geest 2011.
23. Girling 2019, 89.
24. Otto 2013, 169.

25. Jackson 1998; Whyte 1997. Susan Whyte, a medical anthropologist who has worked extensively in Uganda, has studied 'pragmatic' approaches to uncertainty related to money, health, family and relationships among the Nyole in eastern Uganda (Whyte 1997). While based in a different Ugandan context and time period, with specific explanatory idioms and approaches to uncertainty, Whyte's approach is useful in thinking through how people actively engage with the inevitable precarity and ambiguity of life through dialogue, idiom, stories, conversation and 'social problem solving' (ibid.). Whyte's study grounds situated practices which 'produce and reproduce' meaning within the indeterminate wider worlds of social relations and institutions; she argues that it is the task of ethnography to review the patterns (re)produced in the process (ibid.). This anthropological approach to processual sociality and the significance of shared meanings builds from Jackson's concept of 'intersubjectivity', the parallel and porous relationship in between the personal and contextual, particular and universal (Jackson 1998; 2002), which is taken up by Finnström in his study of 'meaning as lived' in wartime Acholiland (2008, 78). Jackson depicts how such storytelling implicates the relational processes of seeking what Giddens has termed 'ontological security', which is defined as a sense of continuity and control over the shifting objective domain (Jackson 1998, 71, ref Giddens, 1991). Storytelling as a 'quest for ontological security' (Finnström 2008, 80) might include ritual, or, of particular relevance to the monograph, practical forms of co-existence or 'togetherness', which also offer meaning and a 'degree of control over the forces of destiny' (Jackson 1998, 71). As Finnström argues in his ethnography of life in the Acholi sub-region during the civil war, there is an 'anthropological duty to understand meaning as lived' (Finnström 2008, 80), and to consider how it (re)produces social relations, institutions and politics.
26. Porter et al. 2015.
27. Ahlin 2018; Pols 2012.
28. Kusimba, Yang and Chawla 2016; Maurer 2012.
This exemplifies the moral embeddedness both of money (Bloch and Parry 1989; Zelizer 2018) and of phone use. This monograph therefore contributes to anthropological literature on the 'social shaping of the mobile phone' (de Bruijn 2013, 3), the ways they are embedded within existing relationships, networks and socio-cultural preferences (Archambault 2017; de Bruijn 2013; de Bruijn, Nyamnjoh and Brinkman 2009; Horst and Miller 2006; Vokes 2018).
29. The appropriation of 'dotcom' for care across distances can be understood in relation to Cati Coe's concept of 'family repertoires', which is based on her anthropological research about ageing in Ghana. Where families are increasingly 'scattered' around the world (Coe 2014; Sigona et al. 2015), existing family expectations or 'repertoires', 'ways of speaking, thinking, and feeling about the family – that mobilize material resources and people in ways that are considered normal and natural' (Coe 2014, 5) are shifting. 'Family repertoires' draw from a history of kinship practices, such as family roles, care norms and intergenerational reciprocities, which have long been established and adapted to economic change and migration (Coe 2014, 41). With a limited ethnographic timeframe of 16 months, historical family repertoires are in part accessible through 'stories of the past' invoked by various research participants, such as those about home-based intergenerational care, ideally in rural areas, with older people surrounded by an extended family network who take up different care roles based on their gender and position. Earlier ethnographies also shed light on family repertoires as they are invoked, enacted and adapted; in particular Parkin's 1969 ethnography in a housing estate near Lusozi demonstrated how Luo people from western Kenya and northern Uganda draw on kinship networks and 'ideologies' in Kampala, especially given shared economic interests based on bridewealth, patrilineal inheritance and customary land tenure (Parkin 1969, 133). Parkin also notes the fluidity with which kin ties and customs are employed, and their adaptation to 'new and specifically urban patterns', not least the ethnic diversity of the city and the political uncertainty of the post-Independence period (Parkin 1969, 191). Through these processes of social change in a migration context, there are patterned but not yet discursively normative ways that people uphold intergenerational expectations such as care obligations which form what Coe and Alber term 'age inscriptions' (Coe and Alber 2018) – a useful terminology and perspective for thinking through the re-configuration of elder care norms among participants in Lusozi. This builds on Bourdieu's theories of 'habitus' and 'social reproduction' (1977), whereby existing power structures are inhabited and reproduced through embodied practices. Coe's concept of 'age inscriptions' offers a more applicable, processual conception of social trajectories, which allows for the possibility of indeterminacy and change over time.

30. Coe 2020.
    This analysis thereby contributes to the existing literature in critical medical anthropology on ageing and care which seeks to radically contextualise intimate and everyday care practices (Buch 2015; Fassin 2009; Kehr, Hansjörg and van Eeuwijk 2018; Nguyen, Zavoretti and Tronto 2017; Kleinman 2015). Care for elders invokes the ambiguity of moral contradictions, of self-responsibility both promoted and undermined, of increasing frailty and financial precarity in later life, and of transfigured 'constellations of care' (Nguyen, Zavoretti and Tronto 2017, 199).
31. Nyamnjoh 2017.
32. Nyamnjoh 2017, 261–2.
33. Wallman and Bantebya-Kyomuhendo 1996, 28.
34. Source concealed to preserve anonymity of research location.
35. Randall and Coast 2016.
36. Southall, Gutkind and Sempa 1957; Fallers 1960; Nahemow 1979; Parkin 1969; Wallman and Bantebya-Kyomuhendo 1996.
37. There is a story of two brothers, Gipir and Gifol, who had a conflict that they were unable to resolve. Gipir then moved to live on the West Bank of the Nile, which is thought to be the origins of Alur people as separate from Acholi. I was sometimes told the story to evoke the similarities between Alur and Acholi people, who share a common language and ancestry. Okot p'Bitek wrote that it is 'a vivid story that "explained" the separation of the Luo rulers in Alur from the rest of the Luo peoples in Bunyoro and Acholi, and thus also established a strong link between them' (p'Bitek 1970). Whyte, Meinert and Obika (Whyte et al. 2016) also wrote on the significance of the story's message about the consequences of refusing forgiveness.
38. MacNeil 1996, 16.
39. Uganda Bureau of Statistics (UBOS) 2014. 'Uganda national census main report'. Accessed 8 June 2021. https://www.ubos.org/wp-content/uploads/publications/03_20182014_National_Census_Main_Report.pdf.
40. Ukah 2018.
41. Allen 1988, 49.
42. Fallers 1960, 16.
43. Fallers 1960, 23.
44. Achol 1987, 150.
45. Finnström 2008, 53.
46. Finnström 2008, 89.
47. Mamdani 1996, xiv.
48. Finnström 2008, 89.
49. Mamdani 1996, xiii.
50. Tamale 2020, 2.
51. Finnström 2008, 53.
52. Finnström 2008, 95; Mamdani 1996; Nakirya and State 2013, 35; Nyamnjoh 2012a.
53. See Karugire 1980, Kasozi 1994 and Pringle 2019 for further background on the political history of Uganda, particularly around the decolonisation period.
54. Karlström et al. 2004, 598.
55. World Bank 2017. 'Data for Uganda'. Accessed 26 May 2017. http://data.worldbank.org/?locations=UG-XM.
56. UBOS 2020. 'Uganda national survey report 2019/2020'. Accessed 15 June 2022. https://www.ubos.org/wp-content/uploads/publications/09_2021Uganda-National-Survey-Report-2019-2020.pdf, 115.
57. World Bank 2016. 'Uganda poverty assessment report'. Accessed 2 July 2017. http://pubdocs.worldbank.org/en/381951474255092375/pdf/Uganda-Poverty-Assessment-Report-2016.pdf.
58. National Labour Force Survey (NLFS) 2018. Accessed 18 November 2019. https://www.ubos.org/wp-content/uploads/publications/10_2018Report_national_labour_force_survey_2016_17.pdf.
59. Ferguson 2006; Hart 1985; Wallman and Baker 1996.
60. GEM 2014. 'Economy profiles: Uganda'. Accessed 18 November 2019. https://www.gemconsortium.org/economy-profiles/uganda.
61. The word 'tribe' is referenced here only as an 'emic' term, in the way it is used meaningfully by participants. In etic terms, the use of the word 'tribe' has been problematised by various

theorists, including Mamdani, who critiques the colonial imposition of fixed, one-dimensional definitions of people and customs in Africa – instrumentalising and segregating cultures, impeding their organic development and assimilation (1996, xiii). Nyamnjoh (2012b, 68) has also stressed that scholars' acceptance of colonially imposed labels is problematic and underplays the multiethnicity of societies.

62. UBOS 2017, 7.
63. UBOS 2017, 28.
64. 'Sub-regions in Uganda (as of 12 May 2020)', https://reliefweb.int/map/uganda/sub-regions-uganda-12-may-2020. Accessed 16 June 2020.
65. p'Bitek 1971.
66. Uganda Bureau of Statistics 2017. 'The National Population and Housing Census 2014 – Area Specific Profile Series, Kampala, Uganda.' Accessed 23 April 2018. http://www.ubos.org/onlinefiles/uploads/ubos/2014CensusProfiles/KITGUM.pdf, 17.
67. Doom and Vlassenroot 1999, 7.
68. UBOS 2020. 'Uganda national survey report 2019/2020'. Accessed 15 June 2022. https://www.ubos.org/wp-content/uploads/publications/09_2021Uganda-National-Survey-Report-2019-2020.pdf, 110.
69. Doom and Vlassenroot 1999, 7.
70. Meier 2013, 39.
71. The Refugee Law Project Working Paper, 2005. 'Peace first, justice later: Traditional justice in Northern Uganda'. Accessed 10 March 2021. https://www.refugeelawproject.org/files/working_papers/RLP.WP17.pdf, 3.
72. The Refugee Law Project Working Paper, 2005.
73. World Health Organization 2005. 'Health and mortality survey among internally displaced persons in Gulu, Kitgum and Pader districts, northern Uganda'. Accessed 28 April 2020. https://reliefweb.int/report/uganda/health-and-mortality-survey-among-internally-displaced-persons-gulu-kitgum-and-pader.
74. The violence of the war and the duration of insecurity in the IDP camps has disrupted social institutions and the social legacies of war have been studied extensively by anthropologists (e.g. Akello 2019; Allen 2007, 200; Finnström 2015, 2008; Meinert and Whyte 2017; Porter 2019; Whyte et al. 2016; Whyte and Acio 2017). As Holly Porter put it in her paper on the impact of war on the Acholi 'moral landscape', '[m]any mourn the profound ways that war is seen to have unsettled the moral foundations of Acholi ways of life' (Porter 2019, 1013).
75. Obaikol 2014. 'Draft final report of the implementation of the land governance assessment framework in Uganda'. Washington, DC: World Bank Group. Accessed 23 May 2022. http://documents.worldbank.org/curated/en/611841504873425190/Draft-final-report-of-the-implementation-of-the-land-governance-assessment-framework-in-Uganda.
76. Dieterle 2022.
77. Nzabona and Ntozi 2017; Whyte and Acio 2017.
78. Nzabona and Ntozi 2017, 3694.
79. Hopwood 2015, 392.
80. Dieterle 2022.
81. Batungi and Rüther 2008; Mwebaza, 'A historical perspective of the land problem in Uganda', HRAPF Uganda. Accessed 23 May 2022. https://hrapf.org/images/researchpapers/a_historical_perspective_of_the_land_problem_in_uganda.pdf.
82. Mamdani 1996.
83. Dieterle 2022.
84. Mwebaza, 'A historical perspective of the land problem in Uganda', HRAPF Uganda. Accessed 23 May 2022. https://hrapf.org/images/researchpapers/a_historical_perspective_of_the_land_problem_in_uganda.pdf.
85. Whyte and Acio 2017.
86. Whyte and Acio 2017, 33.
87. Bloch and Parry 1989.
88. Whyte and Acio 2017.
89. Whyte and Acio 2017, 20.
90. Hopwood 2015, 402.
91. Porter 2019; Whyte and Acio 2017; Allen 2007.
92. Hopwood 2015, 402.
93. Allen 2007, 1988; Whyte and Acio 2017.

94. This is also evident in Hopwood's study of women's land claims in the Acholi region, which noted a tendency for elders and communities to provide land for women who were unmarried or divorced (Hopwood 2015, 403).
95. Obbo 1980.
96. Nzabona and Ntozi 2017, 3694.
97. p'Bitek 1970, 7; Imbo 2002, 4; Mamdani 1996. To outline further important critiques of the 'development' industry: as an institutional legacy of colonialism, the development binary re-establishes a linear conception of history which defines and exoticises Africa as underdeveloped (Mamdani 1996); this thereby reinforces colonial power relations, including neo-imperial demands on policy. In this political context, structural issues such as those related to public health are framed as development issues, for example the ways in which the growth of NCDs is characterised by WHO and the World Bank (Reubi, Herrick and Brown 2016). In this way, development discourses and interventions fit the neoliberal narrative of poverty, responsibilising individual 'lifestyles' and de-responsibilising the state from social welfare and protection, and further exposing poor people to the 'vicissitudes of market' (Ferguson 2015). Related development initiatives, often funded through international aid programmes, tend to manage and problematise the symptoms of poverty or other structural problems, rather than the cause (Mercer 2006, 243), contributing to a fragmented 'projectified landscape of care' (Meinert and Whyte 2014). This can be seen to undermine existing local infrastructures (Allen, MacDonald and Radice 2018, 149) and government accountability. In particular, development often draws on normative stances and conceptions of personhood, promoting Euro-American ideals of individual independence, with an aversion to interdependence and dependence (Nussbaum 2000, 247; Englund 2008). As relevant to this monograph, in relation to technology and in particular smartphones, related developments are often wrongly assumed to lead to development in relations or power dynamics (Archambault 2017; de Bruijn 2014), leading to an emphasis on techno-deterministic fixes. At an interpersonal level, 'development' initiatives run by white European or American staff reinforce conceptions of 'white saviourism' (Cole 2017); see also Uganda-based activists nowhitesaviors. There is also often an over-reliance on narrow quantitative research in development programmes (Hampshire, Hills and Iqbal 2005), a metrics-driven 'development rationality' which can undermine existing forms of care work (Qureshi 2022).
98. Meinert 2009, 167; Onyango-Ouma 2006, 393.
99. Meinert 2009, 166.
100. Meinert 2009, 163.
101. Tamale 2020, 265, 270.
102. Bukuluki and Mubiru 2014, 42; Ferguson 2006, 16; Tamale 2020, 50.
103. Nyanzi 2015, 131.
104. Bourdieu 1986; Meinert 2004; Nyanzi 2015; Onyango-Ouma 2006.
105. Hampshire et al. 2015.
106. Onyango-Ouma 2006, 394; Honwana 2012, 3.
107. Nankindu, Kirunda and Ogavu 2015.
108. Ngũgĩ wa Thiong'o 2005, 12.
109. Ngũgĩ wa Thiong'o 2005, 17.
110. Nyamnjoh 2012a; 2013, 128.
111. Finnström 2008, 16.
112. Pype 2016, 215.
113. Nyamnjoh 2012b, 68.
114. Ibid.
115. Ibid.
116. Jackson 1998; Moore 1994.
117. Coe 2020.
118. Collins 2000; Collins 2019.
    This approach to intersectional gender analysis relates to the foundational work of Black feminist theorists such as Patricia Hill-Collins, who centres the 'distinctive angle of vision' offered by Black women's experiences, particularly single mothers, on the 'intersecting systems of oppression' of white capitalist patriarchy as it operates (and is resisted) through the family, household, neighbourhood, community, society and beyond.

119. Ibid.; Nyanzi 2009; Obbo 1980.
120. Nyamnjoh 2017.
121. Nyamnjoh 2017.
122. Fetterman 2010.
123. Obbo 1980, 160.
124. Golaz, Wandera and Rutaremwa 2017; Nankwanga, Neema and Phillips 2013; Nyanzi 2009.
125. Finnström 2008, 9; Gupta and Ferguson 1997, 34.
126. Golaz, Wandera and Rutaremwa, 2017.
127. de Bruijn 2014.
128. Hampshire et al. 2015, 91.
129. Hampshire et al. 2015, 91.
130. Nyamnjoh 2012a, 68.
131. Nyamnjoh 2017.

2
Elders in the city

Introduction

This chapter considers values of ageing as they are brought to life both rhetorically and through practice in the city. The stories retold here emphasise the fluidity of values adapted to 'dotcom' lifestyles in the city, which in turn are adapted to existing experiences and expectations of ageing. This depicts the everyday, practical relevance of ageing ideals based on intergenerational respect and relatedness, often with reference both to continuity with the past and relevance for the future.

'Stories of the past' encountered ethnographically offer insight into the ways people characterise and experience the present, and how these inform and reflect values as they are meaningfully invoked and practised day to day;[1] as p'Bitek puts it 'making the world intelligible'.[2] As Finnström found in his 2008 ethnography of wartime Acholiland, Acholi values are 'lived and mutable'.[3] This emphasis on the 'aliveness' of values has particular implications in the historical context of Lusozi, briefly outlined in Chapter 1. Various scholars of Ugandan history and social life have highlighted how social customs and values have been instrumentalised through colonialisation, fixing otherwise fluid and dynamic social processes such as customary land ownership, community justice systems, family roles and hierarchies, cultural practices and identities.[4] The reification of customary justice mechanisms for political ends in the post-war northern region, for example, belies the flexibility of otherwise situated, habitual and unnamed community practices.[5] These hold the potential both to reinforce established hierarchies,[6] such as those based on the authority of older men, and to seek social and gender justice.[7] This therefore supports the need for an approach which seeks to understand the concessional and convivial 'middle ground' between continuity and change,[8] as the elder role is reconfigured and enacted in the city.

Older people in Uganda typically hold authority within their households and communities. However, experiences of ageing in Lusozi are of course multiple. As across Kampala,[9] the population of the neighbourhood is extremely diverse, with mixed lifestyles, ethnicities, religious beliefs and practices, income levels and family circumstances. The perspectives of multiple people cited in this chapter portray the diversity of voices throughout the research and the encounters between them. However, as in the rest of the monograph, Acholi people from northern Uganda represent the majority of research participants and Lusozi residents, many having arrived in Kampala during the LRA war. The violence and disruption of this 20-year civil war is thought to have had a devastating impact on social life in the north.[10] Now Acholi ideals for 'ageing well' may be associated temporally with the pre-war past and geographically with the village.[11] However, in their retelling here, these ideals are also evidently pertinent to experiences today, relocated and adapted to life in the capital city. Home is reconfigured and continuities negotiated between the generations. This is evident in efforts to uphold elder roles and respectability by the older members of 'scattered families'[12] in Lusozi who, despite ongoing uncertainties, seek to educate the younger generation, to mobilise support for their elderly relatives in the village and to heed their advice.[13]

The chapter opens with further context on ageing and intergenerational politics in Uganda. This context is then related to representative conversations about expectations of ageing, how present experiences in Lusozi deviate from them and how people work to uphold them on an everyday basis. This is then expanded through conversations with Ladit, a prominent Acholi elder in the neighbourhood. Ladit read the chapter and offered some additional explanatory notes about Acholi culture and dance, translated by Kilongeni; the most relevant sections are included in the appendix (page 49). This aims to depict a written sense of the ethnography as an ongoing dialogue, and also to stress the relevance of the discussion on the re-affirmation of ideals and practices in the 'dotcom era'. As Ladit writes, 'factors from within and other outside factors like Western culture have greatly affected our life'. In response, he adapts Acholi music and dance for relevance to young people in the diverse Kampala community. Overall this offers nuance to widespread conversations about declining respect for elders in the dotcom era, as well as ethnographic insight into the fluidity of aspirations for later life as they erode, withstand or swell with the 'dotcom wave', sometimes 'with novel outcomes'.[14]

Ageing in Uganda

With health and economic crises, as around the world, care infrastructures in Uganda are under increasing strain. Social support systems are typically reliant on mutual support between the generations,[15] through which parents educate their children, who in turn support them in later life;[16] as one older woman succinctly explained, 'they are supposed to support me because I supported them'. In today's economy, even if they are still motivated to do so, educated children may not be able to afford to support their parents.[17] The HIV/AIDS pandemic has also undermined the possibilities of intergenerational support, having led to the deaths of many people in the 'middle' generation of today, leaving grandparents with orphaned grandchildren and without care for themselves.[18] This situation underlies widely held concerns about the declining experience of older people among researchers of ageing in Africa,[19] advocacy organisations and NGOs, health workers and government bodies, and older people themselves.

In Uganda these concerns are heightened amid a shifting demographic context in terms of population ageing, in which older people are a growing and increasingly marginalised minority. This marginalisation is evident in reporting on these politico-demographic issues, with ageing being an explicit media focus precipitated by political events during the time of the research, debates between the ageing President and his youth-centric opposition reflecting broader tensions between the generations. In January 2018 Museveni, then 73, succeeded in extending the presidential age limit ahead of the 2021 elections.[20] Having already amended the constitutional two-term limit to serve what is now his sixth, this resolution met with much opposition – including corruption allegations, parliamentary chaos, suppressed demonstrations and social media campaigns.

The President and his opposition often referenced age categories, 'elder', 'grandparenthood' and 'youth', evoking a 'social imagination of power' and familial relationships.[21] For example, on his Twitter feed and in public speeches, Museveni addressed the people of Uganda as his '*bazukulu*'[22] or 'grandchildren'. Robert Kyagulanyi Ssentamu, popularly known as Bobi Wine, Opposition leader and proclaimed 'spokesman for Uganda's frustrated youth', termed the age limit debate 'a generational cause'.[23] Older political and economic leaders like Museveni are thought to withhold opportunities from the younger generation, maintaining their positions of power and preventing progress. Intergenerational relationships are thus charged with resentment, frustration, economic uncertainty and structural exclusion,[24] with older people often blamed for the 'hardships faced by the younger generation'[25] and younger people often associated with a sense of societal and moral decline.[26]

The social media tax, named the 'OTT tax' ('over the top tax'), similarly invoked intergenerational tensions in the public and political sphere. Among criticisms of the ageing President and his contemporaries denying opportunities to younger people, social media appeared as a central tool and object of the positioning of the young in place of old. The implementation of the tax provoked various petitions, including 'people power' protests led by Bobi Wine that attracted significant national and international media attention. During a national news item on NTV Uganda recording the protests, a microphone was denied to an older man, who was told by one of the young men, 'you're the people making us suffer'.

This story was of particular concern to a social gerontologist and representative on the Ugandan National Council of Older Persons I spoke with. He believed that the idea of older people as 'outdated is extending down, it's having an impact on people's opinions'. The committee for older persons that he has organised in his district just outside of Kampala expressed similar concerns. One older man exclaimed:

> This is terrible … if people power just means youth. It should be holistic, otherwise it can affect one section of society, and yet we are all in this together.

As in this response, being 'all in this together' is often characterised by the older people we worked with as a concept now disregarded by the younger generation, to the detriment of older people's experiences and society as a whole. The image of the microphone being denied to an older person exemplifies concerns about increasing contempt for older people and their knowledge, hierarchies of age that are discussed in the following sections.

Defining elders

The ASSA study initially proposed a focus on the experience of ageing for people in mid-life, between 45 and 70 years old, neither young nor elderly. In line with the World Health Organization (WHO), various researchers of ageing in East Africa set the boundary for 'old' at 50 and above due to the perceptions of their participants.[27] Some of the participants in this research would similarly determine 'oldness' to apply to those aged over 50 and 'elderly' to those over 60. However, according to many participants, including health workers, researchers of ageing[28] and age-based advocacy organisations in Kampala,[29] age is more likely to be determined by the experience and health of the individual, as well as their income and 'environment'. This has been understood by anthropologists as the 'local biology' of ageing or the 'bio-social' factors, where the body and its socio-cultural environment intersect, re-shaping experience throughout the life course.[30] Various participants consider that poverty, manual labour, alcohol use, poor nutrition and chronic illness can manifest as 'oldness', regardless of a person's age. As Edwin, a 43-year-old plumber, stated during an interview:

> *You know you can get somebody who is 25, but when you don't take care of your life, you drink excessively, you do other things wrong, you become old.*

The founder of The Aged Family Uganda (TAFU), an NGO for older people in Kampala, explained that 'middle age doesn't really exist here', as some people grow old before 45 if their health is bad or their lifestyle 'harsh' due to restricted access to food, medicine and care. 'Oldness' was also considered by some people to reflect a personal mindset or attitude towards life. At an event organised by TAFU for older people, 82-year-old Victor refused to describe himself as old. Despite visual impairment, he keeps in regular contact with his three children now living in West Africa, having made himself a braille phone directory. 'Age is just a number. I'm not youth, not aged, but mature.' He thinks age is defined by what you want to do and he wants to dance. He feels that people over 70 are forgotten; younger people believe that they have exceeded their life expectancy so they are 'already dead and cannot help you'. But he has seen that younger people than him have died, so he knows that it is not only age that kills people. 'Me, I don't believe I'm old – I've still got ideas!' He hopes to start a potato farm, and meanwhile keeps active with his housework and his young grandchildren.

Official and unofficial definitions of age are therefore defined by a variety of factors and are embedded in relationships[31] rather than being simply chronological.[32] As well as relational definitions of who is old, there are flexible notions of what it means to be old in relation to elder seniority.[33] An Acholi elder, for example, can be as young as 40 years old, depending on their life experience and family role. Acholi society is gerontocratic, with elders occupying leadership positions within their family, clan and community;[34] they have the authority to allocate land[35] and to mediate disputes.[36] The elders' decisions are taken on behalf of the collective, to be respected or enforced. Acholi elder leadership is defined beyond, and superior to, material status or level of education. Only respectable older people with applicable experience in their family and community can be nominated as an elder. Okot p'Bitek describes how older people who 'do not behave well, like little children' are derisively called '*la-pang cata*' or 'without direction', in order to encourage them to behave appropriately 'according to the culture'.[37] Equally, young Acholi people are described as '*odoko dano*' once they 'become human', when their personal conduct is manifest and in line with the 'fundamental ideas of society'.[38] Respect is therefore a key aspect of upholding expected conduct based on age, as discussed in the section below.

Respect and respectability

Many of the people we spoke with in Lusozi said that they feel increasingly respected as they age. Respect is shown through greeting, chatting, listening and the manner of approach. As 70-year-old Ssebowa told me, he can assess somebody's respect for him through the way in which they speak to him and whether they approach calmly, do not 'bark at him' and are not rude. Mabel, aged 51, feels respected 'because I'm *Jaja* (grandmother)'; she explained that people show respect by greeting her, talking to her 'when they find me on the way' or keeping quiet when she passes. Generally a humble manner is preferred, which can mean a quieter and slower approach indicating deference, while addressing the person in reference to their age and socially superior position such as '*muzee*' (old person). I saw this in the way Amor would translate my questions to our older participants in this calm manner, with a general question usually posed before mine: 'Muzee, we want to ask you a question about respect. Let me bring it like this…'

In Acholi culture, as in others across Uganda, this deference can also be shown through kneeling while greeting anyone of a higher social status than you, particularly younger people to anyone older or women to men. Kneeling implies respect not only for the other person but also for one's own social role; it suggests that a young person has had a 'good family upbringing' and has been taught how to greet people well. As we entered or left someone's home, Amor would generally do so on her knees, where I would typically be instructed to remain upright, demonstrating the everyday dispensations that applied to me as a guest and as a white person. However, during family meetings I would usually sit on the floor with the women of all ages while men sat on the chairs, starting and leading the discussions. In this way, men occupy physically higher positions within social spaces and also in terms of their public and domestic roles, such as in making decisions and speaking first, demonstrating the gendered dimensions of elder authority at household, community and political levels. This also implicates the 'complex social position'[39] that older women occupy, as will be expanded throughout this monograph.

Older people often said they enjoy being addressed as an elder, '*mama*', '*muzee*' (old man/woman) or '*jaja*' (grandfather/mother), as these terms signify that they are looked up to. As Amor's 57-year-old father Kilongeni explained, 'I appreciate it when they call me *muzee* … I feel great'. According to him and many others, 'anybody older than you, you have to respect'. When he was growing up, he thought people with the white hair he has now

> were the God people talk about … only later I learned that those are human beings like my grandfather. I respect them.

He explained that 'it's the way we're brought up', and that if you spend time with older people and offer them help, you will be rewarded in later life, perhaps even living longer yourself.

> The moral of the upbringing of the family must stand. Whether it is dotcom, old age, historical age, there must be respect for the elders because they say, like the Bible says, respect your mother and father, so that your number of days will be longer and all the other blessings you will get from them. Their long life is a representative of God for you.

Despite the established moral, religious and familial obligation for elder respect, in Lusozi we often heard of a general trend of declining respect for older people – particularly in the city, where it is thought 'today respect is given to people of material possession as opposed to age'. As Ahmed, a younger man prominent in the Muslim community in Lusozi put it:

> These days, they are not respected … by the time we reach the age of 15, we see them as … useless … Even if they try to show you that you do this, you tell them that I can't, are you my mother, are you my father, what?

Often, while identifying this trend 'these days', people would distinguish their own behaviour; as Ahmed commented, *'me myself, I do not do that'*.[40]

Concerns regarding the diminishing social status of older people[41] also invoke their established public authority, often said to be based on their knowledge and experience. There is a Luganda proverb, *'bukadde magezi'*, meaning 'old age is wisdom'.[42] Older people in Uganda have been described as 'repositories of knowledge', storytellers of their wisdom, inherited from ancestors or gained through extensive life experience.[43] This could include the experience of bringing up children or of agricultural insight and supervision.[44] As one younger man said, 'they have been around for longer, so they know what's what'.

A policeman named Geoffrey and his wife Judith told the story of his 'Grand Grand', his grandfather's mother who had recently died. Even though she was immobile, her 'lower part like a kid', from the waist up she was old and knowledgeable; Geoffrey gestured to show her upright posture, lifting his arms. She had 'a chunk of land' and often would give family advice, which 'you should always take seriously'. 'Even if you know more about the world, they have seen more than you and have wisdom,' he observed. As Geoffrey suggested of his great-grandmother, land ownership could influence the respectability and social status of older people,[45] connecting them to previous generations and knowledge of the past, as well as giving them authority over who has access in future.[46]

The proximity of older people to spirits and ancestors, being visibly blessed with long life and closer to death themselves, could also enhance their social status; the 'spiritual power derived from their experience to be feared and respected'.[47] Geoffrey and Judith explained that older people can curse or bless you, an ability that comes to some people, especially women, with age. Usually, it would be women in their seventies and eighties who 'have that spirit'. Their blessings can offer long life, with their demonstrable capacity to attain the same. For example, one older woman we interviewed blessed me by wishing that one day I would *'have skin and hair like hers'*, that I will grow old too. If an older woman curses you, you will 'feel it' until you ask for forgiveness; only then 'will things in your life start moving', suggesting that otherwise things remain challenging, artificially fixed in place and likely to fail. The underlying spiritual threat or opportunity when interacting with older people, especially those with authority and access to land, stresses the importance of showing respect to them, for the possibility of reward or retribution.[48]

The older people who we worked with in Lusozi often explained that younger people in their families and communities seek their advice 'all the time', which signifies respect and the social relevance of their knowledge. Many said that younger people sought their counsel, particularly regarding marital problems and bringing up children. They often explained how they sit with married couples to mediate domestic disputes with the aim of keeping their families together. As in one example of many, 45-year-old Abalo said she finds that people respect and greet her, and that both men and women would come to her for advice. They would ask for help in settling their quarrels, and she often advised women to respect their husbands and to stay in their marriages despite hardship. She would gather all her children together and advise them to follow her, which she expected they would do, advising them to love people, as *'love is the only straight route'*. This includes greeting people with respect, never fighting and always trying to help people, for which she commended Amor.

Some people described how they seek their parents' advice via the phone. Ojok Godfrey's mother uses her neighbours' phone to advise, or admonish, her 48-year-old son:

Ojok Godfrey: OK, parents, elders, are supreme, so there's no argument for most of them … even when you're an adult, parents can order you to stop or do certain things.
Interviewer: And you have to do it.
Ojok Godfrey: You have to do it… My mother will call me, summon me to the village and tell me to stop.
Interviewer: She has a phone?
Ojok Godfrey: She doesn't have a phone, but the people nearby have phones … She will call and tell them to call me. And chase me to the village. She'll tell you why she has called…You will feel it. It happened to me some time … that was nearly six or seven years ago, I used to drink a lot and she heard of it. She wanted to come … she called me to tell me that she was coming and she speaks only one language – Luo. She came to Kampala and looked for me and caught me.

Having been forced to leave his home in Gulu in 1991 ('I was lucky'), Ojok has since been a long-term resident in the neighbourhood. He had worked to become an engineer and his regular income had supported him, enabling him to invest in his own land and to build his home in the neighbourhood. Having been separated from his family home and values at a young age, he described how he now works to re-establish them in the city, for example in following his mother's advice. As a respected elder in the Lusozi community, he described how he would help to enact discipline and enforce respect, for example among Acholi men who had failed to provide for their families or those who were known to beat their wives.

> For us, if you do anything wrong, even when you're grown up to my age, if you are terribly wrong, then they will call men of equal weight or even strength to come and cane you ... If you don't stop, we'll come again one day. Because when we call you for caning, we just call you, rough you up, cane you, and then you must apologise. Even me. In our society, we still have respect, there's certain things you can't do. Especially in public.

This demonstrates how values of respect could be articulated and enacted 'in public'. Evidently, as highlighted by feminist legal scholar Sylvia Tamale and expanded below, such community-based approaches hold practical possibilities for seeking gender justice, such as through the resolution of marital disputes or management of gender-based violence.[49] This can also mean that women remain 'vulnerable when these conventions break down'.[50]

The following section further illustrates the role of Acholi elders in the city, with a particular focus on an elder widely considered to be the key authority on Acholi matters in Lusozi, to whom I would often be referred by others. As an older man with knowledge, status and experience, Ladit is considered to hold a position of sufficient authority to speak on behalf of his community, both past and present. The pseudonym 'Ladit' is the name of senior respected male elders responsible for their household and for resolving disputes and representing the village,[51] much as Ladit does in Lusozi today. He offers an established perspective of Acholi ageing ideals, while also working to bring them to life for the younger generation.

Ladit (elder)

Ojok believes that Ladit is the person responsible for 'maintaining our culture, keeping it alive in town ... he knows a lot, a lot, a lot, a lot about Acholi tradition'. Ladit had lived in Lusozi for around 30 years since fleeing his home in Kitgum during the civil war. He was a willing teacher throughout the research, regularly welcoming Amor and I at the dance group's practice, hosting us in his home, telling us stories. He even allowed us to join as a member of his savings group Togetherness is

Strength (TIS), discussed in Chapter 4. He viewed the time he gave us as fulfilling his role as an elder, to educate the younger generation about Acholi tradition.

Throughout our first meeting cited here Ladit outlined his perspective on problems in the Lusozi community and in Uganda more broadly. He related these problems to the loss of Acholi values and practices, which he believed the government should work to reinstate. He said he finds that people are becoming more individualised and less communal, which was causing problems:

> *In our time we loved people, and a problem affecting individuals would be handled communally unlike today ... Tradition brings people together, we would handle situation communally including children's upbringing.*[52]

Ladit feels that elders are no longer respected. He attributed this partly to some of their behaviours, such as drunkenness or causing disputes: '*They are not trustworthy*'. He said that many young people would come to him for advice due to his good conduct in public, for example asking him about family life and marriage, but he would often find that his suggestions are not implemented.

He described how, in the past, people would congregate around the fireplace every evening for '*wang-oo*': '*the place young ones would receive teachings for life*'. Young girls would be taught by older women and young boys by the older men;[53] as a result '*children would grow up knowing what is expected of them*'. Now Ladit and other Acholi elders in Lusozi lament the lack of available time or space to commit to *wang-oo* meetings. He thought the younger generation had become increasingly 'Westernised' at the '*expense of our very beautiful, peaceful, traditional communal life*'.

> *Today, we are copying everything from the Western world, and you know things you are not used to, you never handle it well ... Children are exposed to funny, funny information on television with all weird characters and we cannot control it. These have led to high moral decay in the African society.*

We would often find Ladit at home watching music videos, nature documentaries, Premier League football and Nigerian soaps, or chatting on WhatsApp on his phone. He said he believes that technology such as television, phones and social media has '*brought the world together on a positive note*', with better entertainment and faster communication, but that it has also 'created more problems' for elders. According to Ladit's interpretation, shared by many other participants in Lusozi, individualistic and materialistic Western values were being broadcast and appropriated by the younger generation, to the detriment of respect for elders and their knowledge. To Ladit, *'over-copying'* was evident in infidelity and sexual promiscuity, alcohol abuse, the growth of the evangelical Church and the imposition of 'child rights'. The last in part venerates men's patriarchal authority over women and children, and in part rejects the universalistic assumptions implicit in Eurocentric 'rights' discourses and initiatives, which can overlook situated priorities and possibilities, discussed further in Chapter 7 on co-operative morality.

Ladit cited increasing land disputes as evidence of declining co-operation. He felt that the formal legal approaches to customary land disputes were *'OK, but the judgements in most cases lack wisdom'*. Ladit explained how elders used to act as an effective law-making council within the community; they would decide an approach, prioritising communal good, and it would be respected and put in place, leading to social harmony. Tamale agrees, finding Acholi community justice to place emphasis on good relations, social cohesion and balance.[54] There has been extensive scholarly discussion regarding customary Acholi justice mechanisms as a way of dealing with the reintegration of former LRA recruits[55] and reconstructing the community following the civil war, to 'promote healing in a culturally sensitive way'.[56] In particular, efforts were made to formalise restitutive ceremonies called *mato oput* or 'drinking the bitter herb', to conclude quarrels, and *nyuouo tong gweno* or 'stepping on an egg', to welcome back those who have been away from home for a long time.[57] I happened upon both of these ceremonies during visits to Amor's home village, evidence that these are habitual and everyday practices, called upon and enacted when useful.

The implementation of these ceremonies after the war has been criticised as an instrumentalisation of practices otherwise fluid and diverse, mirroring earlier colonial efforts to incorporate customs into the indirect administration of British protectorate through government appointed Acholi chiefs or *'Rwodi moo'*.[58] This supports the need for a grounded approach to the articulation and practice of ideals, observing them as they emerge through everyday action rather than reifying or taking them out of context. As Finnström put it in his ethnography of wartime in northern Uganda:

> It is important to note that drinking the bitter root *(mato oput)* is not simply a tradition of some glorious past ... These practices, far from

being dislocated in a past that no longer exists, have always continued to be situated socially. They are called upon and performed to address present concerns ... with time they shift in meaning and appearance.[59]

Ladit shows how Acholi values and practices can be flexibly adapted to life in the city, despite intensifying encounters with the world through the internet, mobile phones and social media. He sees it as his responsibility to educate the younger generation about their *'beautiful, peaceful tradition'* of respect and togetherness, and of storytelling through music and dance, re-contextualised in the city. At 67 years old, Ladit hoped that his children would grow old like him, so they can see what he sees and pass on knowledge of how things are done.

From Ladit's perspective, values of respect and conviviality, enabling ways of living and working together, may rhetorically be associated with the *'beautiful and peaceful'* past, while they are also actively lived and made meaningful. In Figure 2.1 below, he introduces a cultural group he set up to share the knowledge he gained from his ancestors with the children born in Kampala. The group perform Acholi and Ugandan dances at various events and they practise outside his home every Sunday evening. They also use television programmes and social media platforms such as Facebook and YouTube to promote their work. The film shows the group practising in Lusozi. Thee young men play various instruments such as an arched harp called *adungu*, wooden drums or *engoma* of varying size, skin

Figure 2.1 A still from the film 'We as elders have a duty'. https://bit.ly/44P9rHt.

hide forged with rope and pins, while the young women, aged between 13 and 30, dance with graceful and rhythmic movements, praise and ululation. As p'Bitek puts it, Acholi dance expresses meanings attributed to social life and the world, as they are both lived and celebrated here and now.[60] Ladit says in the film that *'each Acholi dance has a purpose'*, as he has outlined in the appendix: the *'bwola'* dance, performed at functions or for Acholi traditional chiefs, described by p'Bitek as 'the most formal and controlled' of Acholi dances;[61] *'larakaraka'*, the courtship dance; the *'apitti'* dance for married women; and the *'dingi dingi'* for young women.

Ladit also explains in the film that *'each Acholi song has a message for people to connect to'*, instrumental in the process of education and remembrance. The lyrics might tell the story of a particular person, containing a message or lesson regarding life events such as marriage, war or family. During the time I spent in Amor's home village, the women in her family sang many songs for us and danced in the evening. Each song had a different moral and meaning; a song of praise for the village; a song celebrating brave decision-making by a youth who had followed the advice of his elders; a love story about a couple who stayed together and became rich. The most popular songs have circulated across villages in northern Uganda and are remembered up to the present day, adapting 'stories of the past in the present'. As another Acholi elder and senior member of TIS described it:

> Ours, people explain to you why people dance, ours it's like the way of recording an event. It is like our book. It's a way of writing our things. So in that dance, there is a meaning to that thing. Instead of going to write down, you just sing about it, and it remains in your head. So that was the meaning of it. It is a recording of an event. And the meaning of what they're saying is there in that time.

Ladit's group would also perform music and dance from across the country, reflecting the diverse backgrounds of the area and group members. At intervals during the Sunday practice, the men playing the music would relocate their instruments or change formation, joined by an *endere* (flute) or *ensasi* (marakas), depending on the Ugandan region the song came from. Some of the other Acholi elders in Lusozi criticised the 'modernity' of Ladit's group, which includes music from all over the country, and does not obligate the dancers to wear traditional Acholi dress. As one 58-year-old Acholi elder said, 'it's coated in some plastic', in contrast with other groups or dancers in the village who maintain a more 'real' or 'pure' tradition. However, as shown in Figures 2.1 and 2.2, Ladit's

Figure 2.2 Ladit's dance group practising outside his former home in Lusozi. Photo by Charlotte Hawkins.

traditional teachings were clearly relevant, popular and productive for the young people involved. This included the young male musicians and female dancers, some of whom had travelled abroad for performances and paid their school fees thanks to money earned through the group. It also included the children from the neighbourhood who would come and watch them practise every Sunday evening, attempting to mimic the moves, and occasionally facing Ladit's discipline. As an older Acholi woman who lives in Lusozi observed:

> They train them … They like it so much …We did not drop it down, even though it's mixed up here.

Music and dance can therefore express social significance beyond ritual or enjoyment, framing both individual identity and group belonging across generations[62] while accommodating the 'conviviality' of diverse urban neighbourhoods like Lusozi. They are a key part of the everyday ways people invoke, celebrate and preserve difference,[63] 'dynamically adapting to the challenging contemporary context'[64] and promoting the mutuality of the continuous and the new.

Conclusion

Ladit's storytelling expresses a sense of loss of the ideals he grew up with: respect for elders, the passing of knowledge between generations, collaboration and togetherness. Like others, he showed how respect would be given to elders who have earned it, by respecting themselves and others, as evident through their personal conduct. Respect is shown to them through greeting, a calm manner and tone of voice, and through seeking their advice. Ladit noted a decline in elder respect and respectability, which he believed had contributed to the 'moral degradation' of their society and the younger generation growing up within it.[65] With declining respect and togetherness comes a worsening experience of ageing, along with disrupted hierarchies of age and intergenerational care practices. This sense of decline would often be related to a shifting context of epidemics, urbanisation, population growth and access to 'dotcom' knowledge. It would particularly apply to the city, being 'mixed up', materialistic and youth-centric.

Ladit's concerns were widely shared among elders in the community, health practitioners, policy-makers and advocates, and researchers of ageing in Uganda and in sub-Saharan Africa more broadly.[66] The debate around the presidential age limit and the 'youth revolution' exemplifies, reflects and reinforces related intergenerational tensions. While a chronological understanding of 'oldness' is too fixed in relation to dynamic personal and social determinants of age,[67] categories of age such as 'elder' and 'youth' are evidently socially and politically significant, invoked to elicit ideas of power and dissent.[68]

In educating the younger generation, Ladit worked to maintain the role of elder in the city. Like others, he would seek to uphold respect and respectability, regardless of the wider trends he observed. Ojok similarly explained how he would enforce respect for the family among his peers, and also how he would seek and respect the advice from his mother at home. Kilongeni and Ssebowa also described how they feel respected by their children and other younger people in the community, despite noting a more general trend of declining respect more broadly. Younger people would similarly differentiate themselves from others they consider to be disrespectful of their elders. Rather than being fixed in an 'idealised past',[69] values of respect and relatedness are actively adapted for contemporary relevance and circulated to 'keep them alive in town', (re)generating meanings for both young and old people.[70] The 'aliveness' is exemplified by Ladit's dance group and their regular practice in Lusozi, 'culture' as it is productively lived in the here and now.[71]

This ethnography therefore depicts the ongoing fluidity of social ideals or customs, adapted to the dotcom era and to which dotcom is adapted in turn. In doing so, it contributes to critiques of the colonial reification of custom, on which fixity has been imposed to serve a language of authority and administration, sustaining inequalities.[72] This ethnographic evidence therefore disrupts a chronological, enlightenment understanding of historical progress or 'development', favouring instead a messier, ever-evolving process based on interconnectedness. As Nyamnjoh shows, such interconnectedness is particularly relevant in 'frontier' urban contexts in Africa that 'represent histories of mobility, cultural encounters, negotiation and flux'.[73] Conviviality, which preserves the possibilities implicit in interconnection through uncertainty, locates a 'middle ground' between 'tradition and modernity', promoting the 'concessional mutuality' of social continuity and change.[74]

As shown in this chapter, present experiences of ageing are understood through shared ideals which are themselves collaborative and in flux, adapted to the city in its diversity. Through this process, 'dotcom' is domesticated within existing ideals, which themselves are adapted to accommodate 'dotcom'. While being a primary tool of dotcom, the mobile phone is actually shown to accommodate this respect. Parents are able to share advice for their children despite distances. As discussed in more detail in Chapter 5, children provide for their parents at home thanks to mobile money remittances, thereby upholding expectations of elder care. In Chapter 3, the focus on older participants' everyday lives continues, particularly in relation to their working routines. In bringing the focus to work, Chapter 3 details the gendered healthcare implications of ongoing care and financial responsibilities that compel older women to reconfigure family roles, both pragmatically and morally, according to wider economic conditions. This again disrupts linear life course expectations, along with the ideal of later life as a time of rest and retirement.

Appendix

Ladit's response

> *In response to reading this chapter, Ladit shared the following written observations about Acholi dance that he wanted to include. Kilongeni worked with him to translate them into English.*

Acholi music acts as a library of books for recording events like love stories, wars, mourning lost relatives, and disasters like '*bonyo*', when the locusts invaded and destroyed all the crops in Acholi sub-region (in the early nineteenth century, almost 100 years prior to the locust invasion in the region at the time of writing in early 2020). The songs about the HIV/AIDS pandemic, the '*lukeme*'/ '*adungu*' songs, are played even in Christian churches found in Acholiland. These songs are meaningful, unlike today, when they copy the Western style of hip hop, R&B, dancehall etc for the dotcom era.

At the end of harvest every year, the Acholi's relax their body and mind with a number of dances like '*dingi dingi*', which is performed by young girls below 18 years. They are extremely speedy and hard to perfect, even at that age bracket. Typical instruments are played by talented men, including the calabash '*awal*', drums '*vul*' and flute '*olere*'. This dance is to prepare the young girls for marriage when they clock 18 years and above.

The *arakaraka* dance is the most popular, enjoyed by people of almost all age group but is meant to be for courtship; if your daughter or son dances for more than two years without getting married, then they must be the ugliest girl or boy in the community or just unlucky and should now settle for an already married man or formerly married woman. Costumes are similar to *dingi dingi*.

Courtship for marriage was then done in a very decent manner, by identifying a girl at dances, on market days and any other organised events. The boy arranges a visit to the girl's home to propose, the process usually takes a period of about one to two years, during which time they can learn background of each other with the full knowledge and advice and guidance of both parents. This can prevent divorce, unlike today where people date on Facebook, WhatsApp and via phone calls. The process can now be as short as one day, a period too short to know each other's status and family background. Premature co-habiting is leading to so many divorces, as well as deaths related to HIV/AIDS.

Other dances include:

- *Apitti* dance (*myel apitti*): this is only for married women, done with very respectable dress '*mirinda*', well-folded African '*kitenge*' to show their happiness in marriage, good harvest, childbearing and upbringing or even the number of domestic animals in their family.
- *Bwola* dance (*myel bwola*): a royal dance performed to the Acholi traditional chiefs either during harvest, at a traditional function or by school going children to enable them to learn and do it when they

grow up in the future. Acholi dances are meant to be original without modification, barefoot, bare chested with nothing to hide, just to show people you are the best and fit. In comparison, therefore, it is almost impossible to mix the traditional dance with the dotcom dance of these days.

This is a factor that brings people together, the Acholi traditional dances and songs. I am not being too proud of it, but I say Acholi have the richest culture in the world like *'bwola'*, *'Lara karaka'*, *'dingi dingi'*, *'apitti'*, to mention a few. It also acts as a way to express happiness, emotions, releasing stress, recording events in good or bad times.

In conclusion, therefore, the world has changed Acholi ways of life drastically. Because of this, the dotcom generation now respect any person with money better than their elders. Even the poor ageing elders have a fear of correcting their children because they can withhold financial assistance from them. These factors from within and other outside factors like Western culture have greatly affected our life.

Notes

1. p'Bitek and Girling 2019, 14; Finnström 2008, 80.
2. p'Bitek 1970, 11.
3. Finnström 2008, 32.
4. Finnström 2008, 82; Mamdani 1996; Nyanzi 2013; p'Bitek 1986; Tamale 2020; Allen 2007; Mbembe 2002.

    This colonial, anthropological 'Othering' has 'denied coevalness' (Fabian 1983; Clifford 1986; Robbins 2013) and falsely codified 'tradition' and difference to sustain inequities (Mbembe 2002, 246).

    For example, Mamdani (1996) has outlined how the colonial framing of the 'customary' in rural areas, such as through chieftaincies and land ownership, ensured the stability of colonial rule. This includes enforced market distinctions between 'urban' and 'rural', direct and indirect rule through 'civilised law' and exclusion thereof. Equally, 'customary' is a language for resisting the institutional legacies of colonialism, meaning it can be both emancipatory and authoritarian (ibid.). Anthropologists working in the Acholi sub-region after the LRA war have analysed discussions around Acholi ideals as a 'romantic' nostalgia for a more communitarian past in the village. For example, Porter terms this 'a vision of a kind of continuous static past' (Porter 2019, 1025), through which people assert their identity, shared values and ideals, reflecting a 'human tendency to think of the past as better, simpler or purer' (Porter 2019, 1027). In contrast, Tamale resists analyses where a celebration of African values represents 'a naïve desire to return to a romanticised pre-colonial past' (Tamale 2020, 21), arguing that instead it represents a 'lived experience' of moral traditions related to human dignity, communitarianism and egalitarianism, which hold the potential for the restoration of social justice and dignity (Tamale 2020, 229). Pype has similarly noted a 'practical nostalgia to restore the esteem of elders and create conviviality' in Kinshasha, DRC (Pype 2017b, 169).

5. Allen 2007.
6. Allen 2007.
7. Tamale 2020, 161.
8. Nyamnjoh 2017.
9. Wallman and Bantebya-Kyomuhendo 1996.

10. The Refugee Law Project Working Paper, 2005. 'Peace first, justice later: Traditional justice in Northern Uganda'. Accessed 10 March 2021. https://www.refugeelawproject.org/files/working_papers/RLP.WP17.pdf, 3.

   As one research paper on 'traditional justice' towards the end of the war put it, 'the social infrastructure of the north has been almost completely destroyed'.
11. Allen 1988; Porter 2019.
12. Coe 2014; Sigona et al. 2015.
13. Changes to the social ideal of 'wise and respected elders' has been studied extensively by anthropologist Sjaak van der Geest in an area of rural Ghana (1997a, b; 2011). He argues, as do participants in this research, that the social value of older people is declining and is increasingly measured in terms of their financial capacity. In a 2011 study on 'loneliness and distress in old age', he found that 'the young rarely come to them [old people] for advice … they are not interested in their knowledge' (2011, 71). Van der Geest terms this 'a social death prior to death' (2011, 73), an indicator of the isolation and marginalisation of older people. In contrast, as outlined in Chapter 2, many participants in this research explained how they had many younger people coming to them for advice, signifying the social relevance of their knowledge. This contrast initiated further enquiry into the ways the elder role is upheld in the city.
14. Nyamnjoh 2005, 40.
15. Golaz, Wandera and Rutaremwa 2017.
16. Caldwell 1976; Hampshire and Randall 2005.
17. Whyte 2017, 246.
18. Hoffman and Pype 2016; Kuteesa et al. 2012; Nankwanga, Neema and Phillips 2013; van der Geest 1997a, b.
19. Nankwanga, Neema and Phillips 2013; Maharaj 2020; Aboderin 2004; Nzabona, Ntozi and Rutaremwa 2016; Oppong 2006; Whyte 2017; van der Geest 1997a, b; Maniragaba et al. 2019.
20. *The Economist* 2018. 'Museveni ratifies bill to remove presidential age limit'. Accessed 7 October 2019. http://country.eiu.com/article.aspx?articleid=1456285329&Country=Uganda&topic=Politics&subtopic=F_5.
21. Durham 2000.
22. Twitter, Kaguta Museveni. Accessed 11 March 2020. https://twitter.com/kagutamuseveni/status/1321147670849867778?lang=en.
23. Generational struggles are said to have frequently characterised politics on the African continent in this way. Recent political movements in particular draw on the social category of youth as not only a symbol of the future, but also as the 'makers and breakers' of nation building (Fredericks 2014). For example, in Senegal, youth opposition movements successfully overturned a constitutional amendment which would have allowed the elderly incumbent President Abdoulaye Wade's son to inherit his power (Honwana 2012, 9). Chants were heard at the protests during the 2012 elections; 'Enough of the old man, the old man is dead and buried … The old man must go' (Fredericks 2014). As with Bobi Wine in Uganda, the movement was popularised through music.
24. Thieme 2018.
25. Hoffman and Pype 2016, 47.
26. Whyte and Acio 2017.
27. de Klerk and Moyer 2017; Kuteesa et al. 2012; Velkoff and Kowal 2007.
28. Thanks to Dr Annet Nankwanga, Dr Betty Kwagala and Dr Abel Nzabona at Makerere University for introducing categories of age in the Ugandan context.
29. The Aged Family Uganda (TAFU), Uganda Reach the Aged Association (URAA), HelpAge Uganda, Health Nest Uganda (HENU).
30. Lock 1994; Livingston 2003.
31. Anthropological literature on 'age-grades' and initiation rites in pastoral East and Southern Africa also demonstrate the cultural constitution of social categories of age, and contradictory elements such as power conflicts that arose thereof (Durham 2000, 115). For example, Evans-Pritchard famously described the age group characteristics of the Nuer, the 'age-set system', and how lineage organisation was established through age initiations based on the father's authority and the need to show respect to older 'age-sets', which regulated social interaction (Evans-Pritchard 1967).
32. See Livingston 2003.
33. Hoffman and Pype 2016.

34. Finnström 2001.
35. Whyte and Acio 2017.
36. Parkin 1969, 144.
37. p'Bitek 1986, 28.
38. p'Bitek 1986, 28.
39. Burgess and Campbell 2016.
40. Porter and colleagues have identified a similar tendency in their study of 'intergenerational encounters' via the phone in various fieldsites across Africa, where young people differentiate their own more respectful behaviour from others (Porter et al. 2015, 44).
41. Porter et al. 2015, 44.
42. Nyanzi 2009.
43. Nahemow 1979.
44. Livingston 2003, 25.
45. Nzabona and Ntozi 2017, 3694.
46. Livingston has also shown how physical infirmity is particularly associated with wisdom, authority and proximity to ancestors in Botswana, suggestive of a capacity to give blessings or curses (2003, 212). See also Whyte and Acio 2017, 25.
47. Van der Geest 2011, 71.
48. Elsewhere this social and spiritual power of elderly women derived from their experience has also been associated with fear, suspicion and a resulting precarity and marginality, as shown in Livingston's work in Botswana (2003, 226), and in Pype's work in Kinshasha (2017, 162). Finnström has also shown that Acholi women in general are considered to be particularly exposed to spiritual forces and therefore dangerous (Finnström 2008, 184).
49. Tamale 2020, 161.
50. Burgess and Campbell 2016, 50.
51. Girling 2019, 75.
52. NB This interview is translated, as indicated with italics.
53. Girling 2019, 75.
54. Tamale 2020, 160.
55. Allen 2007.
56. Whyte et al. 2016, 46.
57. Hovil and Quinn 2005, 24.
58. Allen 2007, 1991b.
59. Finnström 2008, 297–9.
60. p'Bitek 1986, 22.
61. p'Bitek 1986, 37.
62. Neveu Kringelbach 2013, 207.
63. Gilroy 2009.
64. Nyamnjoh 2017, 261–2.
65. Kyaddondo 2008.
66. Nankwanga, Neema and Phillips 2013; Maharaj 2020; Aboderin 2004; Nzabona, Ntozi and Rutaremwa 2016; Oppong 2006; Whyte 2017; van der Geest 1997a, b; Maniragaba et al. 2019.
67. Freeman and Coast 2014, 1138; Hoffman and Pype 2016, 4; Kyaddondo 2008, 27.
68. Durham 2000.
69. Livingston 2003; Porter 2019.
70. Finnström 2008; Pype 2017b.
71. p'Bitek 1986.
72. Finnström 2008, 82; Mamdani 1996; Nyanzi 2013; p'Bitek 1986; Tamale 2020; Allen 2007; Mbembe 2002.
73. Nyamnjoh 2017, cf Ekechi, Kopytoff and Falola 1988, 3–17.
74. Nyamnjoh 2017.

3
Age and work

Introduction

Long-standing categories of age in an 'industrialised world' assign certain activities of economic production to particular life stages:[1] education and childhood, a time of dependence; work and adulthood, a time of independence; and retirement and rest in old age, which in Uganda is said to be ideally a time of interdependence.[2] This chapter will show the complexities of this linear conception of ageing and work, disrupted both by socially negotiated categories of age, as outlined in Chapter 2, and the wider economy. In particular, this chapter will address the typical assumption of old age as a time of rest and retirement.

Many of the people I worked with in their forties, fifties, sixties and above have ongoing care and financial responsibilities for both older and younger generations – their children, grandchildren, their elderly parents and themselves. They often discussed plans to move back to their rural homes to retire as soon as possible, in the meantime maintaining regular phone contact with older relatives living there. Despite providing care for both older and younger generations, many people stated a preference to avoid 'becoming a burden' on their children's already stretched time and resources, a familiar refrain encountered by the 'Anthropology of Smartphones and Smart Ageing' (ASSA) team in their various fieldsites around the world. Like the majority of people living in Kampala, many of the older people we worked with ran self-owned businesses started with personal savings, generally based on trade and relying on physical work. This limits their access to formal social protection, meaning that livelihoods can compromise health and health can compromise livelihoods – a particular concern as people age and their health declines. Sometimes people referred to their work as 'gambling', depicting a sense of risk and improvisation, and blurring traditional boundaries between 'work' and 'games'.[3]

This chapter demonstrates that work is not necessarily distinct from socialising or domestic life, and businesses in fact often depend on both. Throughout the chapter the narrative shifts between various activities to emphasise the diversity and interconnections between people's livelihoods. This depicts the everyday 'social texture within which the informal economy operates',[4] and the (gendered) relationships within households and across the community on which it often depends. There is a particular focus on the experiences of older women who continue to work and provide for their families in later life, contrary to stereotypes of ageing and work in the city.[5] This 'holistic, small-scale perspective'[6] on everyday self- and mutual support through work is situated within the wider political economy, which relies heavily on informal networks or 'social infrastructures',[7] as participants themselves often expressly indicate and reflect upon. This shows the active role that older people often play within these urban social infrastructures and in navigating ageing and work in the city. It also implicates the role of wider political factors in everyday lives, especially in relation to community-based co-operation,[8] which is both necessitated and undermined – a tension that will be further explored in the chapters to follow. This in turn offers insight into how people creatively navigate the narrower spaces of urban life, spaces increasingly squeezed and further pressed by ongoing pandemics and cost of living and environmental crises.

While market values have increased in many countries around the world, including Uganda, this has not always led to an increase in salaried employment. This 'jobless growth'[9] excludes many people from involvement in circulations of global capital, disrupts the relationship between people and the state, gives rise to new uncertainties[10] and, significantly here, also relies on unpaid labour. This can include domestic work, assistance from relatives and (self-) care practices.

In this chapter, as throughout the monograph, I focus on older people's situated perspectives on managing uncertainties around health, work, social protection, self and family responsibilities. Arguably this is an increasingly pertinent perspective around the world, as public services are de-funded, and as older populations and cities grow. 'Gambling' in place of formal social security such as pensions is applicable across global economies and urban contexts, particularly in relation to retirement as an increasingly unattainable luxury around the world and for future generations. Amid these global yet situated histories of ageing, the everyday working practices of older people in Lusozi do not represent a differentiated experience. The ordinary, pragmatic and relational mitigation of everyday uncertainties is a shared urban reality across locations and generations, at once a systemic and specific experience.[11]

Work in the city

The ways demographic and socio-economic shifts are disrupting expectations for older people's everyday lives are manifest in various ways around the world. As evident in other ASSA fieldsites, activities associated with old age are being redefined, as in Ireland, where reduced family obligations have increased the capacity of older people to take up independent hobbies.[12] Many of the researchers on the team observed how global and urban migration is 'scattering' families[13] who then increasingly rely on smartphones to remain connected in later life (Otaegui in Chile; Walton in Italy; Haapio-Kirk in Japan). The same is true in Lusozi, where many older people moved to work, and now almost universally aspire to move home to their region of origin, once school fees are paid and enough money has been saved.

As with the youth focus of work and technology, Kampala itself is commonly considered to be 'a youthful place'. As the scholar-activist and medical anthropologist Stella Nyanzi has noted in her work with 'widowed mama-grannies' in Kampala,[14] the capital city is often stereotyped as a place for 'younger, able-bodied people who can hustle and innovate in competition for limited resources'. For the majority of people who participated in this research, Kampala is not seen as a 'home' but as a place to work and for children to get an education, while the village is a place for retiring, to spend time with family and to live off the land. Through the experiences and aspirations of ageing in Lusozi today, certain geographies are assigned to particular stages of the life course, informing an age-based migration from the village to the city and back again. As Ladit explained:

> *I am ageing and so I have very little to do here in town now. I want to go back home... I am gathering some resources now and I will soon go back home. I will not stay here forever, especially when it's safe now to go home. But the young people can still remain here because they are still able to do some work here – not me any more. I have to go back home... In the real context of life, Lusozi can never be seen as a home. Yes, I have my children here and my own family, but I never see Lusozi as a home in any way. A home is combination of things, including having extended families and cultural practices around you.*

As well as a preference to leave behind the economic demands of life in Kampala, there is a social expectation for people to return to their regional home in old age. As a catechist in Lusozi put it, the 'time will come when we have to go to our indigenous home, we have to settle', or as the local football coach said, 'It's where I belong'. Ideally a home and garden will have been prepared and money saved for farming and healthcare. As Nyanzi states:

> Dignity demands a retreat (with pension in hand) to a comfortable home tucked away in some remote rural district.[15]

Yet old age pensions are mostly only accessible for retired government employees on formal contracts or long-term private-sector employees with savings in the National Social Security Fund (NSSF). According to UN statistics, only seven per cent of people over the statutory retirement age of 55 in Uganda are enrolled in a registered pension scheme.[16]

With the exception of 'Social Assistance Grants for Empowerment' (SAGE), there are limited state provisions for those without pensions or savings. SAGE is a senior citizens' grant, awarded to those over 65, which provides 25,000 UGX (£5) on a monthly basis. After the pilot phase in 2010 to 2015, a further phased roll-out was planned with the goal of covering all people over the age of 65,[17] as was ongoing at the time of the research, including many districts in northern Uganda. Evaluations have found the grant to enact positive change in the lives of older beneficiaries, despite the limited coverage and amount and poor accessibility.[18] The Uganda Reach the Aged Association (URAA), an NGO for older persons, monitored the implementation of SAGE and found it to be 'miraculously' successful in preventing extreme poverty in old age[19] – although among some older people encountered in northern Uganda, the requirement to travel to a centre to collect the grant via payment machines, as well as the need for a national security ID card, can limit accessibility. Additional assistance from NGOs, often international or faith-based organisations, is mostly scattered and short-term.[20]

The 'informal economy'

Since the 1970s, what is widely known as the 'informal economy' has been a major source of income in the Global South, particularly in sub-Saharan Africa.[21] 'Informality' refers to a range of activities unregistered by the state, including household and communal livelihoods.[22]

As unregistered and largely untaxed economic activities, 'informal' work can often be characterised as 'deviant' or exceptional[23] – despite the fact that it is intrinsic to the economic system,[24] which has long depended on it. As economic anthropologist Keith Hart notes, the informal includes the 'negation of the form', such as crime or tax evasion, as well as 'variable or unspecified content of the form', such as the completion of established consumer chains via street vending.[25] This chapter will focus on the latter, demonstrating instances in which 'informal' businesses are intertwined with, and supportive of, the official economy.

The 'informal sector' makes up the majority of the economy in Uganda, suggesting that it is the 'real' yet unofficial economy.[26] The National Labour Force Survey 2016/17[27] found that 41 per cent of the working population work in subsistence agriculture; of those who do not, 85 per cent work in the informal sector, which generates over half of national GDP. This contributes to Uganda being ranked the third highest nation in the Global Entrepreneurship Monitor (GEM) in 2014, with 28 per cent of adults owning their own businesses.[28] It also means that Uganda has one of the lowest tax-to-GDP ratios in the region, at 12.6 per cent.[29] In Kampala 78 per cent of the capital's workforce, and the majority of participants in Lusozi, are self-employed within this heterogenous 'informal sector'.

According to the UBOS 'Informal Sector Survey',[30] and as commonly seen in Lusozi, this includes a range of businesses largely based on trade, such as hawking, vending and taxi driving, hotels and restaurants, and manufacturing – including metalwork, tailoring, charcoal distribution and alcohol brewing.[31] The diversity of everyday activities, working routines and access to social protection was often reflected on by participants; as a 56-year-old market vendor put it, *'in our community here, we're all living different lives'*. The informal businesses in Kampala cluster in low-income residential areas such as Lusozi, where they are often household-based, with proximity to customers and markets.[32] In their 1996 study of 'Kampala women getting by',[33] Sandra Wallman and Grace Bantebya-Kyomuhendo have also noted that the informal economy provides opportunities for women in particular. In Uganda 65 per cent of informal businesses are started with personal savings, 19 per cent with outside contributions and seven per cent with loans from family, friends or Savings and Credit Cooperative Organisations (SACCOs).[34] Like those introduced here and many others, people risk capital to set up their own business. Only two per cent of people working in the informal economy have written contracts,[35] reflecting a shortfall in protection policies such as paid holiday, sick leave and pension schemes. This can mean that healthcare requirements pose a threat to income – a particular consideration as people age and their physical health declines.

Informal employment in Uganda is primarily a source of livelihood for the urban poor. The median income of formally employed people has been found to be twice as much as those informally employed, and recent World Bank calculations suggest that 93 per cent of informal firm owners in Kampala are below the international poverty line of $1.90 income per day.[36] They have concluded that informal work is not a form of tax evasion, as incomes are generally below the national tax bracket of 10,000,000 UGX (£2,135). Furthermore, studies conducted in street markets in Kampala, considered 'hubs' of the informal economy,[37] find that they represent a 'hybrid' economy, with formalisation through ground rents and also through the required registration of mobile phones. The latter are found to be invaluable for communicating with clients and suppliers, and for managing payments via mobile money.[38]

This situation challenges the political amalgamation of the 'informal sector' and the strategic employment of certain policies of (de)regulation. For example, in Kampala, central government sporadically supports the resistance of informal economic groups to formal city regulation as a way of gaining votes before an election.[39] The opposite is also true: in recent years there has been a clampdown on roadside vending, which is subject to punitive measures including imprisonment and fines. Older women hawking fruits, for example, could face the night in jail and the loss of their investment and earnings. As shown below, others in the community would often condemn this criminalisation as evidence of an unjust government willing to worsen already challenging circumstances, as figureheads of a system that fails both to provide formal economic opportunities and to protect those required to make a living outside of them. As this chapter will show, 'social infrastructures' often make up for the shortfalls in public provision, such as through care, reciprocal support between neighbours and connections for seeking work and resources.

Gambling

This sense of political neglect was a concern of the 'Parliament' in Lusozi – a group of men aged between 30 and 60 who would congregate on plastic chairs in a sheltered area by the main road. They think theirs is better than the real parliament of Uganda because they consider the 'common man': 'they say we're OK. But we're not OK'. From their vantage point, they watch people in the busy Lusozi community going about their daily business: the many *boda bodas* (motorbike taxis), people walking to get the nearest *matatu* (bus) to work, hawkers carrying fruit and materials to sell, men preparing chapattis and food for passers-by, children in school uniforms. Trade takes place on the street opposite, in the restaurants and in the open doorways of tailors, cobblers, carpenters, barbers, butchers, charcoal sellers, mobile vendors and general retailers.[40] As we sat in Parliament one afternoon amid the daily buzz of traffic, radios, music and laughter, they pointed out a man carrying a sack of plastic bottles. They explained that he collects six kilos of 'wasted bottles' every day, for which he's paid 400 UGX (£0.10) per kilo. He used to be a professional soldier for Uganda People's Defense Force (UPDF), but now:

> If he fails to get something to eat, he comes to the community ... see everyone here, how they struggle... This is a national problem.

Kato is the elected chairman of Parliament in Lusozi. Formerly a qualified technician, a self-employed civil engineer, he injured his wrist at 40 and was forced to quit. Now, aged 61, he continues to work as a property broker, waiting for commissions to arrange the sale of plots of land. 'It's chance, not constant money ... a gambling business'. Most of the men in Parliament, including a retired soldier, a driver and a pastor, do the same work. They use their phones to communicate with other agents around Uganda, for example if someone is looking for land, and they get commission from there. But:

> Jobs are rare ... You can spend a week or even two months without a customer. Then you can get 5 million shillings when they buy a house.

In Parliament, the men explain, 'we combine knowledge and see how we can survive... Someone brings an idea here and we study it'. People would come to discuss their business plans. 'Others come and say "I'm looking for work", so we try to connect them.' In the past they had an office, but the cost of rent and tax was 'too much'. It was technically illegal for the men to sit and work in this area as none of them were paying taxes, so sometimes they get arrested; 'we're gambling now'. Kato felt the government should 'put up houses for us' like he had heard they do in the UK.

> Everything we buy is taxed, sugar, airtime, even mobile money, even water. But they don't see it. They get a lot of money, but they

can't assist the people, that's the problem here. It's just for the people at the top. We need to leave the city completely. We'll go to the village and get there two cows, one goat ... I produced six kids, they need to study; will they survive on that cow? I need to gamble.

To Kato, the financial situation faced by the members of Lusozi's Parliament reflected a lack of national social investment. This depicts a common rejection of economic policies and wealth disparities, viewed as immoral and extractive – further evidence of the selfishness of the political elite.[41] Lusozi's Parliament showed how 'anti-social' policies could be mitigated through 'pro-social' mutual support within their network.[42] At the same time, while waiting for scarce jobs, they observed the way others made their living in Lusozi, appreciating their hard work and sometimes their need to rely on others in the community. *'In Uganda, it's not what you know, it's who you know.'*

As they waited for work, the men would sometimes gossip, talk football and play games. Often groups of men would be seen outside homes and bars in Lusozi watching sports and playing games like Ludo, drafts and pool throughout the day. We were told that originally games were played to pass the time, but people have since tended to pay between 500 UGX and 5000 UGX (£0.10 and £1) 'to make it more interesting'. Games are also thought to relieve stress, to create friendships with people and to offer the potential of small monetary gain, as well as the social benefits of generating friendships, relaxing with others, 'taking soda or beer' and even potentially getting contacts of people who come to play, as 'some of them have good jobs'. Ludo is strategic, competitive, serendipitous, tense – like life and business. It can draw small crowds to watch over the hunched players as the dice rattle and hit the board. Mathematical games like draughts are played 'to keep your brain at its best'. Occasionally the boards are replaced with smartphone apps. This is not just about having fun: games are an opportunity to engage with other aspects of life, work and money, and to interact with people. With work and job-seeking often compared to 'gambling', and both games and gambling recognised for their economic potential, the distinction between work and play is further blurred, the 'open-endedness of work and productivity of play'[43] both requiring a disposition 'characterized by a readiness to improvise in the face of an ever-changing world'.[44]

Gambling was also an everyday activity in Lusozi, as became evident during studies of phone use. Five people out of 30 interviewed about the apps on their smartphones had sports betting apps. During a survey of 170 people who attended a specific mobile money vendor over the course of three days, Amor asked who they were sending or receiving mobile money from and for what purpose. Primarily, we were interested in mobile money practices for caring for older relatives at a distance, which were highly prevalent, as will be the focus of Chapter 5 on phone practices and Chapter 6 on health and care. However, we also found that 28 of the exchanges were for coin gambling or sports betting. Two people explained that they were without work, so instead depend on betting for an income. Amor was shocked to see some men 'losing their children's school fees or lunch money' in one of the gambling halls in Lusozi. This reflected a general condemnation of gambling habits as unproductive and wasteful of family resources. At one point during the research, the police had come to remove all gambling and gaming machines in Lusozi. I spoke with a local leader at the time, who said he agreed with this movement as 'gambling had become a serious problem' – especially for young people, who would 'try their chances with money given to them for other household things'. With gambling a moralised activity in Lusozi, as elsewhere, the use of the term to describe work in later life infers a sense of controversy and subversion invoked in its usage, which expresses a sense of the real physical, financial and social risks that are necessitated by the economic status quo, putting people's lives and futures on the line.

Mobile money

In contrast, Obama thought government banning of gambling and sports betting is short-sighted. For him, it represented a failure to recognise that, just like running a business, it is a way of making money and 'keeping minds growing'. Obama was then 40 years old and, despite having arrived relatively recently in Lusozi in 2011, he was considered one of the most successful businessmen in the area. He provided financial assistance for his family in Kampala and in his home village in Alur. Obama valued his smartphone for the same reason that games were popular; it offered an opportunity to keep in contact with friends and to build a social network, including with people abroad. He saw many business opportunities in WhatsApp in particular and is part of big WhatsApp groups 'with people outside', offering the potential to network and make money.

His business success started when he opened a shop in Lusozi, soon realising that mobile money or 'momo' was his most profitable product and focusing on that. At the time Obama was one of only two mobile money vendors in Lusozi, so 'by then we were really making money, like 5 million UGX (£990) a month'. Business had since changed, due in part to the many branches that have since opened, with 33 competitors providing mobile money services in the Lusozi area alone. As a result:

> We have a problem of copy and paste in business, so the customer is divided… It's the cheapest business that people can set up for themselves.

Other mobile money vendors said they had set up their business as they wanted to be self-employed, and it was one of the most viable businesses available to them. However, there was evidently still demand for their services, with 10 vendors having an overall average of 94 customers per day. Obama estimated that across his three shops, he still had 500 to 600 customers a month. Some mobile money vendors in Lusozi, like the mobile money agent seen in the short film below (Fig. 3.1), emphasised the importance of friendliness and maintaining good relationships with customers in order to ensure regular business despite competition.

In the film below, people explained how they would use mobile money as a personal savings account, as it is accessible within their own neighbourhood. It is possible to pay for various services using mobile money, including electricity bills and school fees. Mobile money would also support business owners, facilitating payments to suppliers and from customers. A study conducted in a Kampala market found that mobile phones are used extensively to pay for services, bills, taxes, rents

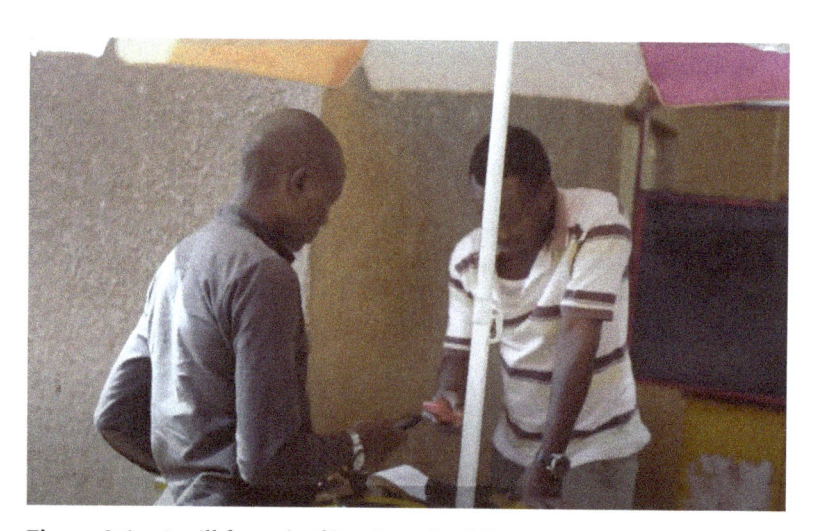

Figure 3.1 A still from the film about 'Mobile money'. https://bit.ly/46ZquIS.

and supplies conveniently and safely.[45] With the registration of SIM cards and mobile money transactions, the researchers argued that this is contributing to 'hybridized formal/informal markets',[46] again reflecting the complex interrelationships between sectors. In the following section, various working routines are described concurrently, that of a market vendor, a hawker and a *boda* driver. This emphasises the inter-reliance between businesses, and the sociality of work.

The market

The conversation with the men in Lusozi's Parliament depicted the everyday association made between economic scarcity and a neglectful government, characterised by extractive self-interest and 'disregard for the common good'.[47] It also introduced the significance of social networks for seeking livelihood in this context. Like the mobile money vendors encountered above, business owners in Lusozi would often emphasise the importance of being social and chatty with people, to ensure customers enjoyed coming back to buy from them. In order to get the best prices in the market, long-standing regular customers were needed to overcome increasing competition, and trust and friendship across the community were seen as integral to this. Some shop owners explained how they would sometimes help customers by giving them items on credit, showing trust and flexibility to accommodate their neighbours' financial constraints.

The men in Parliament also demonstrated how people living and working in Lusozi would observe each other in this regard. Often, during conversations and interviews, people would reflect on the everyday life experiences and routines of others around them in the neighbourhood. These conversations would often similarly emphasise uncertainty, the need to 'gamble' and work hard, the shortages imposed by a removed and uncaring political elite and the role of the community in supporting people in need. The older women who hawked fruits in town were those most often subject to the concerns of others. They would work over long hours and distances, with high risk and little reward, facing theft and criminal punishment. As this woman, a local leader for women's affairs in her forties, explained:

> On the street you have seen many of them selling bananas... For men, sometimes you find it is not also easy for them. So that's why you find women also suffering... You go in the morning to look for

bananas, then from there you proceed to town... You go and sell your business and what you have got from there, you have to come back again, you see the family has not taken breakfast, lunch is still also in that basket you're carrying... So by the time you reach home they tell you food is not there. Then that little money which somebody has come back with, you find she has to go and buy beans, posho ... pay rent, school fees are also there. So it's really very, very difficult and you find women are still suffering.

In her position as a women's leader, she is a crucial figure within local care networks, someone people would go to with their problems who can mobilise support for them. At the time she was particularly worried about widowed grandmothers, many of whom needed to engage in risky working practices in order to pay for their grandchildren's school fees, exposing them to punitive local authorities. She gave the example of Ayaa Palma, who had lost her son and daughter-in-law to a motorbike accident the year before and was then responsible for her three granddaughters, providing for them by selling bananas:

This Jaja told me that now they want to chase her away from the house, she has no money, she lost all her children, she has nothing to eat ... the kids have to go to school and the girl is growing, by the way ... so those are the people we need also to recognise in the community mostly, more than any other person ... and in fact we have been supporting her; when I get little posho, I take it to her... Can you imagine a woman of 65 moving with bananas in town? She was even one time knocked with a *boda boda*, at that age! You move around, city council disturbs her, they chase her, they arrest her ... they take all her things.

During an earlier interview with Ayaa Palma herself, we found her cracking groundnuts on her front step to prepare dinner for her granddaughters. She explained to us how she had moved from Jinja to Kampala to live with her uncle when she was widowed 20 years ago – her family network, like that of many others, enabling her to move to the city to seek work and provide for her four sons. She noticed people carrying produce on their heads and thought she could do the same. Three of Ayaa Palma's sons have since died, leaving her with the responsibility for bringing up their children and paying their school fees on her own. In return, the girls cook, wash and clean for her; while we sat on her step, her 13-year-old granddaughter arrived with a jerry can full of water from a nearby tap. When Ayaa Palma got sick it would be a serious problem for the household, but her neighbours would take care of them, bringing them money, food and water. She pointed at the door adjacent to hers, explaining *'that lady has really taken care of me; God should bless her and give her everything she wants'*. Sometimes, when Ayaa Palma had recovered, she would give them food to thank them. Other young women in the community would also come to seek her advice, for example when facing similar life experiences, which she considered to be the main sign of respect for her age.

This shows a dynamic of reciprocal mutual support between neighbours, particularly in the absence of marital and intergenerational care networks or formal welfare provisions. It would involve checking up and keeping an eye on one another, seeking and sharing advice, providing food and care, helping to solve problems. Clearly, as the women's leader suggested, Ayaa Palma was 'recognised' by her neighbours, who support her through the otherwise insurmountable challenges she faced in the city – the care burdens, working conditions, school fees, health risks, criminalisation, threats of eviction and inaccessible health services. Her uncle's family also continued to provide for them, his son who worked for KCCA sending her money and his wife buying her a house in Kampala. As well as help from her relatives and neighbours, Ayaa Palma felt it was her job that had kept her healthy, as well as the fact that she had *'stayed away from men'* since her husband died. But she is now 65 years old and had *'moved for 30 years'*, so she was already tired. It was her aspiration to have her own market stall where she could *'sit in one place'*.

Amor's mother Adul felt grateful to have had a stall selling vegetables in Lusozi market. When she first arrived in Kampala in 1994, fleeing the rebel and government attacks in their home village in Palabek, she said she was *'living in hardship'*. At the time Amor's father Kilongeni was living in the house of his stepsister, but was still searching for a job. Lusozi *'was still bush'*, with few houses and a lot of space. She said she was scared as she only spoke Acholi and *'feared the different characters from different places'*, hardly leaving home for the first two months. There was no money and she wanted her kids to go to school. After a while a friend introduced her to the market business and Adul became the first person to sell greens, which she sourced from the district market 1.5 km (just under a mile) away. Kilongeni got a job as a security guard, but the pay was *'very little'*, covering only school fees and rent, whereas Adul's earnings paid for food and other requirements. Occasionally they *'ended up in a bad condition'* and neighbours had to intervene, bringing food or paying medical fees.

Now Adul prefers living in Lusozi as she can support herself. Her oldest kids are well educated and at the time of the research all had paid jobs, enabling them to support their parents in buying their home in the neighbourhood, as well as other properties next door which they rent out. Once she has finished paying school fees (the youngest two boys, Smiley and Chol, are still studying in college and searching for jobs), and when the house is built in the village, she will go home.

In the meantime, as she explains in the film below (Fig. 3.2), she would work from 5.00 a.m. to 9.00 p.m. every day, 'Monday to Monday', even on Christmas Day. She would go to the district market first thing by *boda* to buy her greens (*bor, malakwan*), silverfish (*lakede*) and okra (*otigo*), spending 180,000 UGX (£38.75). She can then make up to 100,000 UGX (£21.50) profit on a good day, but from that she needs to pay for the ground rental of the stall to Kampala City Council Authority (KCCA), which costs 15,000 UGX (£3.25) per month, as well as the everyday costs of running the home including charcoal, water and food. This taxation again emphasises the 'hybridity' of formal and informal economic activities, with the market as a 'hub' or 'microcosm' of the 'real informal' economy.[48]

If the market is the 'hub' of the economy, *boda bodas* are the spokes, being crucial to the city's transport infrastructure, to family livelihoods such as Adul's and to the drivers themselves. The *boda* industry is said to generate livelihood for seven per cent of the population, with an

Figure 3.2 A still from the film 'Everyday life'. https://bit.ly/3OmXqni.

estimated 50 to 300,000 drivers in Kampala.[49] *Boda* drivers occupy an important political role, with collective power to 'protect livelihoods' and resist attempts at regulation or taxation of the industry, strategically leveraged for political support.[50] *Boda bodas* are also considered dangerous, with 7,000 deaths from accidents recorded over three years from 2014 to 2017;[51] health workers in Lusozi Hospital also reported the frequency of patients with *boda*-related injuries. This means they occupy a 'complex moral position' being 'vital but pathologised',[52] also evident in the stereotype of 'money hungry' young men who sell family land to buy a *boda*.[53]

While exemplifying the wider economy based on competition, transaction, uncertainty and risk, the *boda* industry is also embedded in relationships, helping the drivers provide for their families and relying on affiliations with customers and solidarity between drivers. The drivers have a 'stage system',[54] co-operatives to establish trust and accountability and provide them with a community of support. In the short film shown below (Fig. 3.3), Adul's *boda* driver Samuel explained that he was in charge of defence at his stage in Lusozi. Having worked there for 10 years, he feels he is '*so social with people*' there, ensuring regular customers. The phone is of course crucial to maintaining a network of regular clients, who can call to request services, or even use the ride-hailing apps that are positioned within 'stage' and gig economy logics, establishing a trusted online network.[55] This demonstrates how digital platforms can become

Figure 3.3 A still from the film '*Boda boda*'. https://bit.ly/3XXKAPw.

'embedded in prior social infrastructure'[56] while also 're-shaping activities', as with the use of mobile phones in the markets.[57]

Samuel thought having a stage was a good thing because they could become part of a community, recruiting others to work with them and *'building each other'*. Adul's whole family preferred to go with him as they knew and trusted him, and he would often also drive me home. He has been a *boda* driver for 10 years, since saving for a motorbike from his previous bicycle delivery business. He works from 6.00 a.m. until 9.00 p.m. every day, starting by taking Adul to her market suppliers and taking only Sunday off when he goes to church. As Samuel explained in the film, he would take children to school and transport food for hotels in town. He could take about 30 to 40 people each day, which made him between 30,000 UGX to 40,000 UGX (£6.40 to £8.50) per day or up to 600,000 UGX (£128) per month. He felt that he had to thank God as he rides a *boda* for a living, but God would still protect him from all those cars. *'Why wouldn't I thank Him?'* If he gets an extra 1,000 UGX (£2.10), he would take it to the church as an offertory on a Sunday.

Samuel explained that he was 'trying to solve the problem of school fees'. He had three children, two of whom lived in the village in western Uganda with his wife, so he was regularly sending them money – a typical arrangement for people who live in the city for work and support family at home.[58] He was the only person providing for his family, and if he needed money in an emergency, he could only turn to money lenders, who charged interest of between 10 and 20 per cent. Samuel's son had been sick, so he had to send mobile money for transport to the hospital (4,000 UGX or £0.85 each way) and treatment. His 70-year-old mother also lived nearby and his kids were sent to help their grandmother in their school holidays, fetching water and helping with other household chores. The rest of the time Samuel's family at home had a live-in maid to whom they paid 50,000 UGX (£10.60) each month. This is an overlooked yet increasingly common household system in Uganda, as families distribute care responsibilities to adapt to economic change.[59] In particular, paid carers accommodate mothers' demanding full-time working routines alongside responsibilities for domestic work. Maids are typically young women who provide childcare, assistance with housework and care for elders.[60] Adul's business also relied on help from the girls at home, her three daughters in their late twenties and the teenage maids, fostered female relatives brought from the village. They would help to divide the big bunches of greens into smaller portions for selling, as well as taking care of the house, cleaning and cooking, bringing Adul lunch in the market and looking after the grandchildren. In return they were given food, a home in Kampala and, when possible, schooling or apprenticeships.

Care work

Like domestic chores, work related to family care has historically been divided along gender lines. As around the world, this is often still the case in Uganda today,[61] where 'caregiving is viewed as a woman's role even if she has full time employment'.[62] Women in Kampala are often largely responsible for the day-to-day management of health and illness in their household.[63] Daily nursing of older relatives, including washing and feeding them, is often the responsibility of wives and daughters, who are also primarily responsible for the care of their own children.[64] Additional burdens of care on mothers and grandmothers, responsible for the health and advancement of everyone in their households, applies 'pressure' which is associated with health problems such as hypertension, as discussed further in Chapter 6. Women tend to turn to home treatment and self-prescribing,[65] buying painkillers or antibiotics in the pharmacy rather than visiting hospital, which would incur fees and interrupt working routines. Amor has often worried about her mother's health since doctors have told her that her regular headaches were from over-medicating with Panadol; she would rather buy medicines than take time away from the market and spend money visiting hospital. Adul's decisions on seeking treatment and healthcare are therefore dictated by her work. Where she might seek treatment for her children or husband, the hospital or clinic is a last resort for herself; she would prefer to self-medicate, a process which has been described as 'the ultimate privatisation of health'.[66]

Mego is 63 years old and also said she would avoid going to hospital, as there was not much room for sickness in her monthly budget or schedule. Whenever she had to go to the government hospital, as she did recently when she got malaria, she could *'spend the whole day'* waiting and *'they just write for you a sheet. Sometimes you don't have a coin, so you walk away empty handed'*. She believed that *'if you have money, it finishes all your problems'*. To find money herself, she would hawk greens and mangoes. This had been her job for the 20 years she had lived in Lusozi, since moving there from her home village in Kitgum. Her mother was still there in the village and Mego called her regularly to find out how she is, sending her 10,000 UGX (£2.15) once in a while. Normally she would start every day by selling greens in the morning, before selling her mangoes from 10.00 a.m. She would carry 40 mangoes in a basket on her head, which weighed up to 5 kg (11 lb) as well as extra reserved in her bag. She would walk all the way into town, a distance of 5 km (3 miles). At the time, Ugandan mangoes could be sold for between 1,000 UGX and 2,000 UGX (£0.20 and £0.40), depending on their size. Kenyan mangoes, which are bigger and weigh 0.5 kg (1.1 lb) each, she would sell for between 1,500 UGX and 3,000 UGX (£0.30 and £0.60). The latter could generate a lot of profit, and on a good day Mego could take home up to 30,000 UGX (£6.30). But there were times she found the whole box contained only rotten mangoes *'because there are many people who are after those boxes'*. As she explained:

> *The problem is that many people are doing the same business, so you can move the whole day and they only buy a few.*

Mego would come home with her legs tired and with pain in her chest. She would take Panadol and then go straight back to the market the following morning. *'All this hustle is to raise children and buy other requirements which are needed like food.'* She had learned how to take care of herself and her health, avoiding fried food and sachets of liquor. *'If you don't you will get physically and mentally sick,'* she said, although she does allow herself to have one beer to relax every evening and more on the weekends for fun.

In contrast, other participants felt that their physical work had helped them to maintain their health through fitness. Two older people we visited referred to their housework as a way to stay fit; one commented, 'I wake up in the morning and I do all the housework. When they cut the grass outside, I sweep it all myself'. Others would go dancing weekly for exercise, and I would often see people jogging up to the top of the hill. Grace, aged 64, had been selling milk at a stall near the entrance of Lusozi market for many years. We met her in her son's home, where she spends time with her two-month-old granddaughter during her breaks. She was following doctors' orders to put off her retirement, as her work was keeping her fit and healthy. She would work from 6.00 a.m. until 10.00 p.m. every day, 'Monday to Monday', taking just the afternoon off on Christmas Day.

Kasolo similarly considered his everyday working routine to be keeping him healthy. He is from western Uganda and had lived in Kampala for 15 years, ever since his boss had brought him here. He had a bicycle which he refers to as his 'Prado'. Walking through Lusozi at the time, you would be likely to find him on the way, pushing the 'Prado' and its daily deliveries. He said he felt his work kept him healthy and occupied. 'My bicycle here, is there anything else that is better than that gym?' Kasolo's friends called him Mr Wise, as he had seen a lot and had a clear understanding about life and other people. He had even had his (currently broken) smartphone registered under the name Kasolo Wise. He was pragmatic about his daily life and that of others within the community. Although he was reliant on physical work, he would refuse to work too late every day and would turn down certain jobs:

> You cannot do something that is heavy for your life, it means you are spoiling your life… You have to work within your strength.

Kasolo took this literally, and would only ever carry what he could manage. He had concerns for the people in the community who were without work, such as young people who take '*njagga*' (drugs):

> You know, when a person fails to get a job he gives up on life and becomes a careless person.

Kasolo also said he wanted 'those elderly people to be ok, even to get some business', as there is a certain age after which they can no longer work and do jobs like his. As he observed:

> Sometimes when you get sick, you can't get money, can't provide for yourself. If you have kids at least one will take care of you.

If not, like one elderly man known in the community, it becomes hard to survive on people's generosity. 'The neighbours help him a lot, shelter him, otherwise he wouldn't be alive up to today'.

Social insurance

The everyday lives of older people in Lusozi are inevitably diverse. What is harmful to someone's health may be beneficial to someone else. As Adul puts it:

> *Everybody in Lusozi is living his or her own lives. They do their own thing depending on what they can afford.*

Without social insurance such as pensions, sick pay or free health services, work can compromise health and health can compromise work. During three months of research in the physiotherapy department at the nearby government hospital, the focus in Chapter 6 on health and care, the health workers said the most common problems they see are back related. The physiotherapists attributed this to the 'nature of work', with people needing to bend to clean, dig and wash. With surgery costs often being unattainable, their role is crucial in ensuring people manage their injuries while maintaining their income.

At Lusozi Hospital, the Head of Physiotherapy was hopeful for more research and advocacy to support provisions for older people working in the informal sector, and therefore contributing to the economy. Older people working in the city were evidently overlooked in terms of service provision, with health needs presenting some of the greatest challenges in their everyday lives. Social insurance schemes can therefore potentially draw on existing co-operative ways of managing uncertainty in the city. This has proved successful in other regions of the country, with over 21 Community Based Health Insurance (CBHI) schemes, based particularly in western Uganda.[67] The largest is in Kisiizi Hospital in south-west Uganda, where a health insurance scheme was founded in 1996 to provide access to health benefits, protect members against catastrophic health spending and poverty and ensure consistent funding for the hospital.[68] It was based on existing 'platforms of cultural solidarity' such as burial societies. In 2019 the National Health Insurance Scheme was approved in parliament after 17 years of planning; excluding Social Assistance Grants for Empowerment (SAGE), it will be one of the first social protection schemes to cater for the majority of the population who are self-employed in the 'informal' sector,[69] based on an annual contribution fee of 100,000 UGX per year.[70] Although this national scheme has been said to overlook 'community models',[71] the hope was that it could prevent crippling household expenditure on health. It is worth noting that enrolment in CBHI has been found to be income-dependent, with wealthier households more likely to participate;[72] enrolment in the national scheme would also likely be dictated by socio-economic factors, so adequate efforts to promote inclusion will be required. Evidence from the prior implementation of CBHI schemes in Uganda shows that this would be reliant on education programmes to inform beneficiaries and establish their trust.[73] Based on the portraits outlined in this chapter, older self-employed workers in urban settings should be primary targets of these efforts, as health insurance could be particularly beneficial to them, and thereby to those in their households and communities. This is principally true of women, who are generally responsible for the health of their household and therefore tend to avoid seeking treatment for themselves.

Conclusion

This chapter draws on a few participants' descriptions of their businesses, routines and income to show how everyday activities for older people can be centred around making money in the city, just like those of younger generations. Many of the people we worked with, well into their sixties and beyond, continued to provide for themselves and their families, their work funding everyday requirements such as rent, food, water and school fees. This includes various and often interconnected forms of employment, such as hawking, alcohol brewing, market vending, mobile money, *boda* driving and deliveries, highlighting 'the social texture in which the informal economy operates'.[74] This provides livelihoods and social security to navigate the shortfalls of the 'official' economy which it also upholds, as evident in its strategic political (de)regulation.[75] The market, in particular, is a 'hub of Uganda's real economy',[76] with 'everyday mobilities'[77] facilitated by the *boda boda* industry and mobile money transfer, themselves significant sources of livelihood. Their regulation, such as through mobile platforms, SIM registration,[78] taxation and ground rents, depicts the hybridity of informal and formal economic sectors. However, employment in the *boda* or market industries is without formal social protection, necessitating further care work.[79]

All of the descriptions here show how people engage with economic uncertainty pragmatically, socially and as an integral part of life.[80] Many participants are self-employed and sometimes their businesses would require physical work. Some people felt that this had kept them healthy by encouraging them to keep active and stay fit. Others struggled with pain, injuries and chronic illness, all of which are increasingly likely as people age. Women in particular are likely to prioritise the health needs of their family and, like Adul, would self-prescribe to avoid missing out on work or spending money in hospital.

Throughout this chapter, the role of mutual support for seeking livelihoods within Lusozi becomes apparent. Each of the people cited, when describing their own everyday lives, looked outwards at those around them. Obama considered the impact of certain policies on others in Lusozi. Kasolo Wise observed the elderly people who are reliant on their neighbours, who would intervene when things became too difficult to manage. Ayaa Palma thanked her neighbours for taking care of her family when she fell sick, and in turn she was observed and supported by other people. From their vantage point on the main road, Kato and the other members of Lusozi's 'Parliament' surveyed other people's everyday activities and instances of co-operation in the community, something that they themselves enacted within their own organisation. Those seeking jobs or customers recognised the importance of their social network, of being known and trusted in the community, improving the likelihood of gaining a job or maintaining a regular clientele despite increasing competition. Work and job seeking was approached as an open-ended activity within indeterminate circumstances.[81] At the same time, games and interactivity were approached as potentially productive activities in terms of social networks and income. As the men in Parliament illustrate, improvisation and risk could to an extent be stabilised through the support of social networks. Work as 'gambling' also expresses a sense of interconnected agency, the scope for creating possibilities, livelihoods, mutual care and self-reliance, as well as for resistance – for naming unjust circumstances, state violence and neglect.

With the support of social networks to access resources and ease pressure on individuals, strong ties and friendships can be an advantage, while isolation can be a particular risk.[82] Work based in households and neighbourhoods is founded on the support of family, friends, neighbours and domestic servants.[83] Co-operation and mutual support is often promoted,[84] while anything which might take away from that is admonished. Politicians would often be judged according to the same standard, and most often fall short.[85] 'Gambling' in place of formal social security such as pensions is applicable across global economies and urban contexts – and particularly in relation to retirement, an increasingly unattainable luxury around the world and for future generations.

The following chapter extends the focus on social relationships based on participation in three community groups. This considers the scope of co-operative 'economies from below',[86] such as savings groups, in seeking to mitigate the tensions of working towards both self- and mutual interest. It also considers how community relationships can offer an extension of family and provide 'family support', allowing women in particular to alleviate the burdens of both work and domestic responsibilities.

Notes

1. Honwana 2012, 12.
2. Whyte 2017.
3. Malaby 2009.
4. Wallman and Bantebya-Kyomuhendo 1996, 2.
5. Nyanzi 2009.
6. Wallman and Bantebya-Kyomuhendo 1996, 2.
7. McFarlane and Silver 2017; Wignall et al. 2019; McQuaid et al. 2021; Simone 2021.
8. Nakirya and State 2013, 34; Tamale 2020, 231.
9. Harvey and Krohn-Hansen 2018, 12.
10. Ferguson 2015.
11. Ethnographies of work around the world highlight both the 'systemic force of capital, and the historical specificity of how these ever-shifting capital relations play out in practice across the world' (Harvey and Krohn-Hansen 2018).
12. Garvey and Miller 2021.
13. Coe 2014.
14. Nyanzi 2009.
15. Nyanzi 2009.
16. See United Nations, Department of Economic and Social Affairs, Population Division 2015. 'World population ageing 2015'. Accessed 9 February 2021. https://www.un.org/en/development/desa/population/publications/pdf/ageing/WPA2015_Report.pdf, 144.

    See Uganda Bureau of Statistics 2017. 'National labour force survey 2016'. Accessed 18 November 2019. https://www.ubos.org/wp-content/uploads/publications/10_2018Report_national_labour_force_survey_2016_17.pdf, xiv.

    Competition for these posts is high, as reflected in national statistics, although it is worth noting that the standards for calculating unemployment and underemployment from labour force surveys are found to be ill-fitting in African contexts (Alenda-Demoutiez and Mügge 2020; Linsi and Mügge 2019). The National Labour Force Survey 2016/17 by the Uganda Bureau of Statistics (UBOS) found that among those of 'working age', i.e. 14–64, unemployment rates or the proportion of those actively looking for a job is at 10 per cent, while underemployment is at 35 per cent, disproportionately affecting women. The 2016/17 survey found youth unemployment in Uganda, i.e. those aged 18–30 who are actively looking for a job, at 13 per cent, one of the highest rates in sub-Saharan Africa; many more, 38 per cent, are 'underemployed'.
17. Byaruhanga and Debesay 2021, 3.
18. Byaruhanga and Debesay 2021, 10; Bukuluki 2013; Merttens et al. 2016.
19. Thanks to HelpAge Uganda for taking the time to meet and discuss this research on SAGE.
20. Nyanzi has previously recommended that these smaller-scale interventions, such as community outreach and vocational training, are deployed at national scale, incorporating input from the elderly themselves (Nyanzi 2009).
21. Hart 1973, 1985; Thieme 2018.
22. Wallman and Baker 1996.
23. Ferguson 2015, 14; Ferguson 2006, 15.
24. Wallman and Baker 1996, 672.
25. Hart 1985, 57.
26. Thieme 2018.
27. UBOS 2017.
28. GEM Consortium 2014. 'Entrepreneurial behaviour and attitudes: Uganda profile'. Accessed 18 November 2019. https://www.gemconsortium.org/economy-profiles/uganda.
29. Clifford 2020. 'The causes and consequences of mobile money taxation: An examination of mobile money transaction taxes in sub-Saharan Africa', *GSMA Mobile Money*. Accessed 18 November 2019. https://www.gsma.com/mobilefordevelopment/wp-content/uploads/2020/06/GSMA_The-causes-and-consequences-of-mobile-money-taxation.pdf, 21.
30. UBOS 2018. 'Uganda manpower survey report'. Accessed 19 November 2019. https://www.ubos.org/wp-content/uploads/publications/08_20182018_Uganda_Manpower_Survey_Report.pdf, 138.
31. Bibangambah 1992.

32. Wallman and Bantebya-Kyomuhendo 1996, 10.
33. Wallman and Bantebya-Kyomuhendo 1996, 10.
34. UBOS 2018, 142.
35. UBOS 2018, 142.
36. World Bank 2017. 'From regulators to enablers: The role of city governments in economic development of Greater Kampala'. Accessed 18 November 2019. https://development-data-hub-s3-public.s3.amazonaws.com/ddhfiles/143567/119806-revised-public-the-wb-book-2017-report-web-individual-page-layout_0.pdf.
37. Goodfellow and Titeca 2012, 267.
38. Larsson and Svensson 2018.
39. Goodfellow and Titeca 2012.
40. See also Southall, Gutkind and Sempa 1957, 2:22.
41. Ferguson 2006, 77.
42. Ferguson 2006, 77.
43. Malaby 2009, 206.
44. Malaby 2009, 206.
45. Larsson and Svensson 2018.
46. Larsson and Svensson 2018, 537.
47. Ferguson 2006; Wiegratz 2010.
48. Goodfellow and Titeca 2012, 267; Larsson and Svensson 2018, 538.
49. Doherty 2020, 1.
50. Goodfellow and Titeca 2012, 264.
51. Wanume et al. 2019.
52. Doherty 2020.
53. Whyte and Acio 2017, 22.
54. Doherty 2020, 3.
55. Doherty 2020, 6.
56. Doherty 2020, 6.
57. Larsson and Svensson 2018, 542.
58. Ferguson 2015, 95.
59. This could be conceptualised as what Cati Coe terms an 'age-inscription' – not yet a discursive norm of ageing or 'repertoire', but a patterned response to social change (Coe 2020; Coe and Alber 2018).
60. Coe 2020.
61. Gertrude et al. 2019; MacNeil 1996; Wallman and Bantebya-Kyomuhendo 1996.
62. Gertrude et al. 2019, 1555.
63. Wallman and Bantebya-Kyomuhendo 1996.
64. Livingston 2003, 215.
65. Wallman and Bantebya-Kyomuhendo 1996.
66. Wallman and Bantebya-Kyomuhendo 1996, 141.
67. Nshakira-Rukundo et al. 2019.
68. Baine, Kakama and Mugume 2018.
69. Bukuluki and Mubiru 2014, 89.
70. LivingGoods 2019. 'Health for all: Uganda's cabinet approves the National Health Insurance Scheme Bill 2019'. Accessed 7 July 2020. https://livinggoods.org/media/health-for-all-ugandas-cabinet-approves/#.
71. *The Economist* 2020. 'How a Ugandan hospital delivers health insurance through burial groups'. Accessed 7 July 2020. https://www.economist.com/middle-east-and-africa/2020/01/30/how-a-ugandan-hospital-delivers-health-insurance-through-burial-groups.
72. Nshakira-Rukundo et al. 2019.
73. Baine, Kakama and Mugume 2018; Basaza et al. 2019.
74. Wallman and Bantebya-Kyomuhendo 1996, 2.
75. Goodfellow and Titeca 2012.
76. Goodfellow and Titeca 2012, 267.
77. Porter et al. 2017.
78. This refers to the recent regulatory requirement to register SIM cards with personal identification for the purposes of crime detection.

79. Harvey and Krohn-Hansen 2018, 17.
80. Whyte 1997; Finnström 2001.
81. Malaby 2009.
82. Mudege and Ezeh 2009.
83. Coe 2020; Wallman and Bantebya-Kyomuhendo 1996.
84. Nyamnjoh 2017, 261.
85. Ferguson 2006, 77.
86. Mauss and Halls 1990; Hart 2008.

4
Togetherness is strength

Introduction

In Chapter 2, togetherness was introduced as an ideal made meaningful in the urban context of Lusozi, particularly in relation to the role of elders. This was developed further in Chapter 3 on everyday life, which shows how mutual support within the community provides 'social insurance' where health, livelihood, state infrastructure and family support fails for an (older) individual. In response to reading an earlier draft of this chapter, Ladit explained that the origins of *ribe*, unity or togetherness in the Acholi sub-region, derives from the concept of *aleya*, rotational or reciprocal labour for farming.

> Except for a lucky few, most farmers were without equipment like tractors or ploughs, so instead used to hire the service of people in the village. Under the supervision of the *Rwot Kweri*, village elder, about 30 or more who would dig one, two, even three big gardens with hand hoes in one day. This was compensated with *awak*, good meals and local brew called *kwete* in sizeable portions, either that day or at the end of the year when the harvest is ready. This would reduce the amount of time spent digging by an individual who would otherwise have spent a whole month working on the same task.[1]

Aleya, or co-operative labour for accessing productive opportunities and for enjoyment, informs how 'togetherness' – or pragmatic co-operation – is understood in this chapter. This includes conversations about the joy of being together, the extension of family roles to friends and neighbours and the pooling and distribution of resources. This idea is conveyed through a focus on three community groups in which

I participated extensively; descriptions are based on observations from regular attendance at weekly meetings and dialogue between and with members. At times, the dialogue reveals how boundaries are drawn between formal group proceedings and obligations and everyday social interactions. In some instances, the dialogue also reveals norms around social relations with friends and family more broadly. Overall, the analysis shows how togetherness is both necessitated and undermined by the wider economy, and how this tension is managed as part of everyday social life.[2]

In order to give an in-depth ethnographic portrayal of how togetherness works within this urban setting, this chapter will focus on three community groups in which we were able to participate regularly. All three groups discussed here were pointed out to me early on in the research as being central to the Lusozi community, and as being particularly well attended by people over the age of 40. The groups include people of various ethnicities, but Acholi people form the majority, as they do across the neighbourhood. In all three groups, the leadership and members stated objectives of fostering dialogue, belonging and mutual support, and had observable successes in attaining them. The first one I joined, a savings group predominantly for women called 'Who should enrich you?' (WSEY),[3] is run by the Lusozi chairwoman, who invited me to attend the weekly parties. The second, a savings group predominantly for men called 'Togetherness is Strength' (TIS),[4] is run by Ladit; the group agreed to let me join as a participating member for one year of the research. Both WSEY and TIS meetings take place in the central bar in Lusozi, known as Soda Bar. The third group introduced here, with the pseudonym 'Place of Peace', was formed as an international, church-based NGO to support single mothers living with HIV in Kampala. It was considered by local leadership and others in the community to be the only NGO that effectively supported people in Lusozi. Many of the older women who participated in the research were also part of this group. Attending their joyful weekly meetings, which involved school and health education, exercise and having fun, was an opportunity to get involved, to spend time with the women and to learn as a participant. These meetings showed that Place of Peace achieved their aims not only of providing medical and financial support, but also of crafting belonging and friendship. As outlined in this chapter, the discussions during the meetings, and with members during individual interviews, offered insight into family and community expectations, especially regarding the role of women.

The other two groups, TIS and WSEY, are primarily savings groups or Savings and Credit Co-operative Organisations (SACCOs), of which there are many in Lusozi as around the world. Place of Peace also has an optional savings association among members. This introduces money into the discussion about co-operation, and how people formulate both self and mutual reliance through 'economic movements from below',[5] participating in world markets through what has been termed 'the human economy'.[6] In savings groups, people save money collectively as a way of rotating or accumulating funds and providing a financial safety net for members. Three of the other researchers in the ASSA project – in Yaoundé, Dublin and Al-Quds – also encountered or participated in savings groups. They are especially prevalent in Africa, where it is estimated that 9 million people are members of a savings group.[7] In Kampala, they are found to be particularly popular among low-income mothers who are responsible for their household.[8] In Lusozi specifically there are an estimated 20 SACCOs with between 30 and 50 members in each.[9]

During the research, I heard many stories where groups' leadership had disappeared with collected funds, stealing members' hard-won savings. Inevitably, therefore, (rotating) savings groups are founded on mutual trust, reciprocity and hierarchical organisation.[10] Savings groups come in many diverse forms,[11] as evident in the different saving and distribution mechanisms of the two groups discussed here. While many wealthy elites engage in savings groups, they are particularly important in the absence of accessible 'formal' credit systems[12] – demonstrating how the 'human economy' bridges the gap between everyday personal experience and wider society.[13]

The vast majority of TIS members are men. The group is primarily organised around the accumulation of funds, with members expected to save 30,000 UGX (£6.40) in their personal account per month. The pooled funds thereby provide an emergency resource of 'mutual insurance'[14] for members to seek emergency loans, and the 10 per cent monthly interest on their return is then redistributed among other members annually. This interest ensures the annual growth of the group's account, but it does pose a risk to borrowers' financial stability.[15]

Groups like TIS, which focus on the accumulation of funds, as shown in the section to follow, have received less attention from anthropologists than rotating savings associations[16] like WSEY, the second, primarily female group. Ardener defined rotating savings groups such as WSEY as:

> an association formed upon a core of participants who agree to make regular contributions to a fund which is given, in whole or in part, to each contributor in rotation.[17]

With these rotations, there is often a 'ceremony of exchange',[18] including gift giving and dancing. With the groups being founded on both official regulations as well as members' everyday relations, boundaries would be drawn between formality and informality during the meetings. Informal conversations would be paused to allow the formal proceedings to commence, accompanied by more prescribed interactions, such as turn-taking in meetings or knowing when to dance and when to sit down.[19] Long-term participation within these groups revealed the challenges of maintaining these boundaries, and the complexities of striving communally for individual gain. However, in line with the logic of *aleya*, and with Nyamnjoh's concept of urban 'conviviality', it also shows how individuals can become self-reliant through a 'framework of collective action'.[20]

This supports the relevance of 'conviviality' as a research methodology in Lusozi. As in open-ended and relational anthropological research, a convivial methodology compels active participation in community environments as a way to meet people and learn about the relationships between individuals and groups,[21] as well as the codes of conduct which seek to provide autonomy through interdependence.[22] To depict an ongoing sense of learning through dialogue throughout the chapter, I draw from descriptions and cited transcripts from the meetings, as well as short films made with the groups, which hopefully help to bring the ethnography to life.

Togetherness is Strength organisation (TIS)

Four years ago a young couple's child was stillborn, and they struggled to fund the transport for the burial in the husband's home village. During the night, people across the community worked together to find the money required. A 53-year-old man named Tolit, who is now TIS's auditor, had taken the young man and his wife first to Lusozi Hospital in his car and, failing to find available health workers, on to Mulago National Referral Hospital. Tolit witnessed first-hand the difficulties the young couple had faced in seeking treatment and raising the necessary funds for hospital fees and the burial. Tolit took the issue to Ladit, and assembled other Acholi elders including Obalo, the vice chairman. They decided to set up a shared fund that could provide support to the community and to young families such as this one. Like many other organisations in Lusozi, they started to pool their resources in a savings group, whose Acholi name means 'Togetherness is Strength'. As the vice chairman explained, it is:

a means of assisting ourselves, in times of grievance or happiness. We thought we should come together to form an association and make light the heaviness on one person.

In particular, the elders formed the organisation to facilitate productive savings among younger people in their community, as well as to provide them with a fund to turn to in times of both emergency and celebration. Furthermore, they hoped that their weekly meetings, from 10.00 a.m. until 12.00 p.m. every Sunday, would give younger people an opportunity to sit with their elders and learn from them, seek advice and spend time with them, as they would have done more regularly in the past. As Tolit explained:

Tolit: [Now] there's no time to sit together as a family. People don't sit together. We used to have what you call '*wang-oo*', a sitting room in our place, a fireplace in the evening. That's where you get to know some of those things. But of late it's not much. But I think it's even the way the society is progressing, and the resources, because to make a fire you need even some space, a log to put in it, and then the commitment.
Interviewer: Is there ever a fireplace in Lusozi?
Tolit: Instead of making a fire, there's a designated place where we meet every week. It's like a fireplace but without fire on Sundays. So that you come and get ideas at that meeting … every Sunday morning, you close off the activities in the bar, and you leave the restaurant, but there's space that we can use for our gathering.

In Soda Bar, the weekly 'fireplace without fire' aimed to build solidarity and communal identity in the city. In 2018, when I first encountered the group, TIS had 20 million UGX (£3,990) saved and 15 active members. The organisation was run by an 'executive committee', which follows a hierarchy based on age: Ladit the chairman; Obalo the vice-chairman, with authority to act as leader in Ladit's absence; Okello the secretary, who would take the minutes, report meetings and decide on agendas; Tolit the auditor, who worked as an accountant for an NGO; Onono the treasurer, a prolific businessman in Lusozi, who collected the funds and kept the books; two 'security' monitors, responsible for policing misbehaviour and enforcing discipline during meetings; an 'advisor', the owner of Soda Bar where the group would meet; and six other members.

I was also permitted to join as a member, in order to learn from the proceedings about how togetherness, belonging and mutual financial support are forged among men in the city.

At 10.00 a.m. Ochido, one of the older members at 51, is the first to arrive, as he is every Sunday. Known to be a humble person, he usually spoke little throughout the meeting, keeping his arms folded and sometimes falling asleep. The secretary, a younger man in his thirties, was also often early, with his registry books in front of him, preparing to update the records (Fig. 4.1). Over the next hour the rest of the members would arrive, greeting everyone, sometimes shaking hands one by one, starting with the oldest person present. The tables were assembled in a line in the centre of the bar. Mama Juliet, the wife of the owner of Soda Bar, sat in the corner. Often a few other men sat around the tables against the walls of the bar and she would serve their beers: Nile Special, Club, Guinness. People would come and go throughout the morning, sometimes hawking clothes. Denis and other members of WSEY would come in to set up the bar for their Sunday meeting, starting later that evening. Outside smartly dressed parents and their children would walk to and from church services. By 11.00 a.m. most of the other attendees would have arrived, the last few to a chorus of complaints and threats of fines for lateness. Jokes

Figure 4.1 TIS members at a Sunday meeting in the bar. Photo by Charlotte Hawkins.

and gossip about national politics or people in the community would be silenced in order to start the meeting. The conversation mostly fluctuated between Acholi and English, and Amor would translate for me where necessary. People who are visiting relatives in the village, or otherwise engaged outside of town, were granted exemption.

Each month everyone is meant to contribute 30,000 UGX (£6.40) to their own savings account; this is saved collectively in Ladit's bank account and noted in the secretary's records. Ladit's account was chosen in order to avoid the costs involved in opening a separate account and because of the group's trust of Ladit. This was an unusually trusting arrangement, as savings groups in the area would typically save cash in a shared box with three keys held by three trusted group leaders in order to mitigate the potential for temptation and theft. For each weekly meeting members would contribute a 'sitting fee' of 2,000 UGX (£0.40), for access to bar and drinks, and another 2,000 UGX (£0.40) to the 'chairman's basket', which would be added to the account for ad hoc group requirements. New members would pay a commitment fee of 120,000 UGX (£25.40), which was put in their account, as well as a non-refundable joining fee of 15,000 UGX (£3.20). A fine could be charged for lateness or other 'misconduct', in the sum of 2,000 UGX (£0.40) for members or 5,000 UGX (£1.05) for the executive committee. Absence from meetings also earned a fine unless a good reason was given, for example work or sickness. There was a 'soft loan' scheme for people who are facing financial problems or looking to expand their business, for which a 10 per cent interest would be levied each month. Typically the loan would come from personal savings accounts, excluding 'special cases'.

The treasurer would keep records of all money put in and taken out of the shared account with the organisation's printed receipts. In 2017 the organisation bought a *boda boda* motorcycle for one of the younger men to set up his business, originally on the basis that he would pay it back over 18 months with interest. Even those with regular salaried incomes sometimes drew on the savings to request loans; for example, the auditor is an accountant for a well-known NGO, but his employer can be late in paying him, so he would request a loan in the meantime. The group would also pledge contributions for various life events of other members. During my one-year membership we each gave contributions of 10,000 UGX (£2.10) for Ladit's 67th birthday, for the wedding of Obalo's daughter, for the treasurer's university graduation and the hospital bill of Amor's husband as well as for condolences, such as when a member lost one of his brothers. The contributions signify commitment to these relationships.

TIS has a constitution, which lays out the rules and principles of the organisation, to help 'ensure the quality of their affairs'. This defines the association's objective to 'promote social and economic welfare', bring together members and 'provide for opportunities to examine issues affecting their lives and the community in which they live'. The constitution maps out their rules and regulations, including a duty to participate, attend meetings and pay monthly contributions, as well as any fees required. Disciplinary aspects of the groups' meetings are established for stability and trust in the regulations, but with enough lenience for anticipated nonconformity. Meetings were typically focused on collecting outstanding balances, monthly contributions, loans and fines for various members. Discussions in meetings circulated around the conflicting principles of the group, both to follow the constitution and to be fair and lenient to members. Deadlines for loan repayments sometimes needed to be extended and monthly contributions were often postponed.

After the opening prayer, Ladit would give an opening summary of group concerns. Topics for discussion were raised in the agenda by the diligent secretary and each item would be discussed with the relevant members. If a group decision needed to be made, each member would be called to state their opinion, initially in order of the group hierarchy. As meetings progressed, comments could become more personal and voices more raised. Here is an outline of a typical discussion, which demonstrates the tensions between maintaining both lenience and constitutional order.

> Meeting on 16 December 2018
>
> [VC made a loan request of 1 million UGX for his daughter's wedding and pledged his pool table as collateral]
>
>> Secretary: If repayment is over three months, that would be a total of 1.3 million UGX (£275.40). This is bringing interest money for everyone…
>>
>> …
>>
>> Member 1: But what about member 2 and his loan for the motorbike? The repayment is not complete.
>>
>> …
>>
>> Secretary: It was Ladit's decision that we won't share the interest from last year until all loan repayments are complete.

Vice chairman: This group is very calm and the secretary is very kind – but there's a limit.

Member 2: Let us follow the constitution. Three months without payment and you're automatically out. Being kind should have a limit. I suggest next year in February.

Vice chairman: Let me be the chairman of deducting contributions from the accounts. Secretary, forcefully or peacefully, let's do it kindly, technically and constitutionally.

....

[Discussion of contributions to a member who had lost a relative. All members pledged 5,000 UGX (£1.05) for M's husband's hospital bill, 10,000 UGX for member 1's WSEY party, 10,000 UGX (£2.10) for vice chairman's daughter's wedding ceremony (introduction for family members)]

Secretary: Even if it's not in the constitution, as a human being, as a point of togetherness, it's not for us to say how close a lost relative is…We're here for unity, so someone can present anything and then we can decide if a member is responsible for those challenges… Condolence is already a must.

As shown in this transcript, regulations were sometimes shifted to accommodate individual financial situations and late repayments. Responsibilities for managing repayments by absent members would be delegated among the executive members, whose airtime costs were covered by the group. Boundaries are drawn to encourage compliance with the regulations, deliberately distinguished from friendships outside the group,[23] despite these relationships being the motivation behind the group's original formation (Fig. 4.2). As with *aleya* rotations, the savings and loans are founded on trust, 'anchored in personal ties and guided by collective rules and expectations';[24] failure to comply compromises the arrangement.

Throughout my membership, there was an intensifying discussion that things were being let slip and loans were being granted too freely and without sufficient consultation of the group, with members able to easily exploit the group's kindness. The *boda* bought by the group for one of its members was a source of pride when I first joined. But after his repayment was frozen due to sickness and family responsibilities, they felt the recipient was no longer taking it seriously, and there was an ongoing conversation about whether the money should be taken from his account or his *boda* confiscated. There were also common disputes around the

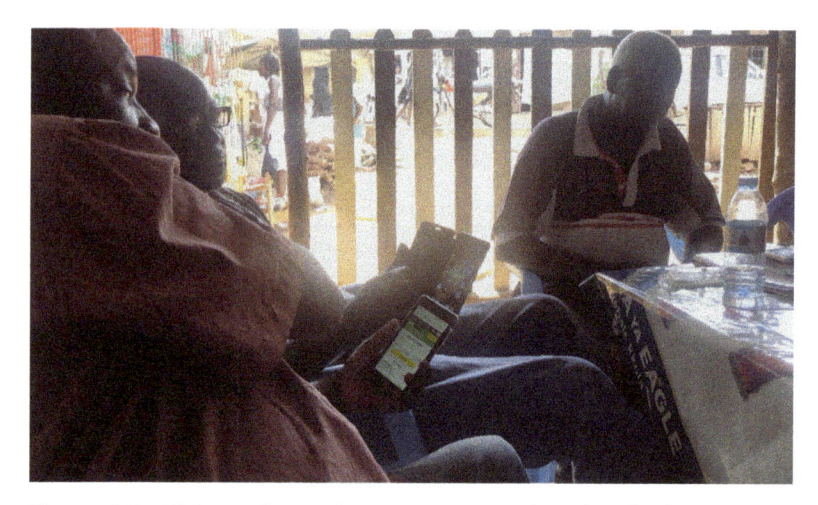

Figure 4.2 TIS members using a sports app. Photo by Charlotte Hawkins.

records, which were sometimes queried and distrusted. At the time of my leaving the group, the secretary stated that monthly contributions were 'very poor' – not even halfway complete for the current financial year.

In addition to the main savings group, a rotating fund called 'Lottery'[25] operated alongside the group. This was founded by TIS as an optional part of membership and was being run by Ocen Matthew. He would come on time to every meeting to prepare his registry and collect cash throughout the meeting. There are 17 members of Lottery, some from within and outside TIS; each contributes 50,000 UGX (£9.90) each week, 40,000 UGX (£7.90) for cash and 10,000 UGX (£2.00) for soap and sugar, chosen as they are important items for household cleanliness and nutrition. The Sunday TIS meeting would conclude with the Lottery beneficiary receiving the total 680,000 UGX (£135), accompanied by applause from the group. Each week the rotation would continue quietly, without much discussion or issue. However, some of the same members who failed to pay their monthly contribution to TIS would continue to make contributions to this smaller rotating fund. At one point the owner of Soda Bar and advisory member suggested they should 'kill the group of Lottery' so that TIS could stand firm.

> This would stabilise the group and make us concentrate on the group office. You can go to the shop and buy sugar and what! We should contribute on the group office… Those who can't afford to be in both sides should switch to one. The small group is overweighting the big one. Should we wait for the big one to die?

It seemed that the rotation mechanism with shorter-term individual household benefits offers greater incentive for investment than the longer-term savings mechanism with collective and personal benefits. The more the members began to subvert the TIS procedures, the greater the group's instability, and the less motivation there was for others to follow the rules.

Participation in the group showed how the members work to balance both self- and collective interest – a tension that Hart argues is a 'prerequisite for being human', on which human institutions are founded.[26] The discussions outline the pragmatic and moral efforts made by the TIS group towards the 'constitutional' and the 'kind', to reassert reciprocity and co-operation within pervasive economic self-interest, competition and inequality.[27]

The TIS savings group, like many others, demonstrates possibilities within the 'human economy',[28] highlighting people's active participation in the economy from their particular personal and contextual vantage point. For example, as well as financial ideals, the group enacted ideals about intergenerational relationships; the older TIS leaders founded the group in order to support younger men and their families, and to offer the opportunity for different generations to spend time socialising together, the 'wang-oo without fire'. Following on from the discussion in previous chapters, this again demonstrates how older people would adapt ideals and experiences of ageing for relevance in urban settings like Lusozi, playing an active role in providing 'social infrastructures'[29] of mutual support. The creative appropriation of open-ended technologies such as money and smartphones to ageing in the city will be a key discussion point in the rest of the book, with Chapter 5 on the 'domestication of dotcom', Chapter 6 on the role of money in health and care and Chapter 7 on co-operative morality.

First, in what follows here, the format and process of the rotating savings fund 'WSEY' are described as a point of comparison to TIS. Both groups use the same space in the Soda Bar in central Lusozi for their meetings, TIS in the morning and WSEY in the evening. Decorations for the WSEY meeting would often be put up during the TIS meeting, colourful drapes to conceal the walls and ceiling, as shown with the blue wall hanging in Fig. 4.1 above. WSEY meetings are expressive and celebratory, but the rules of accountability within the rotation are more rigidly enforced than those in TIS; at some point, TIS members attended the WSEY meeting and were inspired by how organised they appeared. The order of events was not explicitly outlined but must be learned through participation – I was often told to 'wait and see'. As well as practical 'family support', the group encouraged enjoyment and self-expression,[30] with the weekly joy and stress-relief of dressing up, dancing, celebration and being together.

Who should enrich you (WSEY)?

This name roughly translates an Acholi phrase meaning 'Who should enrich you?' – implying that in answer, you should enrich yourselves, together. This savings and family support group was founded in 1997 by a group of women who had been displaced from their homes in northern Uganda, and who agreed that they should come together and deal with their problems collectively. WSEY started with small contributions and loans, which built up sums of interest to be shared annually by the group. Since then it had become a registered community group with Kampala City Council Authority (KCCA) with 78 members – mostly older women, but also a few younger women and men. This registration helps them to access government grants for women's groups around the city. The members would support each other and their families with household items such as soap, sugar and even furniture, as well as 'revolving contributions' of cash.

Each week there was a new beneficiary, who would receive contributions during the weekly meetings. The giver and receiver would have discussed and agreed the amount of the contributions in advance. A strict record was kept by the group secretaries to ensure that the recipient would then give the same amount in return. If contributions were less than the amount agreed, the beneficiary would notify the secretaries and the chairwoman to ensure that it could be rectified. This rotation meant that the recipient would have access to a lump sum of money for investments 'to support the family'. A few members had mentioned that at first many husbands resented the group and the fact that their wives were away from their home on a Sunday evening. Over time, however, they saw the benefit of the 'family support' rotations, with their wives able to bring home extra food and household items.

The Local Councillor 3 (LC3) for Lusozi hill had been the chairwoman of the group since being elected in her position by the members in 2000. She would be supported by Denis, whose mother was one of the founding members, and he would help to run the group as an MC at each of their meetings. They also had four secretaries who would manage the books. Every Sunday evening the WSEY group would meet to celebrate the beneficiary or *'mugoole'* (bride) (Fig. 4.3). The Soda Bar would be decorated with white material hung over the roof and walls, as well as ribbon draped in the colour of the beneficiaries' choice, often to match their outfits. The DJs would set up the sound system for the party and sodas arranged on the top table. The group secretaries would come early to update the records in notebooks, calculating and storing the contributions in a locked box. A few members would then start to arrive, wearing

Figure 4.3 Group members enjoying the Sunday party. The week's beneficiary and two honorary members are in the foreground of the photo, where they face the other women dancing throughout the evening. Photo by Charlotte Hawkins.

smart, colourful dresses. They would greet each other and take a seat, waiting for the party to begin.

Once a small crowd of members had gathered in the bar, the beneficiary would make her entrance. She would be flanked by two 'honorary members' wearing matching dresses chosen by the beneficiary and often made to order. The women's hair and make-up would be immaculate for the event and they would sometimes have matching jewellery. Their entrance would be marked by a song of their choice and all the women celebrating '*ojili*' or 'ululating'. They would walk slowly through the bar in time with the music, coming to a halt by their chairs at the front of the room. Here they would face the rest of the members, who would circle and dance around them. Once the song had finished the honorary members would sit either side of the *mugoole* and their guests, including family and friends, who would take their places at a table behind them. Late arrivals would kneel to greet them, starting with the chairwoman and followed by the beneficiary.

The party could only begin once the chairwoman had arrived, to more *ojili*. The women would kneel to greet her as she took her seat at the end of the top table. Denis, the MC, would manage the proceedings with his microphone, inciting enthusiasm where it was lacking, hurrying late members and nominating someone to give the opening prayer. 'Let's keep the spirit as usual'. Most of the group's members are Acholi, but some are from elsewhere, so he speaks mostly in English, but also slips into Luo, Luganda and Kiswahili. He would then call each member, divided into groups A, B and C, to contribute one by one. They would bring the cash and lead the procession of members from the entrance to the front of the room to dance with the beneficiaries. Typically each member would choose their favourite song each week. The music would come from different regions in Uganda, and sometimes further afield, especially the Democratic Republic of Congo, Kenya, Nigeria and South Africa; each song also would have a specific style of dancing. As a song ended, everyone would quickly sit down for Denis's public counting of the contribution, the cash held up note by note by a chosen member for the purposes of transparency:

> 10, 20, 30, 40, 50 THOUSAND! Can we have a round of applause please for the *mugoole*, our sister and beloved member!

I saw contributions vary between 10,000 UGX (£2) to 2 million UGX (£396), to a total of up to 12 million UGX (£2,377) throughout the evening, the biggest sums for the most wealthy or popular members.

Beyond the financial gains for 'family support', many of the members explained how much they enjoy the weekly opportunity to meet, talk, dance and forget their problems at home; they often commented that 'it makes life a bit interesting'. Denis said the dancing 'takes the stress out for women', helping them to mitigate the challenges of daily life, and find wellbeing; 'it means that in Lusozi we are happy', with dance being an 'emotional resource'[31] to alleviate the stresses of everyday life and to gain joy in its place. Aliel Christine is 45 years old, a single mother of seven boys and a long-standing member of WSEY. She explained how she has benefited from being in the group:

> *I saw WSEY some time back and I realised they had happiness, which attracted me to join it. So I joined. When I joined I saw happiness in me and all the thoughts and stress I had went away. When I go there on Sunday, I get happiness and come back home with it... It has given me what helps me. I have built a house at home* [in Palabek, Kitgum] *and now I can even go to my own house. I left saucepans there and other things, so when I enter I can just start to cook ... I will go back home when I retire because I'm still working right now... I have gotten a lot of good things* [from WSEY]. *I got joy from it because I had many thoughts of being alone, but now I am very good and don't think of anything. Every week in and week out, we are always very happy.*

Even if you leave your home with some anger, when you reach there joy starts coming out of you… WSEY is like my father, mother and sister, which brings people to associate together.

The same sense of friendship, stress relief and mutual support was widely reported by other members. Their WhatsApp group is filled with the photographs of the *mugoole* each week (Fig. 4.4), as well as videos, messages, memes and prayers. The group was created by the chairwoman who is probably the most active member, regularly forwarding updates of news from the community and beyond, such as photos from meetings, public health updates and job opportunities. Other members would also share season's greetings, prayers and parables, news articles and videos, often focused on current affairs and popular media from the Acholi sub-region.

Of course there is occasionally contention within the group as well as harmony. The chairwoman herself admitted that she would get frustrated when she had sent something via the WhatsApp group and nobody would respond: 'it's disheartening'. She and Denis are deeply committed to the group meetings, which come with regular obligations, leaving no time to rest from their already busy political schedules. They sometimes

Figure 4.4 A member taking photographs of the *mugoole* and her honorary members. Photo by Charlotte Hawkins.

expressed their frustrations about this, particularly when the members failed to uphold time commitments. Originally, when I started attending, the meetings would start at around 5.00 p.m. and end by 10.00 p.m. Towards the end of that year, most members failed to turn up until 8.00 p.m., with the party going on until 1.00 a.m. on Monday morning – putting more pressure on Denis and the chairwoman and demanding more of everyone's time.

Popularity was on public display at the parties, with some members having a much bigger turn out, a more excited reception, more photographs and more enthusiastic dancing. Greater popularity could correspond to greater wealth, as these members were both the givers and receivers of greater sums of money. This could exclude the poorer members, creating additional pressures rather than relieving stress as intended. As Denis remarked, 'poverty makes people lose confidence, they have a feeling of inferiority'. He observed that his good friend, a younger member, had a smaller crowd at her party, with smaller donations and with no family members in attendance – yet he felt that she would be someone who would benefit the most from having a special evening, with all eyes on her. In contrast, members with more money such as Rihanna, 'a friend to many', had to take down the fencing of the Soda Bar in order to accommodate all of her guests. She invested in elaborate decorations, including a throne, and had a red carpet rolled out. Rihanna's contributions were much larger and included additional gifts from other members. As with earlier *awak* working groups, the production of resources through co-operative practices can be determined by existing economic access;[32] those with more fields can yield more crops through co-operative *aleya* farming, just as those with more money can yield greater reciprocated contributions through rotational savings.

Part of the appeal of the parties was the opportunity for the members to dress beautifully (Fig. 4.5). On occasion, the beneficiaries designed dresses for themselves and their honorary members, expressing themselves and receiving recognition. As the chairwoman observed:

> They want to be the best dancers, you want to be the most beautiful, your hair should look so smart. So that happiness ... sometimes I sit and say eh eh! I have done my part.

Other community members felt that this way of dressing up could cause competition and bitterness, as in this conversation between two women:

Figure 4.5 A still from the film 'Who should enrich you?' https://bit.ly/3NWU1dn.

Speaker one: The whole community cannot join WSEY. Maybe I want to talk to the chairwoman to see if she can again develop another WSEY for low-income earners… But now this one people fear because you see how they dress… You would buy a dress like you are competing, you have to put on more smartly than others.

Speaker two: Those people buy dresses! My auntie bought *gomesi* (dresses) for 300,000 UGX (£63.50) … how much?!

Speaker one: You see that's another loss, we want something which you cannot inject a lot of money into it… Now if for your week you have cooked, next week I will also want to compete, I will put on smartly, now you end up buying expensive clothes, yet you're going to get less money because you're competing with others. And if you do things that are not nice to people they will even start talking about you, 'ehh for this one it was just like that', so people fear that… There are those who come to show off, she gives 600,000 UGX (£127) and then 120,000 UGX (£25.40) [laughing], so a person who has brought 10,000 UGX (£2.10) feels very small and you don't fit in the whatever… They select – if someone has money, they will come to your party…You have money, they will come!

Then because of your dress, because you cannot afford nice shoes, they still talk of you [laughing]. And the worst is that the little that you contribute, they have to announce it.

While the group can put individual members under certain pressures, in general it was clearly successful in financially supporting women and their families in Lusozi, providing a place for members to express themselves and to make friends, dance and enjoy life, leaving their problems at home. This provides 'connections to sustain urban life', helping people to navigate and cope with uncertainty.[33] As in Aliel's account of her membership, this joy or enrichment is something you can actively seek by taking part, while leaving stress behind. In this way, while drawing from the idiom of family responsibility within the group and providing 'family support' beyond, WSEY is distinct from family life, offering an escape from the pressures it imparts on women in particular. The group would recognise and celebrate the beneficiary, who could gain as an individual from crafting self-expression while being together in enjoyment with others. Who should enrich you? Yourselves, together.

Place of Peace had similarly achieved the aims of creating a sense of family support through hierarchy and sisterhood, both in being together and in offering tangible forms of assistance. Many of the members of WSEY, including Aliel, also attended Place of Peace; it provided school fees for many of the single mothers in the Lusozi community, as well as access to healthcare and education for themselves. Beyond that, members stated that they had found 'sisters, even mothers' thanks to Place of Peace, an extended family within their neighbourhood to guide them and to share their problems with.

Place of Peace

Place of Peace[34] is an international, faith-based NGO set up in 1992 to support mothers in Kampala. The group in Lusozi is one of a few branches around the city. Many participants, including local leaders, consider it to be the only NGO that has really helped the Lusozi community. Their mission statement includes the following:

> The greatest need of a human being is the need for belonging, which gives stability and certainty in all aspects of life… The person who belongs becomes a protagonist because he receives a face and receives a consciousness that unites him with the reality… Belonging to a design that is not yours, that is to say, belonging to somebody else, you become free.

Since 1992 Place of Peace had supported members with medicine and education in health, literacy, finance and skills such as beading. They had visited national parks in Uganda and had also made trips to Nairobi, Rwanda and Italy. They even guaranteed that the children of their members get a good quality education, either in their own school or by paying their school fees. As most of the women are living with HIV, they would visit the Place of Peace staff for antiretroviral (ART) medications, as well as free testing and counselling. A nurse was freely available for consultations and prescriptions every day, and there was also a doctor every Saturday. Any cases too complicated would be referred to the relevant hospital. Every Monday and Wednesday, Place of Peace would hold their meetings and classes, which the directors of Place of Peace Uganda and of the Lusozi branch permitted me to join on a regular basis: 'Go and take part, maybe you can shake your bones – this is what we do!'

During the first meeting we attended, the director explained that she was proud of what the organisation had achieved and was grateful for the friendship Place of Peace offers its members. She felt that it had 'given them back life' as it had helped them to 'discover themselves'; 'before they were miserable, but now you can't even tell they're sick' (Fig. 4.6). The nurse later explained that they teach the women that they have personal value, reminding them that *'sickness, including HIV, doesn't mean you're not like other people, who will also inevitably one day suffer*

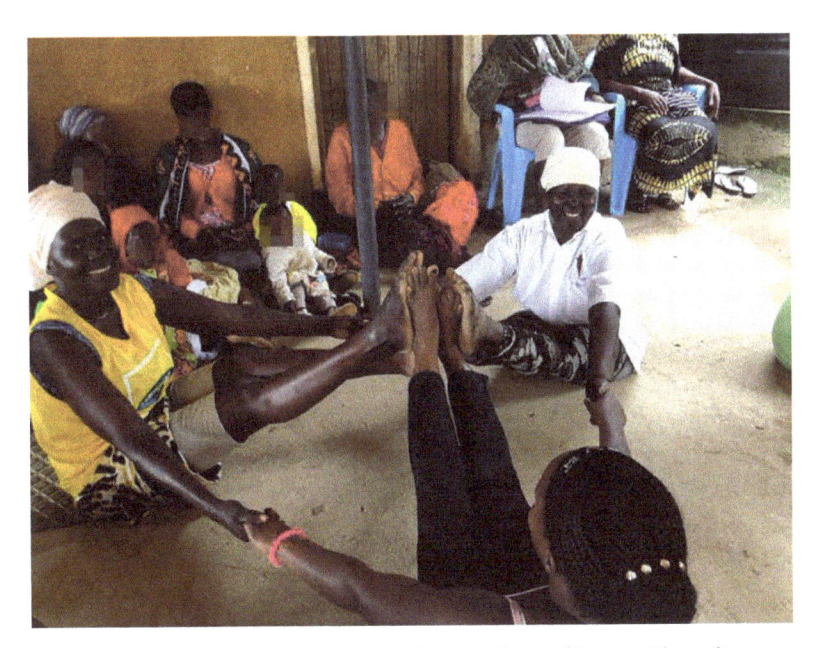

Figure 4.6 Women in an exercise class at Place of Peace. Photo by Charlotte Hawkins.

sickness themselves'. In the past HIV was more stigmatised and isolating, but *'they're now free thanks to Place of Peace'*, as evident in the health and happiness of their weekly meetings. The conversation below demonstrates the agreement between the Place of Peace director, nurse and Amor about the importance of the friendship offered by the group:

> Director: They feel they're sisters.
> Nurse: Being together…
> Amor: Unity is good.
> Director: You have it, get friends, go back free.
> Amor: You can't just finish your problems yourself.
> Director: Talking about problems, you learn that mine is the same…

As with WSEY, these sisterly friendships within the group, sharing problems and laughter, were evident both during the meetings and in conversations with individual members. Amor's aunt said she was happy with Place of Peace as it had helped her to pay the children's school fees and also meant she had met many friends. She herself grew up with boys and at first found it hard to cope with women, something that Place of Peace has helped her with. She has gained 'sisters, even mothers', who tell you off after a quarrel and help guide you. Problems shared 'kill stress'. They teach them that all people have equal value, 'you're all the same', whether you're rich or poor, healthy or sick. Amor's aunt had also become physically fitter thanks to the training, a weekly exercise class run by a group of young men.

As well as paying for the school fees of their children, Place of Peace would also provide education for the women themselves. Every Wednesday a teacher would come to give lessons in English and maths. Many of the women had limited or no schooling so the focus was on primary level education, with the group split into ability, from Primary 1 (P1) to Primary 7 (P7). As the teacher once reminded them, 'if you want to learn, you have to forget about your age and think of yourself in P3'. Lessons would be delivered in a 'repeat after me' style, the women responding in chorus; 'when you want to learn, you have to speak,' the teacher explained (Fig. 4.7). Most members speak Acholi, but not all of them, so lessons were also translated into Luganda or given entirely in English. Some of the women joked that they had been in P1 for 10 years as a result, demonstrating how the emphasis on the English language can present an obstacle in education in Uganda.[35] But many said they were now happy to be able to spell their names, meaning they could give signatures when required.

Figure 4.7 An English lesson at Place of Peace. Photo by Charlotte Hawkins.

As well as English, the teachers sometimes focused on a particular theme for discussion such as family, finances and sexual health; the women would bring forward their ideas or questions. One lesson was about family responsibilities. The transcript of this conversation below reveals consensus on the roles of fathers, mothers and children, and a sense of changing duties in line with 'world needs':

> Teacher: The mother cannot do the duties of the father, but of course it depends on the situation. What a man can do a woman can also do, these days women have overtaken. That one comes as a result of disorganisation in the world. But in accordance with the setting, there are specific duties. Can anyone tell us what your husband does? Some of what the father does at home?
>
> [Laughter]
>
> Member 1: Producing children!
>
> [Laughter]
>
> Member 2: Pay rent.
>
> …

Teacher: The father is the head of the family. Do we all agree?

Members: Yes.

Teacher: In case of any issue at home, who is responsible? Who stands forward? It is the man who comes out, not so?

Members: Yes [chorus].

Member 3: A man caters for basic needs – rent, food, shelter, school fees.

Member 4: Those days yes, but these days no…

Member 5: Nowadays they put on trousers for nothing!

Member 4: They only come for graduation.

Member 7: If you ask for money, they will slap you. They blame the women.

Member 8: You have to fulfil the point of marriage to produce children as in the Bible.

…

Teacher: What about the role of the mother?

Member 9: Cooking food.

…

Member 3: Washing clothes.

…

Member 10: Teaching the children. Men have little time to stay at home, so you find that most of the time mothers stay at home with their children. The behaviour of a child always reflects training given by the mother.

Member 11: When greeting, people don't kneel any more as sign of respect. It is a sign of Dotcom. Let us revive it. At the moment there's no respect.

Member 14: The work of a woman and also man is producing children.

…

Teacher: What about the role of children?

Member 14: Respecting parents.

…

Member 15: They need to perform well at school. That was not here initially, but because of world needs we are now taking them up.

Member 16: The world is moving forwards, it's not going backwards.

While this conversation was humorous in tone, with answers often followed by a chorus of laughter, the jokes also expressed the 'complex social position' they occupy as women,[36] many of them facing marital uncertainty and domestic violence, and bringing up children on their own. This role imparts additional – often sole – responsibility for the children's wellbeing, education and behaviour. The conversation clearly highlights the perceived role of the wider 'world' in altering the distribution of family responsibilities, intensifying the responsibilities of women. The women show how they are expected to mitigate this 'disorganisation' of gender roles[37] by managing childcare and domestic responsibilities, as well as earning money to provide for their families.

Participation in Place of Peace showed how the group overlaps with members' family responsibilities beyond, demonstrating how community-based support groups can intersect with households and provide them with a wider support network. This support – and its limits – was also continually negotiated. For example, during a discussion about fundraising for a member who had lost her sister, the director encouraged the members to attend her vigil, even if they had not known her personally:

> It's not about money, it's about presence. We all know how it feels to lose someone, to have that gap.

Another member had recently lost a husband. Someone responded that 'every second, every moment, people are passing on'. A discussion arose: who should we help first? Who should we give money to? How do we decide if a relative is close enough? The consensus was that if it's 'within the circle' of immediate family – a mother, father, husband, brother, sister, son, daughter – they will contribute 'as many times as needed in the month'. They agreed they would not contribute for those outside the circle, such as grandparents, uncles or aunts. The director concluded the discussion:

> Death is not all about money. Presence is more important. Money is dividing us. Going to see somebody is more precious than anything you will carry ... but give a contribution of 1k if you can. Visiting a member who has lost her sister doesn't need transport, you can just go by foot.

Responsibility towards family and friends in times of sickness and death, in terms of both presence and money, will be further examined in the subsequent chapters on mobile money, health and care and co-operation respectively. As the director suggests, money can be considered both a divisive and relational entity, which can either undermine or contribute to relationships.

Conclusion

The three groups outlined here seek togetherness, understood in this chapter in relation to Ladit's description of *aleya* or communal farming in Acholi: digging that could take one person a month to finish takes 30 people just one day, followed by *awak*, a meal and celebration that can be enjoyed together.[38] This idea of togetherness depicts the pragmatic potential for a collective to alleviate burdens and create joy for an individual. The collectivisation of individual endeavours also affords self-expression and self-reliance, interdependence an 'insurance against dependence'.[39] This is evident, for example, in the income from the *boda* purchased by TIS, or in the financial independence gained at WSEY, or in the friendships gained at Place of Peace: 'belonging to somebody else, you become free'.

Across all three groups, a sense of belonging was compared to that of family, providing elders or sisterhood to turn to for advice or assistance. The groups were all particularly well attended by older members, demonstrating their active role within networks of community support.[40] Distance between relatives, as well as limitations in formal urban welfare systems, may necessitate these family-like ties and obligations among friends close by in the city, as in the conversation among Place of Peace members emphasising the need to be 'present' for others in times of mourning. Perhaps the burden of family responsibility could then be managed through these extended community ties, offering the opportunity to leave the stresses of family life at home while supporting the household. TIS members gained social insurance through pooled resources; WSEY members gained happiness at their Sunday parties, as well as benefits of the 'family support' rotation; Place of Peace members gained accessible health services and education for themselves and their children, as well as a sense of belonging. Compassion and fun were observable in these groups, as well as inevitable pressures and obligations, indicative of the tensions that arise in communally striving for individual gain. TIS's intention to 'make light the heaviness on an individual', and the existing friendships between members, can make it easy to ignore the rules or refuse to repay a debt. In WSEY financial obligations could place a particular burden on its poorer members, the same stresses the group intended to alleviate.

Savings groups in particular present an interesting context to consider the co-existence of seemingly conflicting aspirations within community relationships: formality and informality, self-interest and mutuality, independence and belonging. Other anthropologists who have studied savings groups[41] observe similar paradoxes in self-organised groups 'formalised from below'.[42] In TIS, for example, there is a continual debate about the need to act both 'constitutionally' and 'kindly'. Savings groups can represent an 'economy from below',[43] that integrates particular social priorities of co-operation, mutual support and collective gain, within and against an economic context which propagates self-interest and inequity. As evident in this chapter, the 'above' and 'below' are interrelated in complex ways. However, a situated ethnographic focus on co-operative efforts 'from below' affords emphasis on the array of creative practices which seek to bridge the gaps.[44]

This also applies to the concept of 'smart-from-below'[45] – an idea central to the wider ASSA project for highlighting the creative appropriation of global smartphones according to specific personal and contextual needs. As in the example of savings groups as a self-organised response to financial hardship and inaccessible healthcare, 'smart-from-below' also emphasises the agency of older people in bridging their personal lives and wider society while 'ageing with smartphones'. Although smartphones are often associated with social rupture, the next chapter will show how the phone allows older participants to enact ideals of ageing and to forge continuities in their relationships, despite the flux and instability which threatens them. A key example is the use of mobile money remittances for elder care, which repurposes money and the digital to uphold care at a distance.

Notes

1. As shown in Opira Otto's 2013 thesis on 'institutional arrangements for agricultural labour' in a predominantly Acholi village in midwestern Uganda, farmers 'pool their labour to work on each member's farm in succession' (Otto 2013, 169). Such an arrangement facilitates the work pragmatically and in line with co-operative moralities. Girling's 1960 ethnographic survey of Acholiland similarly depicted *awak* or 'work parties', also emphasising the need to work together due to the short time frame available for planting after the dry season and before the rains in the region (Girling 2019, 89). Girling also shows how *awak* is not egalitarian due to disparities in land access (Girling 2019, 130).
2. Otto 2013, 29.
3. Acholi name redacted for anonymity.

4. As above.
5. Hart 2008.
6. Hart 2008. Hart argues that all human institutions are founded on the conflict and inseparability of self-interest and mutuality. 'There are two prerequisites for being human: to be self-reliant to a high degree and to belong to others' (2008, 1–2). In line with Mauss's work on 'the gift' (1990), he advocates for a particularistic, pragmatic understanding of how economic institutional possibilities and co-operative movements have historically been integrated.
7. le Polain, Sterck and Nyssens 2018, 162.
8. Nakirya and State 2013.
9. This 'community-based microfinance model' has been widely promoted and implemented by the government and international NGOs as part of a 'development' agenda, 'as a way of pooling resources together in order to facilitate development' (Green 2019). Geertz originally conceived of savings groups, specifically rotating funds, as a 'rung on the ladder between agrarian and modern economies' (Green 2019, cf. Geertz 1962). Geertz's assertion fits with the dominant narrative of 'development' as a linear process towards highly industrialised neoliberal economies of the Global North; 'modernisation imaginaries' (Green 2019, cf. Geertz 1962). This linearity implies the advanced nature of these regions and assumes that their social economies are the norm to which those in the Global South should strive. Ardener has since contested Geertz's notion with the prediction (1964), and later the evidence (Ardener and Burman 1995), that in fact rotating schemes have continued to proliferate in the contemporary global capitalist economy. This 'development' agenda also encourages people living in poverty to take responsibility for their finances through such microfinance schemes (Ferguson 2015, 2) within an economic model of 'distribution' pervasive in the region, in which resources are shared across social networks, as in community-based savings organisations.
10. Nakirya and State 2013, 34.
11. Ardener 1964, 222.
12. Ardener and Burman 1995, 2.
13. Hart 2008.
14. Hart 2008, 4.
15. le Polain, Sterck and Nyssens 2018.
16. Green 2019.
17. Ardener 1964, 201.
18. Nakirya and State 2013, 32.
19. Robbins 2007; Goffman 1971; Green 2019.
20. This aligns with Nyamnjoh's depiction of social action in 'plural and diverse' African communities such as Lusozi 'that represent histories of mobilities, cultural encounters, negotiation and flux' (Ekechi, Kopytoff and Falola 1988; Nyamnjoh 2017): a 'socially predetermined frame … emphasises collective interests at the same time that it allows for individual creativity and self-activation' (Nyamnjoh 2002, 115). This defines individuality within a 'logic of collective action', through which individual endeavours are collectivised (Nyamnjoh 2002, 115). The environment is ordered to foster the best interests of the collective, which also serves the individual (Nyamnjoh 2017).
21. Jackson 2012.
22. Nyamnjoh 2017, 261.
23. Green 2019, 106.
24. Otto 2013, 149.
25. Redacted for anonymity purposes.
26. Hart 2008, 4.
27. Mauss and Halls 1990, 89–90. This exemplifies Mauss's idea that we should seek to draw from historical institutions of exchange in order to 'blend moderately' the economic realities of self-interest and the ideals of generosity: 'Togetherness is Strength'.
28. Hart 2008, 4.
29. Wignall et al. 2019; McFarlane and Silver 2017; McQuaid et al. 2021.
30. Nyamnjoh 2017, 259.
31. Neveu Kringelbach 2007, 1.
32. Girling 2019 [1960].
33. McFarlane and Silver 2017.
34. Pseudonym.
35. See Nankindu, Kirunda and Ogavu 2015; Ngũgĩ wa Thiong'o 2005.

36. Burgess and Campbell 2016, 50.
37. See Obbo 1980, 8.
38. Girling 2019 [1960]; Otto et al. 2013.
39. Nyamnjoh 2017, 261.
40. Wignall et al. 2019; McQuaid et al. 2021.
41. Green 2019; Ardener 1964.
42. Krige 2019.
43. Hart 2008.
44. See concluding discussion in co-edited volume 'mHealth: an Anthropological Approach', a publication forthcoming with UCL Press.
45. Pype 2017a.

5
The dotcom wave

Introduction

The previous chapters have built up a partial or 'incomplete' picture of the diverse social lives of older people in Lusozi. Often Amor and I saw how the older people we worked with sought to advise and provide for the younger generation and themselves through their everyday working routines and, in some cases, through mutual support networks and financial co-operation across the neighbourhood. This chapter extends the discussion on intergenerational relationships and care through a focus on mobile phone and smartphone use. This includes everyday practices such as phone sharing within households, buying phones for older relatives and teaching them how to use them, the practice of care at a distance via phone calls and mobile money transfers, the use of WhatsApp to share information and co-ordinate care across families and community groups and younger people connecting their parents to news, information, networks and entertainment. This chapter adopts a digital anthropology approach, which prioritises the appropriation of technologies within specific socio-cultural and historical contexts.[1] Taken together, this shows how the phone can be used to serve vital social needs, in contrast with public narratives that dismiss the smartphone and social media use as wasteful and unproductive.

Smartphones can be broadly understood as an icon of 'dotcom'. As shown throughout the monograph so far, dotcom can be used to describe the contemporary era and the generation growing up within it, often referring to a broad and complex set of 'world changes' and their impact on values of respect and relatedness. These dotcom trajectories encompass various yet intersecting aspects of the wider world, incorporating, for example, the influence of social media and ICTs, lifestyles in the city and 'development' ideologies. The phone acts as a lens onto efforts to establish continuity within relationships despite these societal shifts, reconfiguring social roles and 'ways of speaking, thinking, and feeling about the family – that mobilize material resources and people in ways that are considered normal and natural'[2] – in this case, the older generation providing the younger with an education, and the younger generation providing care for their elders in later life. Phone practices themselves serve to expand these family expectations across distances, bringing both new conveniences and obligations. And, as some participants show in this chapter, as well as dotcom disrupting intergenerational knowledge flows, the younger generation sharing dotcom knowledge and resources with their parents signifies respect.

In this way, the same dotcom technologies associated with declining respect and care for elders also accommodate them across shifting terrains. In the smartphone, then, the 'dotcom wave' does not only overwhelm or erode existing relationships and social norms, but also originates and becomes domesticated within them. As highlighted in previous ethnographic studies of ICT and phone use in Africa,[3] and the few conducted in Uganda in particular,[4] the phone offers insight into processes of social continuity and change more broadly. This is particularly the case when we consider their 'intergenerational implications' from the often-overlooked perspective of older people.

Throughout the chapter, 'mobile phones' will be used to refer to small handsets without access to internet, known as 'buttons' in Lusozi (Fig. 5.1), 'smartphones' to internet-enabled phones with a touch screen and 'phones' to either or both. Mobile phones are owned by the majority, around 60 per cent of the people we worked with, and smartphones by a growing and significant minority, around 35 per cent. This proportion also reflects national statistics on phone ownership in Uganda. With differentiated access to smartphones, existing social inequities are reproduced through 'digital capital', the distributed advantages of technology and 'the wherewithal to use it', which includes digital literacy and also calling and data costs.[5] Like Bourdieu's concept of cultural capital, 'digital capital' is convertible to other forms of capital for attaining social mobility; connections, knowledge, health, skills and resources. In order to understand how people both use and conceptualise smartphones, we employed different methodological approaches, including an open-ended, story-based approach and more systematic surveys about day-to-day usage based on data within the phone. The latter included an app survey, a mobile money survey and a phone use survey, which considered both phone ownership and daily phone practices.

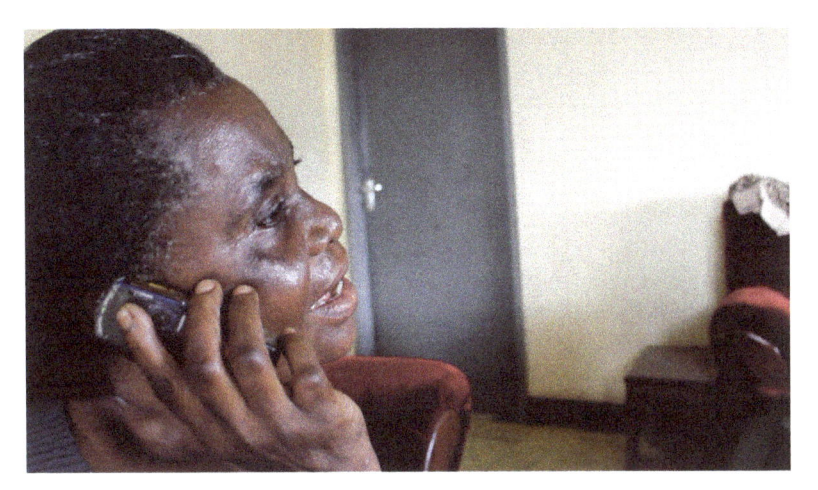

Figure 5.1 Making a phone call. Photo by Charlotte Hawkins.

Bringing the world together

Throughout the research, people would often say that 'mobile phones have brought the world together', an observation that could refer to an expansion of home, or encounters with the wider world. Undoubtedly, they offer people new opportunities for connectivity and with the advent of internet-enabled smartphones in 2011, these possibilities have become even broader.[6] In recent decades, as witnessed by older research participants, there has been an unprecedented 'mobile revolution' in Africa,[7] where take-up of mobile phones has been particularly rapid and dynamic,[8] the fastest rate of growth in the world.[9] This is true in Uganda, where mobile phone ownership continues to increase year on year. A report by the Uganda Communications Commission (UCC) on telephone subscriptions in Uganda at the end of March 2020 found that there were 28.4 million people with mobile subscriptions used in the prior three months, representing a 'tele-density' of 67 per cent of the population.[10] This compares to 53 per cent in 2014 and just 4.9 per cent in 2004.[11] A 2018 report by The National Information Technology Authority Uganda (NITA-U) found that 14.4 million Ugandans (37 per cent of the population) now access the internet on their mobile phones.[12] The Uganda National Household Survey (UNHS) 2016/17, carried out by NITA-U, found that only 3 per cent of households have a working computer,[13] confirming that phones are the primary platform for accessing the internet in Uganda.

Since 1998, the arrival of telecommunications companies in Africa is said to have painted the landscape yellow with branded awnings.[14] Mobile phones have also brought employment opportunities, with vendors selling accessories, airtime and mobile money, as well as providing charging points and phone repairs. There were 33 airtime and mobile money vendors in Lusozi at the time of fieldwork, with many vendors lamenting the rate of growing competition. At a national level, the number of mobile money vendors continues to increase, up by 3.5 per cent in 2018.[15] MTN, Airtel and Africell were the dominant mobile phone providers.

While owned by a significant minority now, it is predicted that smartphones will dominate the market in the near future.[16] The greater penetration of internet-enabled phones in Uganda is partly due to a proliferation of cheaper models being introduced to the market. For example, the Chinese brand Techno were selling internet-enabled phones for as little as 58,000 UGX (£12). Mobile money vendors in Lusozi estimated that about 30 per cent of their customers had smartphones, but that they were 'mostly youth'. This estimation was broadly reflected throughout the ethnography; across a total of 204 individual interviewees, with an average age of 51, 72 (35 per cent) had working smartphones, 116 (57 per cent) had a mobile phone only and 19 (9 per cent) currently had no phone of their own. This might be either because their previous phone was broken or stolen (15) or because they had never been able to afford one (4).

Recent national statistics on phone ownership in Uganda, although quickly outdated, showed that demographic factors related to age, gender and geography influence the likelihood of access to mobile phones and smartphones. A higher proportion of young people own phones than older people. More men own phones than women,[17] with a gender gap of 17 per cent in mobile phone ownership and 48 per cent in mobile internet use reported by the Global System for Mobile Communications (GSMA) in 2020. This is particularly pronounced in rural areas.[18] Overall, more people living in urban areas own mobile phones than their rural counterparts,[19] and in Kampala there is better access to telecommunication, electricity and internet infrastructure than in rural areas.[20] These 'digital divides' are also broadly reflected across this ethnography. According to a household survey of 50 participants between September and December 2018, with an average of 5.6 people in their households, 1 man had a mobile phone compared to 0.65 women, while an average of 0.9 men vs 0.6 women owned a smartphone. The average age of smartphone owners in the household was 31 years old, compared to 38 years for mobile phone owners.

In order to manage these disparities, people in Lusozi would often share phones within the household or neighbourhood. Of the 50 people who responded to the phone survey, only four people said that they were the sole user of their phone, the rest citing an average of three other people who have access to borrow them. This includes their children, siblings, partners, neighbours and friends, who would use the phones to play games, take photos, call friends and play music. During many interviews, phones would change hands in order for relatives or neighbours to make a call. Airtime was also often circulated between family and friends, with 33 of 50 people reporting that they had sent airtime in the last six months, and 30 people reporting that they had received it. 'Beeping' – that is, drop calling someone so they call you back and cover the cost of the call – was also common, with 40 people of 50 in a survey having 'beeped' someone in the last six months, and 46 saying they had been 'beeped' themselves. However, beeped calls can easily be refused, implicating a sense of potential power dynamics that can be reinforced in phone sharing practices – which, as shown in previous studies conducted in Uganda, are not always 'entirely egalitarian'.[21] Phone owners are able to refuse access to others according to their own discretion, such as husbands restricting their wives' usage.[22] As shown below, this can reinforce existing inequities determining access to phones and their capacities.

Phone sharing

Nakito, aged 48, and her son jointly owned and ran a hair salon in Lusozi (Fig. 5.2). While Nakito had her own 'button' phone for work calls, she did not have enough money to buy her own smartphone, so shared one with her son. On alternate weeks they would take their turn to be the main smartphone holder, updating the background photo, Facebook and WhatsApp accounts and even the password. That way, both of them would have periods of independent ownership, but could also use the phone at any time, having obtained permission from the current owner first. Within the phone there were certain apps that only one or the other would use, such as an app called 'Love Quotes' that only her son used to choose messages for his girlfriend. He was the one who knew how to load music on the phone from a memory card, which they would update regularly, especially when they heard something new they liked on the

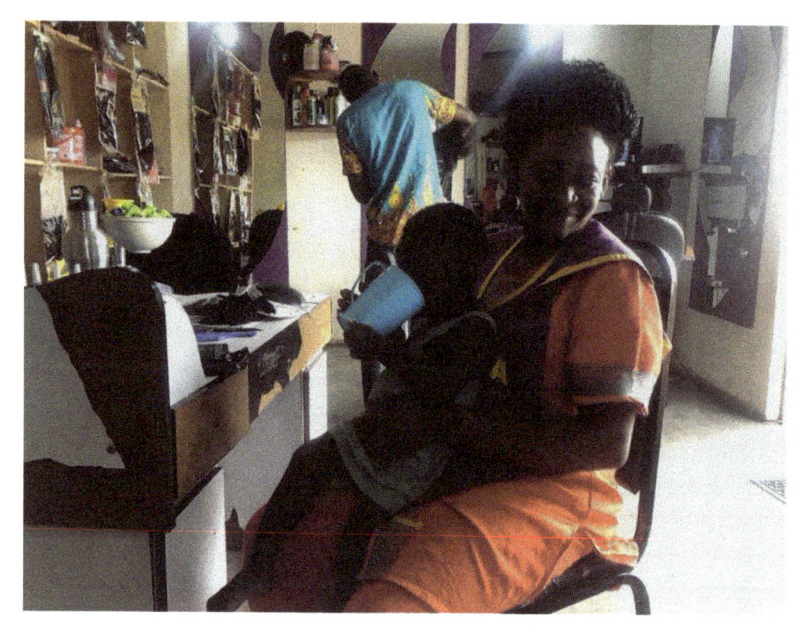

Figure 5.2 Nakito with her son and grandson in their salon. Photo by Charlotte Hawkins.

radio. During Nakito's week she would look for her own music, preferring Baganda songs. They had the same photos, mostly those she had taken of her young grandchildren 'to keep the memories', especially on special occasions like their birthdays.

Other instances of sharing were not so mutual or egalitarian. This was particularly apparent during interviews with people who did not currently have a mobile phone, as was the case for Acen, a 40-year-old mother of three. She had heard of the internet, and that it means you can get to know what was happening outside of Uganda. She would have liked to learn how to use it, but for now she '*doesn't even know how to use a phone*'. Without education, stable employment or support from the father of her children, Acen struggled to pay the rent and school fees, making it impossible to consider buying additional items such as a mobile phone. Occasionally, once or twice a month, she would load 500 UGX (£0.10) airtime on to a neighbour's phone in order to communicate with her relatives in the village. They would show her how to use it, to dial the number and make the call. Normally, she would call to check on her relatives, to find out if everything was stable or if anyone was sick. If they needed to talk to her, they would also call the neighbour's number. The last time Acen had heard from her relatives, they had called to tell her that her mother was ill. She would have preferred to go there physically to check on her, but as she could not raise the money for transport, she sent them 10,000 UGX (£2) instead. At the time of the interview, Acen had not yet received an update on her mother's health as she had been unable to call her relatives again. She had had some challenges when asking the neighbours to use the phone. She had overheard them complain that *'she's coming to disturb us'*, so now she is afraid to ask. She tried to ask a second neighbour, who *'refused totally there and then'*, claiming that her phone did not have any battery and that she was always out. This is one of the problems causing Acen to *'feel totally helpless'*.

The practice of sharing access to phones responds to economic necessity and can therefore reflect existing inequities. As in Acen's case, restricted phone access has direct implications on her ability to take care of her relatives, to gain information and to do so independently of her neighbours. While phones compress distances in an unprecedented way, 'bringing the world together', they can also expand inequalities, bringing the world apart. This illustrates the concept of 'digital capital',[23] which affords access to other forms of social resources. Access to 'digital capital' also depends on various costs associated with using a phone. We found that the majority of smartphone owners participating in this research topped up 1,000–2,000 UGX (£0.20–0.40) on a daily basis, for both airtime and data. This suggests that typically phone calls and the internet were inaccessible to smartphone owners at least once a day.

With these airtime and data limitations, phone services would often be used on a controlled basis. Large WhatsApp groups would be avoided in favour of less data intensive 1:1 messaging, Instagram and YouTube were often used sparingly and data could be switched on and off only when needed. Data and storage shortages on cheaper smartphones could restrict space for new app downloads, or for storing messages and images. With data and storage preservation a priority, the smartphone becomes a tool to be manoeuvred in order to achieve specific communicative ends.

Taken together, these various factors suggest that 'digital divides' do not form a straightforward binary between smartphone owners and non-smartphone owners, as the term implies, but that instead they operate along a more complex and shifting process.[24] This is also evident in variations in phone quality. For example, many people had owned smartphones in the past that had since been stolen or spoiled, and many second-hand phones would circulate and break down. Kilongeni, Amor's father, was my first interviewee, and we had many conversations throughout the research about smartphones, how they are used and their impact on social life. A few months after we first met, his smartphone had broken and the heavily taxed repair cost 150,000 UGX (£31) – as much as a new phone. Either way, he could not afford it at the time. Meanwhile he used a 'button' phone, which he bought for a discount and then found to be ineffective, as it failed to register missed calls. This was causing problems with his daughter, who would often call to check that Kilongeni had picked up her five-year-old son safely from school. While she worked full time, Kilongeni was 'child support', so he found it frustrating that she would call every day.

> She likes calling, but I don't feel good. As a grandparent, give me responsibility. Since I brought her up as a mother, I cannot forget him.

In the following section, Kilongeni's narration about his use of phones and their broader implications introduces how they can be representative of 'intergenerational encounters' (Fig. 5.3).[25] These encounters are considered from the perspective of the 'middle generation' – neither young nor elderly, but with care responsibilities for both. Alongside other

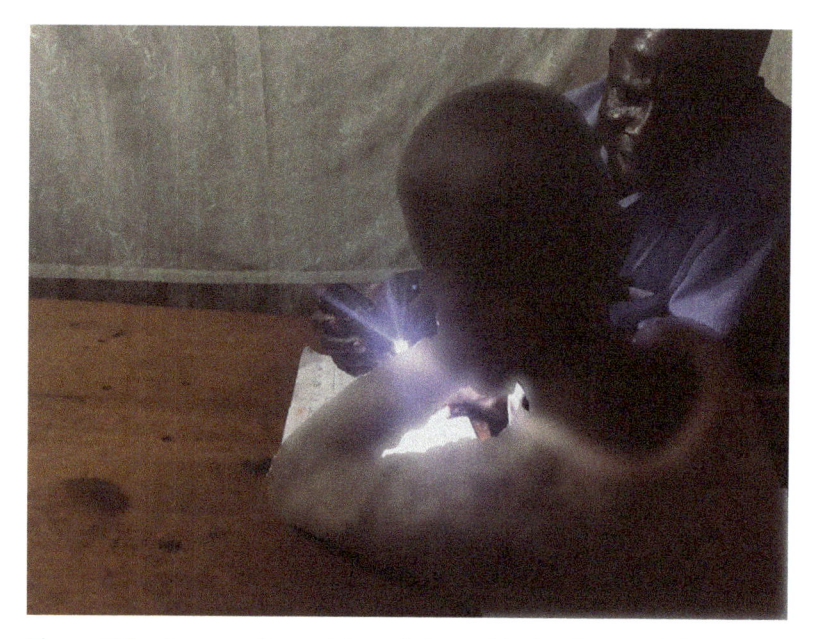

Figure 5.3 A research participant helping his daughter with her homework, using the torch on his mobile phone. Photo by Charlotte Hawkins.

ethnographic examples, this shows how the use and conceptualisation of the phone becomes embedded within existing intergenerational expectations and discourses, even as it reconfigures them.

The dotcom generation

Kilongeni had witnessed how phones have 'brought the world together', having lived without the conveniences of reduced distances between people, faster communication and financial transfers.

> For us when we were growing [in Palabek, Kitgum], information that we normally get is the one inside us, whatever was happening near us we knew. Within the district we knew. What was also happening in Kampala, once in a while, you will also get to know. The only media we were using was sometimes the radio… So, these phones came to Uganda in 1997, 1997… So, you see, this phone has helped people now. It has, it has in fact brought the world *closer*… I used to suffer with school fees when I was still in secondary school. There was a cousin of mine in Entebbe. Whenever I wanted school fees, I would write a letter, stamp and post it through the post office – it would take two months! Two months! For him to write… They chase you when you don't have the school fees, you remain at home. So now you see how it assists people's lives. I can now pick my phone, if I want to call mum, I call mum…

Like many other older people in Lusozi, Kilongeni had bought a 'simple phone' for his elderly mother in the village so that he could call and check on her. This could accommodate emotional, practical and financial support despite the 12-hour journey to her home:[26] 'I always need to call her'. Others, like Lakot, had received a smartphone from their children. She had told her three sons that she was praying for one of 'those phones', swiping her right forefinger across her left hand to imitate a screen, and her sons later surprised her with one as a gift. Lakot explained:

> My children don't want me to be worried because they know I took care of them.

Sons and daughters buying their parents mobile phones and smartphones, and teaching them to use them, can therefore signify respect and reciprocal, intergenerational care. A mobile phone demonstrates a commitment to staying in touch, and also to providing support, news, entertainment and access to wider social networks. This reflects Porter and colleagues' concept of young people as 'family information hubs', able to support the older generation to use their phones and access information.[27] Some of the older people we worked with explained how their children would show respect by educating them about phone use or by sharing knowledge that they have gained through their phones. Omara, for example, has two adult sons who would help him to communicate with people via Facebook and WhatsApp. As discussed in more detail later in this chapter, these were the most commonly used social media platforms in Lusozi, sometimes synonymous with 'the internet' itself.

> Now, dotcom, what does it mean? We learn also from them [young people]… They can do it for me, now I'm learning also from them slowly, slowly, so I will be doing it myself… I was advising them, 'You people, you study very hard, you should know the internet and the rest of the things because the world has changed now, everything is computerised, so you need to know', to keep us in contact with the outside.

With dotcom, the younger generation become the teachers or 'information hubs' for their elders, with the digital capital or ability to share their knowledge and connections with the outside world. As Archambault showed in her research in Mozambique, the mobile phone offers young people a tool to navigate social expectations, providing a platform for 'secrecy and disguise'.[28] This could cause uncertainties and moral 'disquiet' among older people, who found their inherited and experiential cultural knowledge to be increasingly 'sidelined'.[29] Or, as Kusimba and colleagues found in their 2016 study of mobile money use in Kenya, 'among elders, mobile phones are perceived as empowering women and youths to pursue affairs or run away from school'.[30] But as this research shows, rather than representing a pure inversion in the hierarchy of age, the younger generation's tendency to share their 'dotcom' knowledge with their parents can also be incorporated within existing expectations of elder respect, revealing a willingness to 'keep them in contact' with each other and with the outside world.

Younger people in Lusozi would also evidently help their parents to access news and networks, music and entertainment via their phones. A few older people explained how their sons would collect music for them from one of the three vendors in the area, such as Alimo Judith, whose son shows her videos of gospel choirs, and Nakito, whose son brings her Baganda songs. Customers would bring or buy a memory card or 'flash', then choose which genre they prefer for the vendor to download from Google. They pay 200 UGX (£0.04) per song or can buy a bundle of five songs for 1,000 UGX (£0.20). The vendors would try to keep up to date with the latest options on the programme and play the music from their sound system to attract customers. As one vendor explained:

> People come, especially guys who are current... They get interest from outside and they know what they want.

Older customers are 'quite rare … they come once in a while looking for old songs', such as gospel, Lingala or Acholi music: 'it makes them happy'.[31] In a situation where younger relatives – usually sons, nephews and grandsons – are responsible for choosing music and collecting it on flash disks for their families, parents and older relatives could be included in 'dotcom' circulations of music and entertainment. The music travels between generations and media platforms: the radio, the search engine, the vendor's hard drive, the flash drives and mobile phone, the sound system playing on the street and in people's homes. While spanning these spaces and material and digital processes, the content reproduces shared meanings and forges connections.

Although Omara and Kilongeni recognised these advantages of mobiles phones, they had concerns, like many others, about younger people's use of smartphones. Omara imitated young men always looking at their phones, having to charge them up to three times a day, in contrast to his own 'button', which only needed charging once a week.

> If I'm a bit alone at home, I just put it in the ear from here and I can get the music which can entertain me – but I don't keep on disturbing the phone every time!

A few of the older people we spoke with were proud of the longevity of their Nokia 'button' phones, that had survived many years and rarely need charging, in contrast with the frivolity of younger people's preference for battery-intensive, costly and short-lived smartphones like the prevalent Samsung and Huawei brands.

Kilongeni had similar concerns about his sons spending too much time on their phones and being distracted from their surroundings.

He tried to regulate their use of phones, advising them to avoid pornographic images and becoming addicted to their phones.

> I would rather advise them and that is always what I do... When children come back home, they have all their time on screen... For you the father, you don't care whether the pictures they show there are horrors or there is something pornographic... You say urgh!! After all this is the city, and that is not good... You regulate how the screen should be used.... Like I always tell them, I don't like receiving phone calls at night unless it's very serious, it is very important, and then the way you use your phone should not be an addiction... Like am sorry to refer to Smiley [pointing at his youngest son in the room], now he's on headsets, so he doesn't know he is in this environment.

As shown in The Global Smartphone,[32] fears about smartphone addiction and detachment from others are widely held around the world. While the rhetoric about the potential dangers of smartphone use, as something 'addictive, unnatural or harmful', is pervasive, it is then informed by particular contextual values in different places.[33] In Lusozi, fears around the digital would often be informed by broader intergenerational tensions, with older people such as Kilongeni and Omara differentiating their own phone use from that of their children and grandchildren. Other older people in Lusozi shared Kilongeni's perspective on phones and their impact on the younger generation through exposure to 'strange' things like pornography. For example, Geoffrey and his wife Judith both worried that young people would go out and 'copy' the information they find on television and the internet on their smartphones. This comes with concerns about excess, misinformation and a loss of respect, with a damaging impact on younger people and in turn their elders.

'Life's easier now with phones'

Despite these concerns, Kilongeni and Omara recognised the convenience of life with phones. As Kilongeni observed:

> If you don't have limitations, then it ruins someone's life. But they are also very good, they have eased a lot of challenges.

Soon Omara planned to return to his home village, where he would be able to keep in contact with his sons in Kampala. He commented that 'from the village it's very simple. I will keep in contact with my phone'. As found in various studies around the world, the phone provides a 'lifeline' for relationships amid increasing transnational and regional migration,[34] offering the 'perpetual opportunity' of connection and 'co-presence',[35] as well as the obligations that come with it. The primary use of phones among participants in Lusozi was to keep in contact with family members, both those within the household and older relatives at home via phone calls. In a survey of the previous three phone calls made by 195 respondents, a total of 585 calls, 95 respondents (49 per cent), with a total of 135 calls (23 per cent), had made or received at least one phone call simply for the purpose of checking on the caller or receiver, and their family: 'I was checking on how the kids are', 'to find out how he was doing', 'she was checking on me'. A further 122 calls (21 per cent of the total) were for seeking or sending 'help', money or sometimes food: 'he wanted me to help him', 'she called to send money home to my sister'. Thanks to phone calls, continuity in relationships between family and friends can be maintained over distances. The calls offer a sense of 'connected presence', with conversations a sign of an ongoing bond and obligation.[36]

Mobile money was also used almost universally by participants. Various people in Lusozi explained how they were able to provide for their parents and relatives in the village without visiting them as 'you can send money on the phone'. As one woman explained, if she was not sending her parents money, they would have nothing. Her mother had recently had a stomach ulcer, so she had sent her money to go to hospital. And from the perspective of an elder in the village, 'life's easier now with phones', as they were able to communicate family problems with relatives in the city and 'mobilise' the necessary funds. With 33 mobile money vendors in Lusozi alone, as introduced in Chapter 3, the phone would often be the most convenient way to store and send money.

As shown in 'Mobile money', the short film featured in Chapter 3, people wanting to send money would typically take cash to an agent at a kiosk, who then arranges the transfer to the recipient's phone number via their mobile, taking a small commission for themselves. In a survey of 50 people's phone use, only three people said they had not used mobile money in the past six months. Those who had used it sent and received money three times a month on average. We asked for more details of the last three times they had sent or received mobile money: who the recipient was, how much was sent and what was the reason for remitting. Of 130 recorded remittances, the average amount sent was just over 200,000 UGX (£40), with individual sums ranging from as little as 10,000 to 10,000,000 UGX (£2 to £2,000).

Mostly remittances were sent or received by siblings (28 per cent), parents (12 per cent), friends (11 per cent) and customers (10 per cent). Sometimes people had deposited money for themselves, using mobile money as their bank.

The greatest proportion of remittances (28 per cent) were for 'help', which could include money for upkeep, food, 'pocket money' or gifts. This was followed by remittances for health purposes (25 per cent), which could include hospital bills, medicine, transport to hospital and surgery costs: 'my brother sent me to buy medicine when I was not working yet', 'to transport my sister to hospital' and 'I sent money to my grandmother for food as she was sick'. Six of these transfers were received or forwarded by the respondent in a chain of remittances, for the purposes of supporting older relatives. For example, one participant had received 200,000 UGX (£40) from her daughter in order to help her take her mother in the village to hospital; another had received 30,000 UGX (£6.20) from their aunt for their grandmother's hospital bills.

Despite generational shifts, economic change and increasingly 'scattered families',[37] mobile money remittances enable relatives to work together to ensure that the older generation are cared for. Phones are therefore central to maintaining arrangements and delegating responsibilities for care among families split up over long distances and periods of time. Alimo Judith, for example, was 40 years old and had been selling charcoal for 13 years. She is originally from Gulu and moved to Kampala in 1995 to get married. When she first arrived, she thought it was 'better than the village' due to its proximity to the market and hospitals. However, she had since learned that 'life is not easier in Kampala' as it requires constant work and money. Her mother, brother and sister lived in the village in Gulu. Her mother ran her own business, selling food stored in her granary in June, when there is no rain and people are struggling to grow their own. In June, when her mother is making money, she would send some to Alimo Judith via mobile money to pay her school fees, which were due around this time. Later, in September, Alimo Judith could pay her back so her mother can buy food when her stores are empty again. By splitting their household costs, mother and daughter are able to support each other's businesses through annual cycles of cash flow. Sometimes, Alimo Judith would call her mother simply to ask 'Are you badly off?' It is only Alimo Judith who is able to support her mum with money when she needs it for medicine, as she explained:

> She calls me, I send money or go myself so she can go to hospital.

Alimo Judith was preparing to return to the village herself when her children finish school. The possibility of convenient contact and money transfer facilitates retirement in rural areas, ensuring that older people's material and health needs can still be catered for.

This can also intensify the obligations of those living in the city to provide for family at home.[38] Owiny, then 48 years old, had served as a Local Councillor (LC1) in Lusozi for five years. He said that he was always busy, with many people bringing their problems to him. The majority of the work, in which he was assisted by his wife Ada, consisted of mediating in neighbourhood or domestic disputes. People would come to them with a family issue, and Owiny and Ada then bring those involved together to sit them down to try to resolve it. They said their work was almost entirely voluntary, except for a monthly stipend of 10,000 UGX (£2.10) which they found would inevitably be spent on airtime and data. The costs required for continued access to the 'neighbourhood watch' WhatsApp group were covered at Owiny's own expense, as were the costs of hosting and assisting people who move to Lusozi from rural areas in search of their relatives.

Owiny said his motivation to do this work was a desire to help people and to gain their respect, which they would show in trusting him to help solve their problems. This depicts trust and respect as key aspects of public authority in this context, with people holding these positions responsible for day-to-day problem solving within the community. Owiny found that the main challenges faced by older people in the area was being left with responsibility for their grandchildren. As older people they 'struggle to handle the responsibility', as will be discussed in Chapter 6. Like many others, Owiny found that some people still take care of their parents as they become old, but, as in a common idiom of the research, 'it depends on their heart'.

Owiny himself took care of his mother, who was then in her eighties. He had initially brought her to live with him in Lusozi, but she preferred to be in her own home in the village. He said she was very happy there and still productive: 'you will find her with even young people queueing to buy her cassava'. His sister was also there taking daily care of her, while he provided for them financially. Owiny bought his sister a smartphone in order to make communication easier between them, but found that it had actually made his life a bit harder, as it had increased his obligation to people at home. When they have problems, they could let him know immediately, and he is expected to find money for them. He joked that before phones even news of a death could take a week to reach him, by which time he might have even missed the burial.

> Nowadays the problem comes and everybody's aware ... nowadays no dodging!

Mobile money is often lauded as an example of adaptation of technology to requirements 'from below',[39] offering flexible banking and remittances. In particular, health-related transfers can be understood as 'informal mHealth',[40] one of the primary ways in which people creatively adapt mobile phones for health purposes. However, as economic anthropologist Bill Maurer argues, mobile money defies simplistic 'top-down' and 'bottom-up' analyses. Instead it reveals the networked relations between 'human and technological, top and bottom, producer and consumer, person and commodity'.[41] This includes existing 'complex ecologies of money and relationships' such as those described by Owiny, the vast institutional networks of mobile money – as well as the new networks and business opportunities it makes available.[42]

The 'smart-from-below' approach to 'ageing with smartphones' takes these institutional networks and 'complex ecologies' into account, while prioritising the everyday appropriation of ubiquitous technologies according to specific contextual and personal needs. From this ethnographic perspective of phone use and consequence, it is possible to gain insight into how people understand their own 'complex ecologies', in both specific and global contexts. The following section documents social media practices among older participants, giving a sense of the networks that smartphones are embedded in and facilitate. In doing so it presents a clear counterpoint to political narratives at the time of the research, which frequently represented social media use as an 'over the top' (OTT) waste of time and resources.

Taxing *olugambo* (gossip)

As introduced in Chapter 2, in 2018 President Museveni argued that social media promotes 'fake news', misinformation, witchcraft accusations, pornography and addiction, an 'over the top' (OTT) excess. According to the President, social media is a luxury[43] used only for *'olugambo'* or 'gossip', and 'we need resources to cope with the consequences of their *lugambo'*. This justified the temporary introduction of the 'OTT tax' on social media use, a levy collected by telecommunications companies of 200 UGX ($0.05) per day or 6,000 UGX (£1.20) per month for using various social media platforms including Facebook, WhatsApp, Instagram, Twitter, Skype and LinkedIn. When the OTT tax was implemented in

July 2018, it prompted a drop of 2.5 million internet subscriptions and 1.2 million social media users in the subsequent three months.[44] Six of 50 respondents to a survey of phone use in Lusozi reported that they no longer use social media to avoid paying the tax, and 22 said that they found other people less responsive on social media due to the tax. As one 62-year-old grandmother, who previously used her phone to talk to her daughters in the village on WhatsApp, said 'instead of paying tax, I can buy sugar for the children'. This demonstrates the immediate impact of the directives on social media access. They are likely to have disproportionately affected people on lower incomes, especially the older generation with less 'digital capital' to navigate the restrictions. While ICTs offer the potential for open access to information, they are also embedded in existing relations, emphasising the 'social determinism of technology'[45] or the 'domestication of dotcom'. The phone represents and mediates networks between the political and personal, as a key nexus for intergenerational, socio-economic and care relations, and for forms of distributed authority.

The introduction of the OTT tax provoked various petitions and campaigns, including social media campaigns such as #ThisTaxMustGo. Since then, further policies have been imposed and lifted,[46] including the requirement that all blogs should be authorised by the UCC, blocks on internet access during elections and a Facebook ban: what has been termed 'digital authoritarianism'.[47] Protests led by Bobi Wine, the opposition leader and 'spokesman for Uganda's frustrated youth', dominated headlines in Uganda and attracted international attention. Bobi Wine, whose success is linked to social media,[48] frequently draws on the idea of social media as a platform for the emancipation of the younger generation, particularly from the ageing President and older political elite. This invokes the 'dotcom discourse' and its intergenerational implications on a broader political scale. As reported in the *Daily Monitor*, a Ugandan national newspaper, his audio response to the age limit resolution in September 2017 went viral on social media, concluding with a direct address to 'my fellow Ugandans, **especially the younger generation**':

> Now to you my fellow Ugandans, especially the younger generation
>
> […] Let us make use of social media and this modern technology to emancipate ourselves because THE TIME IS NOW. [49]

Bobi appeals emphatically to 'this modern technology' as a dynamic communication tool of the younger generation. In both the content and placement of this speech, social media is positioned as a space to ridicule 'inactive' rulers, a platform for the emancipation of the young from the old. Discourses on increasing internet and social media access thus locate anxieties around broader social changes, their impact on intergenerational relationships and the experiences of older people.

Alongside the ethnographic implications of the political regulation of social media, it is interesting to consider Ivan Illich's concept of the phone as a 'convivial tool', a social device that inherently broadens opportunities for autonomous action undefined by bureaucrats, but that also has the potential to be used for interference, manipulation or control.[50] Illich's idea of conviviality as 'individual freedom realized in personal interdependence',[51] with 'convivial tools' opening up opportunities for connection and self-realisation, also informs Nyamnjoh's work on convivial sociality and scholarship. In many ways, as Bobi suggests, mobile phones and social media have allowed people to overcome the limits of state bureaucracy.[52] The versatile 'convivial' potential of these communication tools,[53] and the need for them, is further credited by impositions of the state on phone use such as the social media tax.

As well as the OTT tax, the Ugandan government introduced an additional mobile money tax of 1 per cent on deposit and withdrawal in 2019. At the time the UCC found that people's mobile money balances significantly dropped at a national level,[54] with many mobile money vendors in Lusozi reporting that they had 30 per cent fewer customers each month. Some of them found that people were using different means to transport money, including boarding the bus to transport larger sums if the fare was cheaper than the tax. Twenty respondents said they reduced their use of mobile money or stopped it completely. However, most said that they still sent mobile money in the same way since the tax was imposed. 'It's stressing me, but nothing to do'.

Ethnographic findings related to social media use among participants in Lusozi suggest that it is used for more than *'olugambo'*, which is itself more than fruitless. For many, social media has now become a basic need, rather than a 'luxury'. For example, researchers have found that phones are a 'lifeline' for people who have experienced strokes in Uganda, allowing them to navigate everyday life and to connect with their families.[55] As Tanja Ahlin notes in her study of migrant families' care of elders through ICTs, phone practices are 'not only about communication, just as remittances are not only about sending money'.[56] What are 'over the top' platforms used for other than *olugambo*? And what is the value of *olugambo* itself, particularly to older people? These questions are considered in the section to follow on the use of social media by older participants in Lusozi, specifically WhatsApp and Facebook.

Social media use

In Lusozi WhatsApp is widely used and is often synonymous with 'the internet' or even 'the smartphone' itself.[57] This reflects the cost efficiency, simplicity and user friendliness of WhatsApp, making it a practical tool for communication around the world.[58] Large WhatsApp groups for information sharing are common, for example in neighbourhoods or among service professions. In 'Who should enrich you?' (WSEY), there are regular messages sent on the WhatsApp group. Almost every week the chairwoman would update the group photo with the week's beneficiary and her two honorary members in their dresses. Updates about members would be shared, for example if they give birth to a child or lose a relative. When a member lost her daughter, the chairwoman announced fundraising to take place at her home that afternoon. They would also update one another about group proceedings, as well as more regularly sending news items, jokes and celebratory wishes.

The chairwoman's brother in Gulu in northern Uganda said he was part of a council WhatsApp group, for which he was able to access Airtel data funded by the municipality at a reduced price. This helped him to find out about council health sensitisation sessions and to mobilise the community to attend. In this way, WhatsApp groups would be used as platforms for information sharing; 'they bring news'. For example, when the OTT tax was announced, the speed at which the news spread to 15,000 WhatsApp users made national headlines. As one 40-year-old man explained:

> Now almost everyone has what they call groups, friends' groups, all these, it could be work groups, these groups are there. And these groups, there is always information that keeps coming around, like what you heard about the [OTT] tax – it went around the country in 10 minutes, 15,000 recipients received the message. If anything that seems to be relevant and affecting the life of people directly, the messages tend to go very fast.

Often these news circulations are health related. In the case of disease management, such as a cholera outbreak in Lusozi in 2018, the Ministry of Health sent radio and television announcements, as well as text messages to people in affected areas, which were then further circulated on WhatsApp. At the government hospital, all of the staff are part of a WhatsApp group where announcements are made. Each department has a smaller WhatsApp group where people can let each other know if they are going to miss work, give updates about patients and medical supplies. Or, as one 50-year-old electrician told me:

> In that group of mine, one is a teacher, one is a doctor ... so any information one of them gets, I have to get it here.

A 48-year-old woman told me she had 'learned so much' about health from WhatsApp, for example how to check for breast cancer and nutritional information. Another older man also learned about the health benefits of beetroot and bananas through his WhatsApp group; he has started eating more of them as a result.

Family WhatsApp groups can support the distribution of tasks related to supporting older relatives. Obalo, the vice chairman of 'Togetherness is Strength' (TIS), is 62 years old. His four-roomed, self-contained home sits behind a gate with an *eskari* (security guard) in Lusozi. He comes from a family of four sons who have all had successful businesses and careers, affording their independence from each other. However, they would still make an effort to come together for family meetings every few months. At those meetings, the older people would advise the younger generation, particularly those who have recently married and who had young children, and are therefore most in need of guidance. His family would use their WhatsApp group for organising the meetings and for sharing news, good and bad, or for asking for assistance and fundraising. Family further afield or without smartphones would be called with updates, as shown in the following transcript:

> We have WhatsApp groups for Togetherness is Strength, and a family group and that can give me trace of what's happening .... The messages are so frequent, because today I received this [shows photo of grandson in school uniform on his first day] and tomorrow I might receive another. Another is that if we have programmes like weddings, graduations, we usually inform them very early so that they can contribute. ... For both good and bad. Like if there is a problem maybe far, we have people over there and we call them and let them know and they also tell us what's going on. ... I call them every week because I need to find out what's going on. Like

now I have an uncle who is sick, and I need to call and find out if he's okay. I usually send using mobile money and, if someone is very sick, we try as hard as possible to send a representative or go there by yourself.

Care tasks can be delegated across distances among siblings and cousins via phones, through calls to check on them, through family WhatsApp groups or through mobile money transfers.

Beyond supporting families and existing networks, social media was also used by older people in Lusozi to seek new friends and broaden their social networks. Facebook would often be used for this purpose, with people explaining how they would search, add and chat with new friends. Some of them attributed this to 'friendliness', enjoying making contact with new people and chatting to them. A few also said they saw it as an opportunity to network and learn from people. Opoka, for example, then 48 years old, had owned a smartphone for five years. He used Facebook to talk to old friends and look for new ones. He said he especially likes finding international people, sending photos and sometimes exchanging phone numbers. He said he likes 'learning from them', explaining that 'when a new face appears, we're eager to talk to them'. Opio Joseph, the 39-year-old secretary of TIS, would also accept or send friend requests on Facebook. In particular he enjoyed:

> creating friends worldwide. ... You see their photos, if you like some and want to make friends ... to take you to a higher level.

Again, he would not meet them in person, however, and generally loses contact eventually. Frederick, only 33 at the time, also said he sometimes likes to find new friends on Facebook by sending requests or receiving them. They are 'outside Uganda and all over the world'. He explained:

> I like chatting to new people and meeting friends. I like people and being friends.

Namubiru is a 45-year-old market vendor. She had old friends she would connect with on Facebook, but also sometimes looked for new ones. Her children would even look for new friends for her, usually women or families from Uganda. She had never seen them 'live' in person, it was *'just to make friends'*. Her children would call them, and they would chat, just asking them how they are; they always wanted to find out how her elderly mother was.

These conversations on the use of WhatsApp and Facebook portray the productivity of social media and *'olugambo'*, particularly for older people. It enabled them to keep in touch with families despite distance, to re-establish and co-ordinate community groups, to provide financial and personal care, and to seek friends and business networks in Uganda and around the world. This shows how technology, while differentially accessed, can 'make movement possible', encouraging mobility and encounters.[59]

These are the open-ended possibilities or 'affordances' of smartphones, a 'convivial tool' which, like Nyamnjoh's theory of convivial social action elaborated in previous chapters,[60] allows for 'autonomous action by means of tools least controlled by others', opening up possibilities for connectivity and self-actualisation which also 'enrich the environment'.[61] These possibilities can also be regulated through the socio-cultural, political and economic status quo, as evident in what has been referred to as 'digital authoritarianism'[62] in Uganda. Digital restrictions can therefore also be interpreted as restrictions on all of the possibilities of 'digital capital' – showing how political narratives and directives can impose themselves in everyday lives and between the generations.

Conclusion

Often ethnographies of phones, documenting how they are perceived and domesticated,[63] find that they can accommodate continuity in social life.[64] This is evident here in the ways that phone use is embedded in long-standing social roles and practices – for example, in the use of phone calls and mobile money transfers to support older relatives at a distance in line with elder care norms, or in exacerbating existing inequities related to gender and income. At the same time there is an understandable propensity for people to perceive mobile phones as 'highly significant agents of change'.[65] In Lusozi people would often say that 'mobile phones have brought the world together', which could refer to an expansion of home or encounters with the wider world. People can seek new friends and connections on Facebook, discover news from around the world and easily keep in touch with relatives at home. These 'compressed distances' have brought both new social possibilities and pressures.[66] Economic migrants, including many of the people we worked with in Lusozi, could face heightened expectations for regular contact and remittances to relatives in their rural homes.[67]

Access to social media via smartphones was considered by some people to be corrupting younger people and eroding co-operative ways of life. The findings here suggest that phones are incorporated in more dynamic social processes, being embedded in pre-existing networks, re-establishing them and at the same time having the capacity to transform them;[68] they both reflect and influence 'relationships, encounters and interconnections'[69] and in turn people's sense of identity and belonging. As Porter and colleagues put it in their study of intergenerational relations and the phone in Africa, with connection to relatives and their resources across distances, there is 'an increasingly sophisticated reconfiguration and re-imagining of family networks, in which new types of cohesion exist alongside old continuities'.[70] Phone ownership and sharing represents distributed social status and access to resources; phone calls or exchanging numbers can be symbolic acknowledgement of relationships in themselves; mobile money transfers offer practical assistance and show care and respect, upholding family roles; music downloads can encourage the inclusion of older people in contemporary popular culture. The phone focuses a lens onto these complex trajectories, a lens that is particularly sharpened in consideration of intergenerational relationships and elder care.

Care is the focus of the following chapter, which considers healthcare responsibilities for older people across the health system, the family and the individual. As in previous chapters, the theme of health and care again allows us to consider how older people's experiences integrate the personal and political to a particularly intimate extent. Care for, and by, the older generation responds to gaps in formal and informal health systems wrought through economic liberalisation, often along gendered lines. Further, chronic conditions themselves are often understood as an embodied manifestation of wide-reaching economic issues. The chapter therefore focuses on prevalent chronic non-communicable diseases such as hypertension, and explores how they are managed and understood. Documenting these discussions can expose how people seek to gain certainty in an ambiguous world, particularly when that ambiguity is exacerbated by long-term illness, economic crises and age itself.

Notes

1. Horst and Miller 2006; 2012. The chapter also follows Science and Technology Studies (STS), which takes a situated, nuanced perspective on the use of 'technological artefacts' such as phones to counter the hype or pessimism of 'technological determinism', instead considering how contextual factors are both shaped by and shaping the use of phones (Larsson and Svensson 2018; Pols 2012).
2. Coe 2014, 5.
3. de Bruijn, Nyamnjoh and Brinkman 2009; Porter et al. 2015; Pype 2017a; Archambault 2013.

4. Burrell 2010; Namatovu and Saebo 2015; Svensson and Larsson 2016; Larsson and Svensson 2018; Vokes 2018.
5. Hampshire et al. 2015.
6. Goggin 2012, 101.
7. de Bruijn and van Dijk 2012, 1.
8. Goggin 2012, 101.
9. Vokes 2018, 274.
10. Uganda Communications Commission (UCC) 2020. 'Market performance Q1 2020'. Accessed 23 September 2020. https://www.ucc.co.ug/wp-content/uploads/2020/08/UCC-Market-Performance-1Q20-Report-FINAL.pdf, 4.
11. Uganda Communications Commission (UCC) 2016. 'Facts and figures'. Accessed 27 November 2017. http://www.ucc.co.ug/data/qmenu/3/Facts-and-Figures.html.
12. UCC 2016.
13. NITA Uganda 2018. 'National information technology survey, 2017/18 report'. Accessed 31 July 2019. https://www.nita.go.ug/sites/default/files/publications/National%20IT%20Survey%20April%2010th.pdf.
14. de Bruijn 2014.
15. Uganda Communications Commission (UCC) 2018. 'UCC sector report'. Accessed 31 July 2019. https://www.ucc.co.ug/wp-content/uploads/2017/09/UCC-Sector-Report-December-2018_260719.pdf, 30.
16. Deloitte 2017. 'Deloitte's mobile consumer survey: The Africa cut 2015/16'. Accessed 29 November 2018. https://www2.deloitte.com/content/dam/Deloitte/za/Documents/technology-media-telecommunications/ZA_Deloitte-Mobile-consumer-survey-Africa-300816.pdf, 4.
The COVID-19 restrictions subsequent to the research are also thought to have precipitated considerable up-take of smartphones across the country, particularly among young people.
17. NITA Uganda 2018. 'National information technology survey, 2017/18 report'. Accessed 31 July 2019. https://www.nita.go.ug/sites/default/files/publications/National%20IT%20Survey%20April%2010th.pdf, xxxi.
18. GSMA 2020. 'The mobile gender gap report'. Accessed 14 January 2021. https://www.gsma.com/mobilefordevelopment/wp-content/uploads/2020/05/GSMA-The-Mobile-Gender-Gap-Report-2020.pdf, 11.
19. NITA Uganda 2018. 'National information technology survey, 2017/18 report'. Accessed 31 July 2019. https://www.nita.go.ug/sites/default/files/publications/National%20IT%20Survey%20April%2010th.pdf, xxxi.
20. Namatovu and Saebo 2015, 338.
21. Burrell 2010, 238; Svensson and Larsson 2016, 210; Porter et al. 2020.
22. Burrell, 2010, 238; Svensson and Larsson 2016, 210; Porter et al. 2020.
23. Hampshire et al. 2015.
24. Hampshire et al. 2015; Burrell 2010, 232.
25. Porter et al. 2015.
26. Porter et al. 2015, 41.
27. Porter et al. 2015, 44.
28. Archambault 2017.
29. Porter et al. 2015.
30. Kusimba, Yang and Chawla 2016; see also McIntosh 2010; Archambault 2017, 2013.
31. As in Pype's analysis of older people and popular media in Kinshasha (Pype 2017b), in an urban environment where entertainment often targets youth, older people can reconnect with contemporary society through their knowledge of earlier music.
32. Miller et al. 2021.
33. Sutton 2020.
34. Kamwesiga, Tham and Guidetti 2017; Ahlin 2018; Madianou and Miller 2012.
35. Miller et al. 2021.
36. Licoppe 2004, 141. As Licoppe argues, perhaps the content is less significant than the fact of calling itself.
37. Coe 2014; Sigona et al. 2015, 131.
38. de Bruijn, Nyamnjoh and Brinkman 2009; Ferguson 2015, 77.
39. Pype 2017a.
40. Hampshire et al. 2021; Hampshire et al. 2017; Hampshire et al. 2015.

41. Kusimba, Yang and Chawla 2016, 266; Maurer 2012, 589.
42. Maurer 2012, 600.
43. Namasinga Selnes and Orgeret 2020, 382.
44. Namasinga Selnes and Orgeret 2020, 392.
45. Namasinga Selnes and Orgeret 2020, 384.
46. Nyamnjoh has previously related government media control in Africa to the colonial origins of print and radio, which would promote Western interests and prevent dissidence (Nyamnjoh 2005, 45).
47. Namasinga Selnes and Orgeret 2020, 394.
48. Namasinga Selnes and Orgeret 2020, 393.
49. Bobi Wine 2018. 'Museveni is as good as his word'. Accessed 4 April 2019. https://w.soundcloud.com/player/?url=https%3A//api.soundcloud.com/tracks/342295943&color=%23ff5500&auto_play=false&hide_related=false&show_comments=true&show_user=true&show_reposts=false&visual=true.
50. Illich 1973, 19.
51. Illich 1973, 12.
52. de Bruijn and van Dijk 2012, 12.
53. Illich 1973.
54. Uganda Communications Commission 2018. 'UCC sector report'. Accessed 31 July 2019. https://www.ucc.co.ug/wp-content/uploads/2017/09/UCC-Sector-Report-December-2018_260719.pdf, 30.
55. Kamwesiga, Tham and Guidetti 2017.
56. Ahlin 2018.
57. Shambare argues that WhatsApp has encouraged the widespread adoption of smartphones (Shambare 2014).
58. Shambare 2014.
59. Nyamnjoh 2012c. 'Fiction and reality of mobility in Africa'. Standard Form for African Studies. https://www.nyamnjoh.com/2012/11/francis-nyamnjoh-fiction-and-reality-of-mobility-in-africa.html.
60. Nyamnjoh 2012a, b, 2017, 2005, 2002.
61. Illich 1973, 18.
62. Namasinga Selnes and Orgeret 2020, 394.
63. Horst and Miller 2006, 7.
64. Miller, D. et al. 2016, 7.
65. Vokes 2018, 276.
66. de Bruijn, Nyamnjoh and Brinkman 2009.
67. de Bruijn, Nyamnjoh and Brinkman 2009.
68. Vokes and Pype 2018.
69. de Bruijn and van Dijk 2012, 2.
70. Porter et al. 2015, 41.

6
Health and care: who is responsible?

Introduction

The previous chapter shows how older people in Lusozi creatively weave mobile phones and smartphones within their everyday lives – informing social life, intergenerational morality and political discourses, as well as an ethics of care across urban and rural areas. In Kampala, smartphones and mobile phones are a platform through which people can express care and respect for their parents, or vice versa. The phone is therefore at the centre of contemporary communities of care or 'social infrastructures' in Kampala, networking people and retooling relationships in the 'dotcom era'. This leads to the focus in this chapter on ageing, health and care in Lusozi: who is responsible for the health and care of older people?

This question invokes the uncertainty that exists around elder care, as something that people negotiate at personal and political levels. It is often answered by families, adapting their roles and routines in times of sickness,[1] as well as by health workers, mitigating shortages in the health system.[2] Answers to this question can also implicate the gendered dimensions of care, with caregiving often viewed as a woman's role.[3] As shown in preceding chapters, older people living in Lusozi may have many responsibilities for themselves, their children and grandchildren, and their neighbours, as 'active and resourceful' givers and recipients of care.[4] Many said they aspire to physical and financial independence in later life in order to avoid being a burden on their children, highlighting the relevance of self-responsibility as an aspect of ageing in this historical context.

As we saw in Chapter 4, sharing responsibilities ideally enables people as individuals.[5] This ideal of distributed responsibility, or 'togetherness', is considered by participants and researchers alike to be undermined by processes of 'Westernisation' and related principles of individualism and self-interest, associated with the dotcom era and urban environment, and the weakening of intergenerational obligations. Elder care is therefore situated within broad global and historical processes, as they are intimately experienced and embodied.[6] The ethnographic focus here on embodied experiences of global socio-economic factors draws from literature in critical medical anthropology on ageing and care,[7] exposing the lived 'intersection between the macro and the intimate'.[8] Articulated experiences of life at this intersection are specific to the individual participants in this research, situated in the health context of Lusozi. However, people also actively reflect on how this uncertainty represents and cuts across a worldwide context of economic insecurity and disintegrating public services, the increasing financialisation of life, wellbeing and care, and the corrosive impact this is having on established relational values.[9]

The role of the global in older people's health and care was often explicitly observed by many of the people we worked with in Lusozi, including both older participants and health workers. For example, an awareness of care norms in other contexts both disrupts and re-establishes existing ideals of home-based intergenerational care.[10] Care homes in the US and Europe are widely disparaged, while health workers at Lusozi Hospital aspire to provide the specialised gerontological services they have seen in Korea and China. Health problems themselves can be understood as the consequence of wide-reaching socio-economic and environmental issues. This chapter will focus on hypertension or 'pressure', which is particularly prevalent among older participants and often understood as an embodied form of economic stress. The various social and self-care strategies employed for preventing and managing 'pressure' will be outlined here, building on the book's central theme of pragmatic co-operation in context.

The chapter is structured around the various levels of healthcare, starting with the public health system and then shifting towards family and self-care. The health system includes medical, religious, social, spiritual, digital and herbal approaches to health and healing, which can be sought 'simultaneously and sequentially'.[11] For example, someone with a health problem may go for prayers and medical advice; if that fails, they may then go to a herbalist or spiritual healer. This depicts the complex 'continuum' of healing – a fluidity actively drawn upon both by health service users and their providers, in what can be understood as a 'pluralistic therapeutic approach'.[12] This 'pluralistic' approach to treatment-seeking is also evident among older people in other ASSA project fieldsites around the world. In Ireland, for example, Miller found that his participants would often seek treatment based on a holistic experience and concept of health, often siloed in the biomedical approach. And in China Wang found that people would use both traditional Chinese and Western medicine simultaneously and on a pragmatic basis.

Concurrent 'pluralistic' approaches to health and care within the neighbourhood, the hospital, the church or mosque, or on the phone, reflect a holistic concept of health and wellbeing and a practical engagement with related uncertainty[13] that can have diverse yet overlapping explanations and solutions. Susan Whyte, a medical anthropologist who has worked extensively on chronic conditions in Uganda, argues that conversations with others can be the only way to seek guidance and control within an ambiguous world, in terms of sickness and seeking prevention, cause and cure.[14] This means that the dialogue, idioms and stories that are drawn on to discuss and define health offer meaningful insight into shared perspectives and experiences.[15] For Whyte, it is 'the task of ethnography'[16] to detail and explain these patterns and to consider how they might reinforce – or occasionally undermine – established social relations, inequities and institutions. This task is taken up here in the subsequent sections on routines and conversations around care for older people, particularly those living with long-term chronic health conditions like hypertension.

Health context

In Lusozi there are various health services available in close proximity, including six private health clinics, five pharmacies, a regional government hospital, and various herbal and traditional healers. The private clinics are close by and considered good quality; they are generally open 24 hours a day, providing outpatient consultations and medicines as well as limited in-patient services. Most of them are run by doctors or senior nurses who also have positions in the government hospitals in the capital. However, given the costs of private services, the older people we worked with tend to go to the government hospital a 10-minute walk away in Lusozi. Here consultation services are generally free, with additional official and unofficial costs for medicines and surgical supplies.

Lusozi Hospital was built in 2012. What was once a small, trusted community health centre is now a regional referral hospital, which at the time of research in 2019 had 100 in-patient beds and 365 staff. During that year 104,010 outpatients were treated, significantly fewer than in the previous year, as three other regional hospitals had opened in Kampala to relieve growing pressure on health services in the capital.

I spent two months observing consultations in the physiotherapy ward of Lusozi Hospital, often visited by older people with attendant relatives to learn how to manage chronic health problems and injuries. Sometimes consultations were in Luganda, sometimes in English, sometimes both. With surgery costs often being unattainable, physiotherapists are responsible for helping people to manage their injuries and continue working. They explained that the most common health problems they treat are back related, due to 'the nature of work'. I also interviewed health workers from departments across the hospital, the people broadly exposed to the health concerns of the Lusozi community and the services available to them.

According to many participants and health workers, provisions at Lusozi Hospital are lacking for older people in particular. This was a major concern that was highlighted by the physiotherapists I worked with, as well as other health workers, including hospital administrators. For example, Nakyanzi, a senior hospital administrator, felt that the health system in which she works needs to have 'better provisions for these [older] people'. With the 'youthful population' in Uganda, she found that health policy and funding often forgets older people, an omission that she felt needed to be rectified as the older population grows.[17] Nakyanzi was inspired by the geriatric services for older people that she observed on a training course in South Korea, which highlighted for her the gaps in Ugandan policies for older people's healthcare. Without specialised services, older people with multiple conditions would need to seek specialist care from various departments. As Nakyanzi put it, they come to the hospital and have to 'roam around' for all the services they are referred to; long queues at each department meant that 'they're lining up around the hospital'.

Many older participants' narrated experiences in the hospital confirmed Nakyanzi's account, with common complaints about the poor quality of services due to inadequate levels of stocks, delays, costs and the attitudes of health workers towards the elderly – suggesting that the hospital and the health system more broadly are falling short of their expected responsibilities for older people's health and care. These quotations are representative of many similar responses:

> The hospital is very bad; they want money and are very lazy about work. They don't care.
>
> You go and line up. You go in the morning at 8, even at this time [in the evening] you still haven't got your medicine.

Two elderly women in their eighties separately explained that they now refuse to go to the hospital. They had been turned away from the queue in the past, having been told that their health problems were 'just old age':

> When they see those old people, they stop them on the way and tell them 'You people go home and wait for your day'.

As the principal physiotherapist explained, many people, including some health workers, think of ageing as:

> a normal thing; they don't understand the other issues that come in and need to be taken care of as medical issues. They say 'pain is just old age'.

This expression is also cited in Nankwanga and Neema's study with people over the age of 60 across Uganda. Some of their participants had also been told that pain was 'just old age', denied treatment and deterred from seeking it in future.[18] Other studies on the accessibility of public healthcare for older people in Uganda also found that they can be overlooked and sidelined by health workers and the health infrastructure more broadly,[19] and they may already face poverty, political marginalisation and a range of health problems.[20]

Typically, older participants in Lusozi were clear that they did not blame the health workers, or even the hospital, for resource shortages and lacking services. Instead, they saw it as part of the wider health system in Uganda:

> I also sympathise with the doctors, they handle too many people.

> It is no mistake by us or medical personnel – it is a problem facing the hospital and us.

Senior doctors at the hospital earn a maximum of 2.6 million UGX (£510) per month. The hospital human resources team explained that these comparatively low salaries in the government sector (the average national salary for doctors is around 6,000,000 UGX or £1,200 per month) meant that, at the time of the research, various positions were still open at the hospital, particularly at senior consultancy level. Despite that, the hospital had three senior consultants and eight consultants, significantly more than most rural regional referral hospitals where the salaries are generally lower. There were 11 medical officers' special grade

Figure 6.1 Health workers preparing to administer vaccinations in Lusozi Hospital. Photo by Charlotte Hawkins.

(trained with a Master's specialism), 10 medical officers (trained at university), 17 clinical officers (with diplomas) and various 'allied health professionals' (including dentists, therapists, eye specialists, laboratory staff, pharmacists and a practitioner of Traditional Chinese Medicine or TCM). Nurses formed the bulk of the 365 staff members, comprising 37 nursing officers, 40 enrolled nurses and 20 nursing assistants (Fig. 6.1).

To supplement their income, health workers would also often run their own private practices, which could take time away from their work in the hospital. They may also act as unofficial brokers for outsourced supplies. Omara, aged 60, was therefore savvy when it comes to seeking guidance from health practitioners in government hospitals, as he knew there may be a financial incentive for the health worker to prescribe certain checks, routines or medications. He would first call one of the medics that he knows, friends that he went to school with when he was young, then would visit the hospital armed with this advice. Based on what they tell him, he would then go to another hospital in Kampala, where he would not share the previous diagnosis:

> Let me step up and try another hospital ... Now the doctor will start afresh with me to compare.

This would mean that he can then read between the lines, taking responsibility to determine the best way forward for his own health.

Omara's approach depicts a relational yet self-sufficient strategy for seeking healthcare and information. Through dialogue with various friends and health workers, Omara attains some independence in his capacity to take care of himself. As with Omara, treatment-seeking would often start with a phone call to a trusted friend or relative, particularly among the older generation. This demonstrates the importance of relationships and trust in making care choices, particularly where this involves managing uncertainties around health.[21] The following section further contextualises family responsibilities for older people's health, outlining representative care routines and conversations.

Family responsibility

Responsibility for maintaining health, providing care and mitigating health crises would generally start within the family, particularly where there is limited access to formal healthcare systems. This reflects resonant discourses on family responsibility, as well as the marketisation of public health services.[22] This family role could also be promoted by state institutions. During hospital outreach programmes, the head of the Community Health department said he would make sure to emphasise the 'big role of families … every family must be able to take care'. He noted that family, as the 'basic unit of community', increasingly denotes a nuclear household with immediate relatives, rather than extended intergenerational family networks with proximity. The heads of each household 'must be able to provide' preventative measures for sickness such as immunisation, food, water and sanitation. In the case of sickness, they must fund and support treatment, as well as transport to hospitals.[23]

This can require a significant investment of time and resources, especially for long-term chronic conditions. For example, as in most hospitals, all hospital in-patients are expected to be accompanied by an attendant relative, typically a daughter, who is responsible for daily nursing, providing food and practical assistance. Taking this time away from work can inevitably have a profound impact on household earnings, which for long-term health problems can be particularly challenging.[24] As the community health practitioner noted, it also means that 'people suffer a lot without children' and that 'having children is an insurance'. Without them, 'elderly people suffer… They may have some kind neighbours, but it's not sustainable'.

As shown in previous chapters, neighbourhood mutuality offers some support for basic needs. For example, Ayaa Palma's neighbours would provide food for her grandchildren when she was too sick to work. Neighbours would check on each other regularly, at least every two days, and would be the first port of call for relatives living at a distance in case of health emergencies. But as participants cited throughout the monograph suggest, including the community health practitioner here, relying on neighbours for care is a less than ideal circumstance for later life, associated with emotional neglect, loneliness, insecurity and poverty. And the prospect of the further institutionalisation of elder care is 'not a good thing. In a family setting you feel better, not with strangers or rude nurses'. Interdependence with children thus forms, in Nyamnjoh's words, 'insurance against the risk of dependence',[25] on 'kind neighbours' or unkind institutions.

The idea of children as a form of 'insurance' has also been noted in an ethnography of migrant family life in urban China,[26] where it was analysed both in relation to a long-standing 'gendered notion of filial piety' and to capitalist speculation, 'pre-empting future risks through private means'.[27] Evidently the adaptation of responsibilities along 'mutually constituted'[28] moral and market lines is a phenomenon occurring across contexts, demonstrating the global and personal nature of discussions about care for the older generation. Family is then promoted by institutions as an essential 'safe-haven' for self-interested individuals, providing protection against risks in the wider world.[29] In turn, as in gendered care expectations for attendant relatives in Lusozi Hospital, for example, further burdens are placed on the 'idealised woman carer', whose responsibility for the provision of unpaid care labour is reproduced.

Care roles

While care for elders ideally involves multiple generations living together in rural areas, and most younger people now need to stay in the city to make a living, there are a few alternatives besides phone-based care. If adult children can afford it, they might pay for a domestic servant to help their parents with daily care, household chores and farming. Domestic workers can be young girls from a poorer household within the extended family network, who in return might receive school fees or an apprenticeship. Another common arrangement of intergenerational family support involves sending grandchildren to live with their grandparents in the village,[30] offering possibilities of daily support at home, as well as a reduced cost of living and education. For example, Mama Eric's parents would take care of her sister's children in Kitgum town. This meant that they could access cheaper schooling and take care of their grandmother, fetching water and preparing food when she was in pain. However, Mama Eric would prefer to have her children at home, as she thought grandparents spoil their grandchildren, letting them off housework, 'they don't learn'. Her concern reflects a broader sense that this informal care option could compromise the grandchild's upbringing and education. Schooling is also considered to be of a lower standard in rural areas, presenting barriers to accessing other forms of 'cultural capital'[31] and demonstrating how social status can be reproduced through forms of care.[32]

Social roles and inequalities are also reproduced through the gendered dimensions of care expectations. Historically, family care tasks have been divided along gendered lines, with sons more likely to be responsible for financial support and daughters for daily care.[33] As 'everywhere in the world',[34] this is often still the case in Uganda today,[35] where 'caregiving is viewed as a woman's role even if she has full time employment'.[36] As introduced in Chapters 3 and 4, women in Lusozi would typically be considered as largely responsible for the day-to-day management of health and wellbeing in their household, which could include earning money to provide food, school fees, clothing and medicine. Daily nursing of older people, including washing and feeding them, would also often be the responsibility of wives, daughters and daughters-in-law, who are primarily responsible for the care of their own children too.[37]

For example, Sobi and her daughters took care of her 90-year-old mother at home, while her brother would provide money for transport to the hospital and medical requirements. Sobi's mother was considered well as she could talk, telling us many stories of Lusozi in the past. However, she had pain in her legs ('*they feel like fire*'), and she lacked energy, '*maybe just because she's old*'. Sobi's mother also suffered from 'pressure', for which she needed daily medication, paid for and delivered by her sons who lived elsewhere. As she could no longer walk, her son made the decision to move her next door to Sobi, telling her to stay where she could be cared for by Sobi and her daughters. This was a subject of contention to which Sobi's mother frequently returned, '*I want to go home; no one is taking care of my house*', and stating that she was waiting for enough energy to be able to do so.

Mostly she stayed inside the house, but sometimes they carried her outside so that she could get some fresh air. She said she would often receive many visitors, which made her '*feel very good*'. If she needed to go to hospital, her sons would pay for a car to take her. Her daughters and granddaughters washed her and her bedsheets every evening. In between working on her various vending businesses in Lusozi, Sobi would bring her food, visiting several times a day or sending one of her daughters. While Sobi's brother decided on this arrangement for his mother's care, it was Sobi and her daughters who were responsible for the daily, intimate care at home: cooking, cleaning, bed making, company and conversation.

Despite the prevalence of such family arrangements for domestic intergenerational care, women's responsibilities could often be overlooked in conversation, or only implicitly recognised. This was evident during an interview with an older woman in her home. She had leg complications related to side effects from her antiretroviral treatment (ART), so was house-bound and unable to continue working in her *waragi* (gin) brewing business. When we asked, 'who takes care of you?', she responded that her first-born son was taking care of her by bringing her money. Meanwhile her daughter was cooking, having quit her full-time job in order to stay at home and look after her mother, providing day-to-day support for her food and hygiene. This exemplifies the differential visibility of gendered care roles. It also reiterates the explicit association between money and care as a significant aspect of family obligations,[38] or the relational embeddedness of money within 'the human economy'.[39] This aligns with the discussion of phone use in Chapter 5, which showed how remittances can be used as a 'care currency'.[40] Paying costs for healthcare also relies on distributive social dynamics, for example in raising money for treatment across families and communities. As Kilongeni explained:

> Sickness just comes by coincidence, sometimes abruptly, when you're not even prepared; you need money to take care of that. So if any sickness, you just have to begin to look around, call a family meeting for any contribution for treatment, 'This one has a problem, we need to…', so we help each other like that.

I often saw how Kilongeni and his children were called upon to support their neighbours in Lusozi and their relatives at home in the village – particularly for his mother, to whom they would send food and mobile money during the increasingly unpredictable dry seasons. While she was cooked for daily by her daughter-in-law, Kilongeni would visit regularly to check on the land and his mother's health, with his children often funding the transport. Most people have similar responsibilities to send money or fund visits to older relatives, which can span extensive distances.

Care at a distance

Nakyanzi said she would check on her mother by visiting her at home in her village, a five-hour drive from Kampala, every weekend. She explained that people are considered responsible for their neighbours' wellbeing and are obliged to check on them regularly, ideally every two days; if they go away for a few days, 'you pass the message on'. Responsibilities for checking on other people can leave 'little time for self'. Even when Nakyanzi would allow herself a day off, at the end of it she would feel it was a day wasted if she had not visited someone. She said she believes this leads people to focus on the 'smaller picture of family units, and sometimes forget society'. She related that to the 'pressure of globalisation', which has reduced the community bond to smaller units based on proximity. In other words, personal pressures imposed by global processes are turning a once more communal outlook inward, to immediate families or within the household.

These 'global pressures' also include the appeal of independent, individualist ways of life in Western countries, observable through social media and global encounters, which she said had the potential to 'make you feel freer than your original cultural norms'. Younger people may be influenced to become more 'independent minded', with 'self' more 'on the agenda'. She said that it is now more common to hear people say 'I'm actually very busy' instead of conforming to expectations that 'you must be there for people, as a team', 'check on your people' and 'be responsible for your community and your own belonging'. In line with many researchers,[41] participants, policy-makers and NGO advocates, she is concerned that this will be a problem for elder care, as institutionalising older relatives is 'not allowed' and often instead 'they would rather abandon them'.

The possibility of abandonment in old age was occasionally mentioned during this research, often considered the worst possible fate for later life. There were some elderly people in Lusozi and in Amor's home village who were known to have been 'abandoned', left without family to care for them; as shown in Chapter 3, they would often rely instead on assistance from their community, particularly for food. National figures suggest that older people living alone in Uganda is fairly common, notwithstanding 'potentially compromised' demographic data on older people in Africa;[42] based on an analysis of the 2010 Uganda National Household Survey (UNHS), Wandera and colleagues have noted that 9 per cent of older people over the age of 50 live alone.[43] Other studies have identified the risks of living alone and loneliness to health, well-being and financial stability among older people in Uganda – notably in urban areas,[44] where they may be 'isolated, dislocated from former social circulation and missing being relevant'.[45]

Established narratives on elder abandonment suggest that this is a contemporary phenomenon,[46] resulting from the growth of the older population, adult children shirking care responsibilities, a shrinking care network and the devastation of the HIV/AIDS pandemic.[47] However, health workers and older participants both in Kampala and in Kitgum felt that this had always been the case: 'it is just a part of life'. This view is supported by Nahemow's 1979 study, which identified social isolation and loneliness among 'the aged Baganda',[48] as well as by Girling's record of some older men living on their own in the Acholi sub-region in 1960.[49] However, where abandonment by the state is already felt by older people today, and where extended family and clan networks are increasingly dispersed, neglect and abandonment by adult children and other immediate relatives presents a significant risk of hardship.

Abandonment could also be associated with institutionalised care.[50] On the subject, many people would ask me in hushed tones if it was true that in the UK 'we put our old people in care homes', thought to be like a prison for people who don't have relatives. In contrast, Cati Coe has noted that despite an established narrative in favour of family care in Ghana, her older research participants were open to old age homes as an alternative form of elder care.[51] As care homes are few in Ghana, Coe argues that this openness is based on a 'social imagination' – which draws on known institutional elder care practices in 'the West', a pragmatic resignation to the idea that home-based intergenerational care is no longer possible in today's economic context, and an ideal of institutional sociality and availability of care based on past experiences in boarding schools.[52] This is similar to Sarah Lamb's work on ideas around care homes in India, interpreted as being 'Western institutions' while also being tailored for relevance in this context.[53] This highlights the explicit role of the global in personal and intimate everyday elder care responsibilities. A 'social imagination' of the dignity or disregard of older people in other countries serves rhetorically to re-establish care norms, which are then pragmatically adapted to suit shifting circumstances.

'Care across distances', a global phenomenon, reflects the relational mitigation of increasing mobility and migration.[54] Home is reconfigured, and existing moral economies and family norms adapted in new locations.[55] This is seen, for example, in anthropological work on 'complex global care chains'[56] or 'transnational constellations of care',[57] such as migrant care workers travelling to Western Europe and North America, leaving their own children with grandparents and sending remittances home.[58] Across various fieldsites of the ASSA project, contextually appropriate practices were employed to support the care of older people at a distance, for example the use of visual communication on smartphones providing affective support for older people in Japan and China, in line with existing social expectations.[59] In Lusozi, as discussed in detail in Chapter 5, remittances accommodate ideals of co-habitation and home-based care in a context of age-based migration between the city and the village. Existing norms and relations could thereby be reconfigured and reproduced, despite complex shifts in economic possibilities and family living arrangements.

Self-care

Various studies of 'successful ageing' in Africa argue that people desire interdependence with family in later life.[60] As van der Geest observes, isolation and loneliness in old age in his research setting in rural Ghana is the 'clearest indication of unsuccessful ageing'.[61] This is contrasted with policy and discourse in Europe and the US which emphasise health as the responsibility of an older individual – for example, through 'active ageing', 'wellness' and exercise and nutrition – to alleviate the increasing burden of population ageing on health systems and families.[62] Susan Whyte goes as far as to say that a 'successful ageing' paradigm 'doesn't exist' in Uganda, where remaining healthy and independent is not 'culturally resonant'.[63] However, this ethnography complicates this claim. Many older people who participated in this research discussed their aspirations to be able take care of themselves financially and physically in later life, to avoid 'being a burden' on their families. As one 67-year-old grandfather put it:

> They also have their responsibilities now, and I don't want to be a liability to them. They also have their families some of them now, so I don't want to burden them too much.

Some people showed how they actively work to achieve this through everyday self-care practices, such as eating well, doing exercise, limiting workloads and avoiding stress and unprotected sex.

This means that self-care can also be an act of care for others. This was also evident in the discussion in Chapter 3 on self-prescribing and home treatment among older women, who tended to buy medicines in the pharmacy rather than visiting the hospital as this would incur fees and interrupt working routines. Many women we met throughout the research were taking drugs that were ineffective or even dangerous, such as irregular doses of antibiotics, or over-medicating with painkillers. This was also noted by Wallman and Bantebya-Kyomuhendo in their 1996 ethnography of 'Kampala women getting by' during the peak of the HIV/Aids epidemic; where women might seek treatment for their children, parents or husbands, the hospital or clinic is a last resort for themselves and they would prefer to self-medicate.[64] Ongoing practices of self-medication among older women in Lusozi, over 20 years later, affirm their sustained relevance within both interpersonal and socio-economic conditions, turning responsibilities inward and determining disparities in access to health and care.

Based on her study of 'resources for health in Uganda', Meinert observes that strength, a 'strong body' in older age, indicates long life, a healthy lifestyle, self-sufficiency and access to other resources.[65] Strength was similarly valued by research participants as indicative of sustained health and resistance to illness; Amor would often compliment older participants on their strength in our initial exchanges. Nutrition and exercise are therefore particularly important aspects of care, both for self and others. Amigo, who is an engineer, said he would take care of his health by keeping active and restricting his diet, following advice by doctors to lose weight in his forties:

> I rarely eat fried foods, meat is restricted. I mainly take vegetables, fruits, no sugar, some bits of honey.

Omara, who as shown earlier mitigates potential hospital malpractice by seeking health advice from multiple sources, was also careful to monitor what he eats:

> I fear to eat these fried things with a lot of oil. I concentrate on eating greens so much … instead of buying juice which is already made, I buy fresh fruits.

While he still enjoyed 'pashing', spending time playing games, chatting and laughing with other men in Lusozi, he would avoid drinking alcohol with them and would advise them to take care of themselves too:

> Especially because nowadays it is not in the least helping, it destroys my bones… At the same time I am doing some exercise, you see it

is keeping me [strong] up to now. Others are saying you are still strong like this while others are getting old, I say you have to take care of yourself.

Obalo, a 55-year-old policeman and football coach, had been told that he was at risk of diabetes. As a result he was:

abandoning some food which I was eating. … Say like *posho* now, I used to eat a lot of *posho* and now a lot of starch is not so good, that's why I have changed a bit. And having daughters at times is good, sometimes you come and find they have prepared other types of food like *mattoke*. I avoid even these oily things … I don't take things with sugar.

The quality of food and cooking methods was often discussed as a significant aspect of health and sickness prevention. Acholi participants would often champion their long-standing cooking methods of pasting and boiling food as a source of longevity. An elderly woman we met in Palabek, said to be 100 years old, attributed her long and healthy life to her diet of millet, greens, peas and pasted food; all of which were included in the beautiful meal she served to us. In their written response to reading a draft of this monograph, Ladit and Kilongeni observed:

Acholi of old age used to have a very good and healthy way of living of up to above 100 years minus serious illness; they had a secret, being boiled food, food mixed with pasted *sim sim* (sesame) or ground nuts called locally as '*odi*', well prepared with millet bread, '*kwon kal*'. Other food varieties like maize, cassava are also added supplements. There was above 50 or more fruit and roots, both grown or wild, available as edible food or medicine, for example oranges, sweet bananas, mango, guavas, avocados, jackfruit for growth, '*kwomo*', '*kongo-ogwal*', '*oywelu*', '*lango*', '*kwomo*' and '*olelemo*', which carry a lot of vitamins and medical value. The current medical doctors still prescribe them for most, if not all, the people visiting hospitals.

Many older people across Lusozi would also emphasise the health risks of processed foods and modern cooking methods, frying in cooking oil or using excess salt and sugar, as evidence of the dangers of 'dotcom' lifestyles in the city, contrasted with the tried and trusted methods they grew up with. Poet and critic Professor Taban Lo Liyong writes of the Luo past:

> [T]here were no onions to be fried with fat or oil; there were no sugars and ice creams; there were no hamburgers filled with everything dear to a child's tongue. With the result that the youths never lost their mothers to obesity, high blood pressure or other such diseases.[66]

As discussed further below, various participants' observations and epidemiological studies have similarly associated urbanisation and processed foods with high blood pressure and related chronic conditions in Uganda,[67] often known in Lusozi as 'pressure'. While public health approaches to the 'rising tide' of non-communicable diseases (NCDs) like high blood pressure are often framed through individual 'lifestyles' and 'risk behaviours',[68] these conversations about urban diets also highlight the role of 'life conditions'[69] and the interaction between broader societal processes and the body. As Whyte shows, a 'healthy lifestyle' of selective eating, following fitness regimes and taking prescribed medicines is not always part of a 'lifestyle choice' but of a 'life condition', embedded in structural and environmental contexts.[70]

Pressure

Non-communicable diseases (NCDs) such as hypertension, diabetes, strokes, cancer and mental health problems have relatively recently become visible in Uganda.[71] NCDs can be some of the most resource-intensive conditions to manage, requiring long-term changes in family life including working routines, regular visits to hospital and meeting ongoing costs of treatment. Uganda's national and international healthcare funding prioritises communicable diseases such as HIV;[72] only 17 per cent of the national budget is allocated to chronic non-communicable conditions, leaving families mostly responsible for these costs. For example, hypertension requires daily medication, which can cost 1,500 UGX (£0.30) per tablet, or up to 50,000 UGX (£10.75) per month. Treatment for diabetes, often co-morbid with hypertension, is even more costly. Mwebaze had type 2 diabetes for 20 years, which she thought she had inherited from her father. She had various daily medical requirements to ensure that she can safely eat a meal, coming to a total of at least 120,000 UGX or £25.80 each month. 'I try, but it's not easy'. Fortunately Mwebaze had regular income from rental properties, as well as three adult sons with good jobs. She said that most people with diabetes in Uganda cannot afford this medicine and have to 'live by God's grace':

> It is an expensive disease ... I pity those who can't afford [the medicine] ... I sometimes ask the doctors in the hospitals, 'Why don't you care for diabetics like the way you care for HIV patients?'

Hypertension or high blood pressure, often known as 'pressure' in Lusozi, is one of the most common health problems faced by older participants. We discussed hypertension in 35 of 210 interviews in the neighbourhood (17 per cent), while 23 people (11 per cent) aged between 49 and 93 years old discussed their own experience of high blood pressure and 12 (6 per cent) discussed the experiences of their close relatives – parents and partners, for example. Their symptoms varied widely, but might include a fast heart rate, difficulty in breathing, headaches, exhaustion, itching, problems with eyesight, limb swelling and pain, overheating and dizziness. For nine participants high blood pressure was also co-morbid with diabetes. Six also had stomach ulcers (the most prevalent chronic condition encountered in general) and two had been told they were at risk of a stroke. We also had extensive casual conversations about 'pressure' during and subsequent to the research, often when people were speculating about unexplained illness or death, suggesting that it is at the forefront as an explanation for health uncertainty.

These figures likely underestimate actual prevalence. Various epidemiological studies have found high blood pressure to be prevalent in Uganda,[73] particularly in central and urban areas of the country.[74] A national epidemiological study noted:

> a region-wide epidemic of hypertension in sub-Saharan Africa, which is probably related to rapid urbanisation in the region.[75]

Hypertension is often co-morbid with other chronic conditions, such as diabetes, strokes and cardiovascular diseases. This is not to mention the complexity of co-morbidity with infectious diseases such as COVID-19. It can be understood as a vector for various biological, socio-economic, structural concerns – sitting at these multiple intersections and interacting in complex ways to exacerbate their outcomes, what might be understood as a 'syndemic'.[76]

As well as diet, financial problems related to family responsibilities were commonly identified as a cause of 'pressure' and even in some cases equated with it. While increasing studies also associate chronic stress or emotional distress with cumulative blood pressure elevation and hypertension,[77] the concern here is less with causal attribution[78] and more with how people link their understanding of changing life conditions to the 'rising tide'[79] of hypertension and related chronic illnesses – what Whyte might call a 'pragmatic approach' in medical anthropology. As some examples outlined here will show, pressure can be understood as embodied stress, a result of 'over-thinking' or 'thinking too much' about social and economic conditions, shown in various studies to be a common idiom of distress around the world. This provides a meaningful language for expressing experiences of embodied social suffering, for making sense of them and communicating them to others.[80] In doing so, people can articulate a sense of the relationship between the mind, body and wider social worlds, a process that can also be employed to convey and mitigate social suffering and 'pressure'.

According to many participants, additional burdens of care on mothers and grandmothers, responsible for the health and advancement of everyone in their households, applies 'pressure' which can result in hypertension. Aida, a 49-year-old mother of eight, explained:

> *I'm suffering from pressure and ulcers. I have pressure because of paying school fees. Pressure means a lot of problems.*

The pressures associated with paying school fees are widespread, and often discussed.[81] In a survey of 150 older people in Lusozi, participants were found to pay school fees for two children on average, spending an average of 760,000 UGX (£151) per semester, only slightly less than the average monthly income of 780,000 UGX (£155). Paying school fees also puts pressure on those with higher incomes, who may be held responsible for the education of the whole family.[82] Otim, a 57-year-old man with 12 children and an income of 5,000,000 UGX (£995) per month, said he is responsible for as many as 20 children's school fees, to a total of 6,000,000 UGX (£1,194) per term. This suggested that a significant proportion of his income was being spent on school fees alone. For many, 'overthinking' about school fees could be explicitly linked to high blood pressure and related chronic illnesses. Mwesigwe Robert, a 45-year-old *boda* driver, also attributes his pressure to 'thinking a lot' about paying for school fees, hospital fees and food:

> There's a lot of things so it becomes hard for you to control your thoughts … and you're just one person, so you can't control your pressure.

While working hard to provide their children with an education, to the detriment of personal health and aspiration, a few people question the value of it. They have seen that jobs for young people are scarce regardless of their education. Many graduates face un- and under-employment[83] in terms of their skills, time and income levels,[84] making it difficult to fulfil expectations of gaining salaried employment and providing for their families.[85] Older people, who likely have made significant investments in education, can then be left without financial support in later life. I interviewed a 60-year-old woman who told me, as she sat among photographs of her youngest daughter's recent graduation, that 'there's nothing good in education'. These days, she said, 'if they don't have school fees, they stress a lot'. Her son-in-law had pressure as he had 'so much stress over the kids … the problems bring the pressure'. She remembered that if you graduated in the past 'you found a place to work, but now it's not there'. She has four daughters who had graduated but could not find employment, so she kept paying for her grandchildren in the hope that it would be different for them: 'every kid has their own luck'. In the meantime she continued to work to sustain her income make up the deficit, a common family arrangement for managing this economic situation.

Structural under-employment can also have health implications for the younger generation. From the perspective of older research participants, many voiced concerns about increasing despondence among educated young people with limited employment opportunities, who turn instead to drugs or '*njagga*' and alcohol:

> No jobs, idleness, peer pressure … some take it [alcohol] to pass the time. They have no work and just want to gain confidence.

Many discussed the impact of '*njagga*' and alcohol on their children's minds, families and futures – as well as on their own lives, necessitating their own ongoing responsibilities to provide for the whole family despite their age. As shown in Chapter 3, if youth is a time of prolonged 'waithood' in precarious urban economies,[86] then this is true for the older generations too.

We discussed the ongoing responsibilities of the older generation for themselves and their children with Achola, a 60-year-old woman. Despite not having had children herself, Achola is a mother to many children, including her own nephews and nieces. She said she is confident that she '*knew how to raise them up*'. Some of their parents had died of AIDS or were killed by rebels during the war, '*some for my brothers, some for my sisters*'. Six of them now live in the village, and five stay with her in Lusozi. '*They are lucky because I am here*'. She is staying with them in Lusozi, where she stayed with them so they can continue their studies. '*I'm their parents, their father and mother are not there*'. Like her good friend Evelyn, she values her independence and her female friendships. These are the women she would turn to if she needed help, or her grandchildren will turn to when she's sick.

If not for the children's education, Achola would have returned to the village by now, '*amero caro* (I like the village), *there's food there you can dig ... I know people are there sitting under the tree now – I can see them from here!*' For Achola, '*Staying here is now difficult, no money, I can't afford rent and food ... I want to go to the village now, I'm old and I can't keep working for money*'. We asked if she hoped to return to the village in the future, and she laughed. '*Bambi, I haven't even anything to dig it all. My money has all gone on school fees here in Kampala.*' Do you expect the children will take care of you in return? '*I want them to take care, but you don't know ... even if you produce many, maybe only one or two will care, but for others, they won't care.*' In the meantime Achola worked hard, distilling *waragi* in the factory at the bottom of Lusozi hill. This is a physically demanding job that is a common form of employment for single mothers trying to pay school fees. As the founder of a *waragi* factory in Lusozi told us:

> *You know very well that this kind of work men cannot do ... If you just sit at home because you're sick, it will be hard to educate your children. And then you find there is no future. So with this business I keep paying school fees. One of my children is supposed to go to university this year. She wants to study medicine. We do it even if it is going to affect your health, but for the future you have to do it.*

Here the responsibility to earn money and provide for the family is carried by women, who are considered more capable of compromising their own health in order to provide for their children and 'the future', and of putting their own everyday lives and aspirations aside. Achola describes how she manages her own 'waithood' and worries about the future by praying at the local Catholic Church every morning at 6.30 a.m., '*too much I like it*'. Sometimes if she stays at home instead, she has too much time to think about her future old age. '*I feel that, what am I going to be when I reach up to 70, 80 years? I will be old, I cannot dig or carry water, so what can I do? If I go to Church and pray, the thinking reduces.*' One day she even had a dream which '*told her to stop over thinking*', which she believes was a vision from God. At the time she '*was so worried, I used to over think as I had seven kids in the house'*. Now she lets thoughts go, realising that *'if not I may build pressure or get a stroke'*. We asked Achola what she understands pressure to mean:

> *Pressure, 'tic tic tic'* [imitating heartbeat], *pressure is overthinking. If you think a lot your heart beats at a high speed to the point that if they bring bad news suddenly you can just faint … it can go to your brain, then it can disturb your brain.*

She advises others to *'stop over-thinking'* because *'pressure is not a disease, it comes from your own thinking'*. This is the same for mental health disorders, which are *'hard, but are from over thinking'*. Rather than downplaying the effects of pressure or mental ill health, which clearly present real health concerns for Achola, this idea that 'pressure is not a disease' further establishes the understanding of pressure as a manifestation of 'too many thoughts', meaning that the symptoms reflect organic effects of stress on the body and can also be considered metaphorical or psychosomatic in themselves.[87] This offers insight into the 'social mechanisms' at the 'embodied intersection of pressure, stress and social conditions', and also the underlying concepts of the relationships between 'too many thoughts', damaging 'the brain' and overworking 'the heart', which are then vulnerable to external stressors like sudden bad news.[88]

What are some of the strategies employed to 'stop over-thinking'? To avoid over-thinking about her own future, Achola goes *'to pray for my soul, so I go to a better place'*. Her grandchildren come to church with her, and two of them in the village even work in the church ministry. She hopes that her grandchildren are all *'going to be very well'* and that one day one of them will be a priest and one a sister, as *'I have seen what they do in Church, it is really something good'*. Stella Nyanzi has conducted research interviewing 'widowed mama grannies' in Kampala city slums. She spoke with grandmothers who seek solace, sanity and strength from prayer, with one 72-year-old saying 'I pray for strength to look after my grandchildren'.[89] For Achola, prayer has been a way of reducing 'pressure' in relation to her present responsibilities and the unknown future. This daily morning ritual is shared by many others, such as Nabasa, who also used prayer to share and reduce her worries, and to ensure that her children have a *'successful life'*. She had faith in prayer since she lost her job; she had prayed to God, and not long afterwards had found an organisation to sponsor her children's school fees. She hoped for *'what every parent hopes for'*, and prays every day for her children to be all right in the future, *'that they can be able to help themselves first, so they can help me after'*.

As soon as Nabasa wakes up, she thanks God, as '*to wake up is a gift*'. She then goes to the local Catholic Church for mass at 6.20 a.m., something that she has done every day for her whole life, excluding special occasions. She would kneel down to thank Him, to carry all her worries in His heart and ask for help. '*It is only God who is able*'. Some of her worries she would only keep for God. Her main concern for her children was that they would not be able to find employment when they graduate. If they come to her complaining of disappointments in their lives, she tells them to '*kneel down and pray*'. She prays that God '*opens ways for them*' so that they can get jobs and also take care of her – then she will be happy.

Through prayer, a daily routine of sharing their worries with God, Nabasa and Achola were able to alleviate the stresses of bringing up and educating many children, offering the hope and strength necessary to fulfil these family responsibilities. This alleviates their worries for the future of their grandchildren, and for their own old age. If their children are successful, perhaps they would also be able to support them in return. This is not just a reciprocal exchange between generations, but a parallel sociality, with shared 'waithood' across the generations. Idioms defining 'pressure' and its management depict a sense of the absorption and re-articulation of economic stress via thoughts, a socially implicated yet self-determined, internal process. This outlines the extent to which an older individual – especially a mother or grandmother – is expected to manage their own health and wellbeing, both in response to economic conditions and to family responsibilities. Self-care can thus be considered another embodied act of familial care, rather than one of 'individualism'.

There are also important examples of 'self-care' through community engagement, ways of seeking out wellbeing, managing personal stress and even collectively organising.[90] Achola, for example, would regularly attend women's meetings, '*to see how life goes, talk about how life is, how age is pushing you*'. If someone there was in need of food for their children, for example, they would help each other. Or, as in Chapter 4, the women's groups weekly parties were often said to help the members to 'kick off stress' and to mitigate the challenges of their domestic and financial responsibilities. Again, 'convivial social action'[91] in the community can enable forms of resistance and self-care, in turn benefiting the household and family. Arguably these are the existing strategies of collective self-reliance that public health responses to the hypertension 'epidemic' and related 'syndemics' should seek to learn from and support.

Conclusion

This chapter began by asking the question 'Who is responsible for older people's health and care?' in order to outline observed social processes involved in seeking an answer. What is the role of the state, the family and the older person themselves, and are they meeting these expectations adequately? Where social possibilities fall short of expectations, which alternative relationships are formed? What is the role of increasing digital connection, of kind strangers with proximity, of 'unkind' or inaccessible institutions? What is the role of relatives, based on which socially determined and embodied roles they inhabit, and on the far more complex and messy stories of our interpersonal relationships? Who will do the cooking, cleaning and conversation? Who will provide resources – and how?

Answers to the latter questions bring to light the narrowing of care possibilities. With greater longevity and global urbanisation, there are widely voiced concerns about the de-personalisation of care, or even the increasing abandonment of elders around the world. The risk of elder abandonment highlights how almost intangible global connectivity between people and others can impinge on lived circumstances, in some cases paradoxically determining day to day isolation and loneliness. There is an increasing public emphasis on the responsibility of older people to take care of their own health, to prevent sickness and avoid becoming a burden on their families and already stretched health systems. This 'successful ageing' paradigm is said to be a preoccupation in Europe and the US, based on a tendency to individualism, an emphasis on economic productivity and an aversion to dependence.[92] In contrast, 'successful' older age in East Africa is said to be a time of 'interdependence', with aspirations to home-based family care.[93] The ethnographic findings outlined in this chapter complicate this binary, with many people working towards financial and physical independence in old age, in order to continue supporting their children and to avoid becoming a burden on them in future.

An understanding of elder care norms in other societies, specifically in conversations with me about imagined institutionalised care in the UK, present a disparaged alternative against which existing family expectations are re-established.[94] Instead families often rely on care practices that tend to be overlooked, including remittances, self-care, the hiring of domestic help or sending grandchildren home, supporting possibilities of home-based care. This maintains the long-standing role of women as family caregivers, even while they work to make money in the city.

As well as reinforcing established gender roles, elder care practices can also reproduce class status,[95] as in the cost-saving approach of sending grandchildren home to the village and limiting access to what is considered a good education.

Literature from the anthropology of ageing has similarly emphasised how later life care, even daily intimate support, embodies sociopolitical and demographic concerns.[96] This also reflects approaches to care in critical medical anthropology, which studies how 'individual and collective health is closely entwined with power relations',[97] especially economic factors.[98] In this way global, social, political and economic factors are implicit in everyday discussions and routines around elder care, which offer insight into how people manage uncertainty related to health; as Whyte argues, conversation with others is one of the few ways of seeking security amid the ambiguity of life. This is especially true in times of sickness, when people seek guidance from trusted people and health experts in various fields.[99] Ways of talking about health can then be understood as insight into relationships between people, and with the world around them. This is evident in the common attribution of 'pressure' to economic stressors and ongoing family responsibilities.

In an economy which promotes self-care while undermining its possibilities,[100] family care underpins a 'moral economy' of ageing which is in flux and under pressure.[101] As Nguyen et al. have noted in reference to literature on the 'global care chain', care is part of a situated moral discourse as well as 'the neoliberal project' which promotes self-determination and self-care in 'the face of growing precarity and widespread uncertainties, conditions that are stripping away the very possibilities for self-determination for most'.[102] They argue that this represents the 'broadest moral contradiction, ambivalence and hybridity of our social and political world today'.[103] This chapter therefore sought to contribute to this theorising on the political dimensions of care by locating the '[c]oexistence of local and global ideas about ageing and care on which young and elderly people draw to survive and maintain relationships in shifting political and economic conditions'.[104]

Care practices in particular offer insight into the management of increasing healthcare shortages, which also promote self and family responsibility along moral lines.[105] As Kleinman states, family care can act as a 'counterbalancing force' to political and economic conditions while simultaneously reflecting moral and religious values, as well as empathy, compassion, respect and love, or endurance, rejection and burdens; he argues that this is what makes us human.[106] Further, as Park and Akello show in their study of the moral experiences of caregiving during the Ebola outbreak in Gulu in 2000,[107] family caregiving can even have a 'distinctive moral logic' based on responding to the 'radical insecurity' of ill-health, sometimes at odds with state policy and biomedical discourse. In this way anthropologists have theorised care as a 'primary locus' for enacting morality, both in relation to caregiving and also to self-care, the 'moral/ethical reconfiguration of selves that is characteristic of many healing traditions'.[108] Care is one aspect of enacted morality highlighted in this ethnography, alongside phone use, work and livelihoods, as well as the 'habit' and 'articulation' of co-operative values,[109] defining and enacting an individual's responsibilities to others. This is the focus of Chapter 7 to follow, which considers some 'moral moments' of the ethnography in the historical context of the 'moral moment' in Uganda.[110]

Notes

1. Kleinman 2015.
2. Hampshire et al. 2017; Hampshire et al. 2021.
3. Gertrude et al. 2019; MacNeil 1996; Wallman and Bantebya-Kyomuhendo 1996.
4. Whyte and Whyte 2004, 90.
5. Nyamnjoh 2017, 261.
6. Buch 2015.
7. Buch 2015; Han 2012; Fassin 2009; Kehr, Hansjörg and van Eeuwijk 2018; Kleinman 2015; Nguyen, Zavoretti and Tronto 2017.
8. Kehr, Hansjörg and van Eeuwijk 2018, 3.
9. Fassin 2009; Han 2012; Kehr, Hansjörg and van Eeuwijk 2018; Nguyen, Zavoretti and Tronto 2017.
10. Coe 2020.
11. Wallman and Bantebya-Kyomuhendo 1996, 113.
12. Wallman and Bantebya-Kyomuhendo 1996, 145.
13. Whyte 1997.
14. Whyte 1997, 27.
15. Whyte 1997, 25.
16. Whyte 1997, 25.
17. See Chapter 1 for demographic data.
18. Nankwanga and Neema 2020, 84.
19. Droti 2014; Mulumba et al. 2014; Schatz et al. 2018.
20. Mulumba et al. 2014; Nankwanga and Neema 2020; Wandera, Kwagala and Ntozi 2015.
21. Hamill et al. 2019; Whyte 1997.
22. Nguyen, Zavoretti and Tronto 2017, 199; Kehr, Hansjörg and van Eeuwijk 2018, 13; Bukuluki and Mubiru 2014, 10.
23. In their study of care during the Ebola outbreak in Gulu, medical anthropologists Grace Akello and Sung-Joon Park term this the 'oughtness of care' for sick relatives, based on the distinctive moral logic of care, that it 'has to be done', regardless of the fear instilled by public health campaigns (cf Kleinman 2014, 119; Park and Akello 2017, 60).
24. The head of physiotherapy has conducted research on the relationship between disability and poverty due to the emphasis on family to provide care.
25. Nyamnjoh 2002, 115–16.
26. Zavoretti 2017.
27. Nguyen, Zavoretti and Tronto 2017, 204.
28. Nguyen, Zavoretti and Tronto 2017, 203.
29. Nguyen, Zavoretti and Tronto 2017, 203.

30. Coe 2020.
31. Bourdieu 1986; Meinert 2004.
32. Coe 2020.
33. Livingston 2003, 25; Wallman and Bantebya-Kyomuhendo 1996, 11, 13.
34. Roth 2010.
35. Gertrude et al. 2019; MacNeil 1996; Wallman and Bantebya-Kyomuhendo 1996.
36. Gertrude et al. 2019.
37. Livingston 2003, 215.
38. Livingston 2003.
39. Hart 2008.
40. Singh et al. 2017.
41. McIntosh 2017; Nzabona and Ntozi 2017; Oppong 2006; Schatz and Seeley 2015; Whyte 2017.
42. Randall and Coast (2016) note that the quality of data on older Africans is unreliable. They find that 'The data available are so problematic that any conclusions about age-related health and welfare and their evolution over time and space are potentially compromised'.
43. Wandera et al. 2017.
44. Kuteesa et al. 2012, 297; Najjumba-Mulindwa 2003, 10; Nzabona, Ntozi and Rutaremwa 2016.
45. Nyanzi 2011, 378.
46. Aboderin 2004; Nankwanga, Neema and Phillips 2013; Sokolovsky 2020.
47. Ssengonzi 2007.
48. Nahemow 1979.
49. Girling 2019, 108.
50. Fassin locates the 'zone of abandonment' as representative of the evaluated 'worthiness of life' (Fassin 2009, 54) – the treatment of individuals considered tolerable in moral economies which construct differentiated values of lives, representing what Fassin terms 'biolegitimacy'. He follows Biehl's ethnography of institutionalised 'Vita', who says 'people forgot me' (Fassin 2009, 54).
51. Coe 2019, 2020.
52. Coe 2019, 2020.
53. Lamb 2017.
54. Ahlin 2018; Oudshoorn 2011; Pols 2012.
55. Sigona et al. 2015.
56. Buch 2015, 286.
57. Nguyen, Zavoretti and Tronto 2017, 199.
58. For example, Ahlin 2018; Baldassar et al. 2017; Horn and Schweppe 2016; Madianou and Miller 2012.
59. Wang and Happio-Kirk 2021.
60. McIntosh 2017; Schatz and Seeley 2015; Whyte 2017; van der Geest 2011.
61. Van der Geest 2011, 67.
62. Lamb 2017: McIntosh 2017, 10.
63. Whyte 2017, 244.
64. Wallman and Bantebya-Kyomuhendo 1996, 141.
65. Meinert 2004, 21.
66. Liyong 2018.
67. Guwatudde et al. 2015; Lunyera et al. 2018; Musinguzi and Nuwaha 2013; Wandera, Kwagala and Ntozi 2015.
68. For example, see WHO 'Global NCD target: Reduce high blood pressure', from the WHO Global NCD Action Plan 2013–2020 and the 2030 Agenda for Sustainable Development, particularly target 3.4.
69. Seeberg and Meinert 2020.
70. Whyte 2014.
71. Whyte 2016.
72. Whyte 2016, 222.
73. Guwatudde et al. 2015; Lunyera et al. 2018; Musinguzi and Nuwaha 2013; Wandera, Kwagala and Ntozi 2015.
74. Guwatudde et al. 2015; Nankwanga and Neema 2020, 82.
75. Lunyera et al. 2018.
76. Singer et al. 2017, 2021.
77. Liu et al. 2017; Spruill 2010.

78. Nguyen 2016, 88.
79. Whyte 2014, 188.
80. Mendenhall et al. (2010) have referred to this as a 'culturally meaningful somatic language'.
81. Vokes and Mills 2015, 331.
82. Whyte 1997, 44.
83. Uganda Bureau of Statistics (UBOS) 2017. 'Education: A means for population transformation. Based on the National Population and Housing Census 2014', 50. Accessed 1 April 2020. https://www.ubos.org/wp-content/uploads/publications/03_2018Education_Monograph_Report_Final_08-12-2017.pdf.
84. Kiranda, Walter and Mugisha 2017.
85. Meinert 2009, 9.
86. Thieme 2018.
87. See also Mendenhall et al. 2010, 222.
88. Ibid.
89. Nyanzi 2009.
90. Burgess 2020.
91. Nyamnjoh 2017, 259.
92. Lamb 2017.
93. Whyte 2017.
94. Coe 2020.
95. Coe 2020.
96. Buch 2015.
97. Kehr, Hansjörg and van Eeuwijk 2018, 4.
98. Farmer 2004; Fassin 2009; Han 2012.
99. Wallman and Bantebya-Kyomuhendo 1996, 113.
100. Nguyen, Zavoretti and Tronto 2017, 206.
101. Livingston 2003, 222.
102. Nguyen, Zavoretti and Tronto 2017.
103. Nguyen, Zavoretti and Tronto 2017.
104. Nguyen, Zavoretti and Tronto 2017, 206.
105. Nguyen, Zavoretti and Tronto 2017.
106. Kleinman 2015.
107. Park and Akello 2017, 60.
108. Black 2018, 86.
109. Black 2018; Keane 2016.
    The former, being intermediate and communicative, is associated with the 'moral' and the latter, being more reflective and conscious, with the 'ethical'. However, given the challenge of distinguishing between the two in anthropological research (i.e. the impossibility of determining whether 'communicative action is reflexive enough to be considered ethical'), they can be used together or interchangeably, as in Black's analysis on 'the ethics and aesthetics of care' and Keane's seminal contributions to moral anthropology.
110. Allen 2015; Baral 2016; Boyd 2013; Doherty 2020; Finnström 2008; Karlström et al. 2004; Kyaddondo 2008; Monteith 2018; Tamale 2020; Whyte et al. 2016.

7
Co-operative morality

Introduction

During this ethnography, many people explicitly discussed how they define 'goodness' and what it means to be 'good'.[1] This has been addressed throughout the monograph so far, which has emphasised the meaningful enactment of moral values: in the 'aliveness' and fluidity of ageing ideals in the city, outlined in Chapter 2; in the sociality and ethics of work, outlined in Chapter 3; in the co-operative associations described in Chapter 4; in phone-based intergenerational support, described in Chapter 5; and in the elder care norms and family responsibilities described in Chapter 6. The expanded consideration of co-operative morality in this chapter also builds on the central concept of *social individuality*,[2] through which autonomy is attained through 'convivial' co-operation – an ambivalence that plays out particularly through gendered and intergenerational tensions.[3]

    Moral categorisations of 'goodness' are of course diverse and inconsistent between individuals, who may also redefine morality on an ongoing basis. Particular distinctions are likely to appear between people of different generations, geographies, ethnicities and religions.[4] However, many of the older people we worked with often commended those with a 'good heart', who are visibly respectful, generous and co-operative with others. A recent study conducted by Oxford anthropologists presents a theory of 'morality-as-cooperation' based on ethnographic records of 60 societies.[5] They argue that this includes a set of universal, well-established moral values and corresponding types of co-operation, including, as relevant here, family values and distribution of resources to family, group loyalty and co-operation for mutual advantage, reciprocity and social exchange, respect and conflict resolution.[6]

This study is part of an emergent focus on morality in anthropology, towards an 'anthropology of the good'.[7] This monograph contributes to this literature by focusing on encountered discussions and portrayals of moral goodness in context, specifically through everyday concepts of togetherness, respect and 'heart'. For example, as discussed in Chapter 2, respect is shown to older people through humble deference, a polite manner of approach, taking time to greet them and seeking their advice. As Englund shows in his review of morality in the anthropology of Africa, upholding moral obligations to others is also a way to demonstrate one's own personal attributes. It comprises an 'ethical self-formation' through everyday co-operative practices which counters the 'imagined social whole' of a 'bounded community'.[8] This infers a morality that can be made visible, or 'publicly articulated'.[9] This kind of observable, enacted respect for family roles and particularly older people's public authority, intentionally shown through a certain disposition, informs an ethnographic understanding of co-operative morality in this chapter. This builds on relevant anthropological work which defines morality as it emerges through social experience and interactions,[10] as well as various studies of the 'moral moment'[11] in Uganda, around shifting intergenerational expectations and wider histories.

It is worth noting here that the articulation and practice of co-operative morality may have been particularly apparent to me as a visitor, initially seeking to understand ways of showing 'goodness' myself and offered ongoing generosity by the many people who participated in this research. As the Lusozi chairwoman put it in a speech she gave at the workshop concluding this research, the hospitality that was shown to me reveals the 'good heart' of my hosts. The idea of a 'good heart' as the superior antithesis to money, a quality that will be reciprocated by God, appears throughout this chapter:

> I want to thank the people ... you've been giving your time. I think this is so great... We in Lusozi, we are very poor. But we are very rich at heart [agreement]... That is how we welcome people. That is how we stay with people ... that is how we brought up our children – they are very good like us, eh? So they know how to receive people in their home, they know how to treat visitors, they know how to welcome visitors. And they even know how to escort them back to their places ... you know surely it is not about money, people, it is about heart. It is not about money. And how you do it, that is how God gives to you.

The chapter opens with a discussion of contextual factors which may contribute to the *visibility* of co-operative morality in Lusozi.[12] These factors include colonialism and conflict, the rise of Pentecostal Christianity, politicised sexuality and economic uncertainty, all of which are highly moralised domains of social life; 'impersonal forces' that are intersubjectively expressed, experienced and negotiated.[13] In Kampala, the conflicts and economic insecurities resulting from British colonisation[14] are said to have exposed a particularly 'moralised environment', reflected in a 'passionate discussion about moral decay in society'.[15] This is also the case in northern Uganda, where the 'moral landscape' is said to have been 'deeply impacted by war',[16] leading to the 'continuous assertion' of shared values and ideals.[17] The chapter shows how defining and enacting 'goodness' can respond to complex lived conditions, while also offering possibilities to act on them. This will be explored through various ethnographic examples around the theme of 'a good heart', including a ritual of forgiveness at Amor's family home in Palabek, and conversations with many people who discussed moral co-operation and respect at length. These conversations and interactions are outlined to offer partial insight into how people relate to histories, to the world around them and to each other.[18]

The moral moment

The growing interest in moral anthropology has been associated with global economic, political and ecological instability. As Muehlebach notes of anthropologists, 'the world is ... speaking to us in a heightened ethical register' – evident, for example, in the language of humanitarian and development discourses, philanthro-capitalism, charismatic religions, political protest and 'human economies'.[19] Anthropologists working in various contexts have noted how neoliberal encounters and social change contribute to a 'heightened sense of moral concern' and a 'moral debate in everyday life'.[20] Arguably, as shown in the previous chapter, these moral debates are particularly exposed in light of intergenerational care responsibilities. As Nguyen and colleagues put it in their analysis of 'global caring', the co-existence of local and global ideas about ageing and care on which young and elderly people draw to survive and maintain relationships in shifting political economic conditions[21] causes moral anxieties around the world, with 'conflicting moral frameworks' exposing 'ambivalence and uncertainty'.[22]

In Uganda, as highlighted by anthropologist David Kyaddondo, shifts in economic activities and reciprocities are contributing to a 'moral debate over intergenerational relations'.[23] Parents unable to fulfil their role of providing financial and care resources are open to criticism from their families, as are children who fail to maintain respect, deference and obedience to their parents in return.[24] Economic conditions overburden moral values of togetherness and respect, simultaneously obliging and undermining related material expectations, making them increasingly difficult to uphold. This is reconfiguring how actions are categorised morally, reflected in many older people's concerns about the younger generation, to what extent they will be able to co-operate with their families and each other in this economy, and the impact this is having on home and community.

In Lusozi, a sense of moral uncertainty was evident in public discussions, often in religious terms. During an Acholi function at the Catholic Church in Lusozi, a pastor opened the event with a long speech. Referring to a recent spate of crime, he told the many attendees: 'We live in difficult times, in a situation of insecurity, the factors of which we do not know ... '. Like the chairwoman cited above, he appealed to 'unity', working together, in biblical and familial terms, 'We must be our brothers' and sisters' keepers, because what happens to your neighbours will also affect you'. In Uganda, 84 per cent of the population reported to be Christian in the 2014 census (a figure to be taken 'with caution'),[25] and a growing proportion of them are Pentecostal,[26] or *Murokole* (Born Again). Pentecostal Christianity originated in North America, and includes ecstatic worship such as speaking in tongues, with belief in miracles or gifts from the Holy Spirit.[27] Doctrines of Pentecostal Christianity include a 'strict moralism', such as the banning of alcohol, indigenous spirits, sexual promiscuity and gambling.[28] As a 'relatively new religion', it is also thought to be responsible for an 'ethical dilemma' – a moment at which previous ways of life are questioned,[29] encouraging a break with the past to allow for a moral and spiritual rebirth.

This is a worldwide movement. Anthropologist Joel Robbins has analysed a situation of ongoing 'moral breakdown' among the Urapmin in Papua New Guinea, who face a clash of values between their traditional, relational concept of morality and their relatively new Pentecostal values, focused on individual salvation and a renunciation of the past. Robbins observes that this results in an ongoing 'moral self-reflection' – evident, for example, in the regular confession of sins. This shows that when conflicts between values arise, an awareness of moral decision-making is foregrounded.[30] Drawing from

Robbins' analysis, Zigon argues that ethics are performed at the point of 'moral breakdown', the moment at which morals are no longer used as unreflective tools[31] but as 'conscious efforts of self-mastery and ethical cultivation'.[32]

The global and situated moral influence of Pentecostal Christianity in Uganda is politically evident. Famously the proposed 'anti-homosexuality bill'[33] has been strongly linked to the influence of the Christian establishment in Uganda and prominent Pentecostal missionaries from the US, who perceive marginalised gender identities and sexual orientations as a threat to 'the family'. A rhetorical analysis of an earlier draft of the bill finds it to be based on a falsely standardised understanding of the 'traditional family' in Africa, which Nyanzi argues can be traced to the binary colonial categorisation of otherwise ambiguous and flexible traditions related to kinship, sexuality and gender.[34] Others highlight pre-colonial complexity and homophobia, as well as a long history of nuanced gender identities and sexualities.[35] There are also critiques which link the current politicisation of homophobia to socio-economic factors; widespread dissatisfaction with the current economic and political reality, grounded in Western imperialism and aid,[36] forms a complex backdrop to the rise of the 'anti-gay agenda'.[37] The resulting threat to the everyday lives of queer people in Uganda, inscribed in hostile political rhetoric, violence and repression, depicts the interplay of global economic, political and moral factors, as experienced and embodied.

'People's hearts are changing'

At times during the research people would discuss how their cultural beliefs clash with their more recent conversion to Pentecostal Christianity, which denounces spiritual beliefs and practices as demonic. As Robbins has noted, this is one reason to account for increasing global popularity of Pentecostalism, as, unlike other forms of Christianity, it acknowledges and incorporates people's existing beliefs, even while demonising them. In doing so, it demonstrates a 'simultaneous rejection and preservation of the traditional cultures it encounters'.[38]

For some, like Namukisa, this has caused problems with their families, particularly with the older generation, their parents and grandparents. We met Namukisa at her stall in the centre of Lusozi where she sold snacks and fruit. Her ancestral Baganda name has some associations with witchcraft, so since she became Born Again she has slightly changed the spelling; it now means 'Blessings'. Her religion had led her to reject various Baganda traditions that conflict with her new beliefs. She would no longer attend funeral rites that appease Baganda Gods, such as cutting bark cloth from the shroud and providing sacrificial offerings. As Born Again, she does not believe in those gods, and has faith that no more sacrifice is necessary as Jesus has already shed blood for humanity. She has rejected her Baganda identity *'totally'*, and is confident that being Born Again is much better. Her husband was pleased, as it meant she had stopped drinking *waragi* (gin), and they were both convinced that becoming Born Again had cured their daughter of epilepsy. The rest of her family, particularly her parents, felt *'bad, heartbroken'* and *'always try to talk to her about it'*, but her decision was made. It means she even has to go against her own mother's advice, particularly when it comes to visiting Baganda healers. She expects that the next generation will be far better people, as more of them will have become Born Again.

Like Namukisa, Aciro Anne said she had stopped drinking alcohol, and that her *'heart has calmed down'* since she became Born Again. She was no longer interested in brewing *waragi*, which she used to do to provide for her seven children after her husband died when they were still young. She said it had been very hard, and that if it was not for her income from the brewery and her faith in God, she would not have been able to manage. We asked how she would advise other young women in her position.

> *First of all, they need to be prayerful and take care of their kids.*

Aciro Anne added that she is *'wealthy in heart'*, meaning that she is always willing to help other people. She would alway check on her older brothers and visit them to see how they were coping. She was concerned that *'it will be very bad for the next generation'* as *'people's hearts are changing – that's why you see people don't care about their relatives'*. This contrasts with the past, locating an intergenerational ideal often discussed and enacted in the present:

> *Our generation and the ancestors' generations were not like this ... Those days people had respect, if it is an elder it is an elder; nowadays there's no respect at all... They do their own things, not bothering whether you're a big person or not.*

Aciro Anne explained that she had been brought up as '*a proper girl, doing the right thing*'; for example, she '*used to kneel and greet people while she's kneeling*'. As was often explained to me, respect is shown to older people through disposition, ways of talking to them, dressing, and conforming to practices such as kneeling to greet them. Young people are expected to speak to their elders in soft and courteous tones, a politeness that should be extended to anyone older than you, including those outside your own family. Showing 'respect' and 'respectability' in this way means that people can be seen to acknowledge the public authority of elders and to uphold family values and roles.[39] It is therefore often considered bad manners to talk back to your family, especially parents and older relatives; if you disagree, you are supposed to wait and 'give an explanation in a low tone' at the right time.

Elder authority is particularly central in Acholi society. During a visit to Amor's family home in Palabek, she had lost her smartphone after we had returned from bathing in the river. A clan elder had visited to talk to us, and the conversation often returned to the issue of the lost phone and speculation as to its whereabouts. Amor and a few others spent time searching around the house, while one of the younger men returned to the river to look for it. She was getting increasingly stressed, worried that the battery would run out. The family sat in a circle, discussing the issue at length in Acholi. One of the women, Amor's aunt, started crying, shouting and thumping her hands in the dirt. Amor's Jaja, the clan leader and Kilongeni admonished her in turn, and the woman became increasingly frustrated. I surmised that the clan leader had asked her if she knew where Amor's phone was and she was trying to defend herself. Kilongeni and Amor were evidently conscious of my presence, apologising to me. 'Let's forget the issue of the phone, we have a project to do'. Kilongeni had planned a tour of the village and a meeting with a few elders. I went inside to pack a bag and found Amor's phone tucked in my suitcase, left there for safe-keeping and forgotten. Meanwhile the argument continued outside with Jaja, now seated in front of her house, admonishing the woman from a distance. I took the phone outside and there was a shocked silence. The accused woman sobbed and ran to a bench under a tree at a distance. Amor followed, asking her for forgiveness.

The clan leader, as the eldest man and therefore most senior person there, nominated the accused woman for the first public apology, enacted through *mato oput* or 'drinking the bitter root'.[40] With a determined expression and tears still on her cheeks, she bit into a piece of blackened wood, took a sip of water and blew pieces of the crushed wood on Amor, her baby and me, the three visitors. She then put some leaves into the mug of water and splashed the water on us. Amor laughed, saying to me, 'you see culture?' Kilongeni then did the same on Amor's behalf, explaining that *mato oput* is performed after each argument; if people refuse, the next day they must try again. The apology serves a practical purpose, visibly 'ending bitterness'[41] and 'untying knots in relationships'[42] by enacting resolution and allowing families to move on from disagreements. The ceremony symbolises the 'end of bitterness', pragmatically and meaningfully emphasising 'reparation, restoration, reconciliation'.[43] Otherwise 'keeping something in the heart blocks the flow of relationships' and of life itself.[44]

In this instance, moral transgression was both defined and managed through public behaviours and orientations towards others; the visibility of Amor's aunt's anger towards elders and in front of visitors, thumping her hands in the dirt, was considered the greater offence. The enacted restoration,[45] 'publicly articulated', was then key to overcoming the disagreement, accepting responsibility and re-establishing co-operative priorities and family roles. As this shows, while serving a pragmatic purpose, the ways that transgressions are defined and acted upon can reproduce existing social hierarchies, such as those privileging older men, urban relatives with smartphones and white visitors such as myself.

A giving heart

Publicly visible behaviours, in the context of existing social relations, are therefore particularly important to how people's moral 'goodness' or transgression is defined and acted upon. This also applies to elders, who are expected to uphold respectability, show respect to others and honour their role in order to educate younger people. As discussed in Chapter 2, Ladit attributed the fact that many young people come to him for advice to his good conduct in public. As shown in Chapter 6, Omara, aged 60, would also often sit with the other men in the evenings, but he always avoided drinking alcohol for the sake of his health and to evade arguments. Like Ladit, he said that he always tried to advise the younger men there similarly to avoid alcohol and crime, and to take responsibility for their wives and children. He complained that recent developments had undermined respect for elders among the younger generation:

> In the past, as our parents were bringing us up in childhood, we were so co-operative and we were really very polite. Even children kept on respecting the elders, not only your parents. And now slowly

> with the development coming in this country, of course things start changing. And we were having religions which we were following. Actually the religions we know, Catholicism, Islam, Protestantism and *Murokole* – *Murokole* came late… So we were trying to co-operate and religion was also involved, so the children were really so polite to each other and everybody; it would become even very easy to teach them from school. But nowadays that has changed. The children coming up have their rights, women have their rights, in the long run you find that even they don't respect their parents. It becomes so difficult, that's why you find these *bayaayes*, thieves, increasing in our country…

Bayaaye is a moral term for young people in the city, especially young men, associated with crime and drug use. It is also re-appropriated as a sign of youth and creativity.[46] Such moral stereotypes about younger people, in some instances intended to infer 'the moral virtue of the speaker'[47] and their generation, also reflect structural unemployment which hinders young people from attaining autonomy, work and marriage, posing broader threats to elder authority and social belonging.[48] The resulting moral ambivalence between autonomy and co-operation imparts a particular expectation on women to 'outwardly comply' with gendered family roles.[49] Young women may be admonished by older people for sexual promiscuity and teenage pregnancy, or for prioritising material possessions over productive love and secure marriage. Young men, especially those unable to find work, can be disparaged as 'idle'; their use of drugs and alcohol would often be moralised by older participants, discussed with concern as well as compassion.

This intergenerational moral concern reflects the 'dotcom' discourses outlined throughout the monograph, related to the corrupting influences of social media, the city, individualism and money, as well as the sense that related social changes are threatening co-operation and family life. This includes the introduction of 'human rights' laws in Omara's lifetime, founded on the protection of individual personhood and property[50] and sometimes considered to be at odds with the respect and relatedness he describes.[51] From this perspective, like 'respect', the moral language of 'rights' can be employed not only to seek social justice, but also to stake a long-standing claim to power over morality.[52] As Omara observed:

> I have seen that they came up with something like the children should have their rights. People did not understand exactly what

> we call rights ... the youth should know where to start and where to end. That's their right. But they should also follow the regulations of the country, and at the same time you need to respect the elders. It doesn't mean that you can do anything with your rights without respecting your elders.

Despite a declining sense of respect for elders and co-operation in the community around him, throughout our conversations Omara frequently noted that his sons were very respectful towards him. He knew that his sons would take care of him into his old age, just as they would help him with 'dotcom', for example, by sending messages on WhatsApp for him and googling for answers about his health:

> They can do everything for me, my children; they respect me.

This reflects the discussion in Chapter 5, which showed how phones would be used to uphold respect and obligations to older relatives, with young people connecting their parents to knowledge and social networks online. Rather than invert the hierarchies of age, involvement of parents in 'dotcom' serves to re-establish respect. Further, 'dotcom' allows younger people to uphold obligations to their elders, even at a distance. Many people explained how they would support their parents' health needs with mobile money transfers to cover transport to the hospital, medical bills or the costs of medicine and supplies. They hope that their children, or at least one of them, will do the same for them in future but, as in a common idiom of my research, 'it depends on their heart'.

According to Omara and many other research participants, 'good heart' is something that can be seen or shown through helping others, talking to them in a certain way and giving them time. Like many others, Omara commended Amor, having known her since childhood:

> She is very good, good character, behaviour and the rest. You see, if you don't, people will not co-operate with you ...

He noted that 'she greets people respectfully, takes time to talk to them and find out how they are'. Omara also considers himself to be a 'good person':

> They see how I talk to them, how I bring them closer to me. I can also help them the way I help them, so it shows this is a good person.

This visible, co-operative goodness can ideally promote social harmony within the neighbourhood, preventing quarrels and promoting mutual assistance. As detailed in Chapter 3, neighbours often intervened to support those in need, such as elderly people living alone or single grandmothers when they are sick, providing food or raising contributions for medical needs. Public mutuality'[53] with neighbours can ensure regular business and support when looking for work, but the reverse can present a particular threat to health and livelihoods.

These urban 'social infrastructures'[54] span household and neighbourhood, for example assisting women to 'support their families'. Omara had worked to pay his son's school fees up to university, often relying on co-operation with others in the community:

> In case I run short of something, I have to cry for help from fellow friends. They can help me with some money and later I can pay them back because money comes and goes.

This kind of financial co-operation within the neighbourhood for 'family support' was the focus of Chapter 4 on Savings and Credit Co-operative Organisations (SACCOs). These organisations provide people with a collective mechanism in which to save, accumulate and borrow money, often with the explicit intention of 'making light the heaviness on an individual'. However, they can also impart financial pressures of competition and inequity, a tension explicitly worked through and addressed through formal mechanisms of accountability. In this way, co-operative approaches to money are paradoxically obliged and disordered by capitalist logics, and the uncertainty with which money 'comes and goes'.

Older people are particularly active within these support networks, as givers and recipients of care across generations and distances. Amor's uncle explained that 'an older person is recognised much more'. Whenever he went home he would take gifts for his mother, depending on what he had:

> The more you give, the more you gain, the more blessed you are.

If an old person gives you something, he advised 'don't ever say no, just take it and say thank you'. It means that their heart was a 'giving heart' and that they hope you will remember them one day, even after they are gone. A gift, kindness or hospitality can be given 'from the heart', with the hope that it will be remembered and maybe even reciprocated in the future, even after death.

Money and morality

A 'good heart' can therefore be enacted in the sharing of money, which can 'transmit moral qualities'[55] and can even be rendered sacred at the time of death and burial.[56] This was evident in Chapter 5, which outlines how older participants often send and receive mobile money between family and friends. Someone's goodness of heart can even be expressed in monetary terms, a 'giving', 'rich' or 'wealthy' heart. This contrasts with the common association of money with the destruction of solidarity and community,[57] or as morally inferior to 'a good heart'; what economic theorist Ferguson refers to as 'moral vocabularies for thinking about money',[58] ways of categorising and discussing money as either pro-social and moral or anti-social and destructive. As the chairwoman quoted above observed:

> It is not about money people, it is about heart.

This highlights the complex role of money in the 'moral moment', as an embedded tool which can both express and corrupt a 'good heart'.[59]

As a proponent of mutuality and showing co-operative 'goodness' within the community, Omara frequently returned to the subject of disagreements between neighbours, some who have 'different hearts':

> There are some situations here, disagreements with neighbours… We come, meet some friends, and we need to co-operate with them so that the co-operation would help us in one way or the other… You see, now, the co-operation, some people have different hearts, are short-tempered… I love all of them, but in the long run others had some habits, you don't know what is in their heart.

Other peoples' 'heart', their internal 'goodness' or intention towards others, can be difficult to determine from the outside, undermining possibilities of trust, reciprocity and solidarity. This paradox brings with it the material risks of balancing, as Nyamnjoh puts it, 'intimacy and distance'.[60] As with Omara, others similarly suspected their neighbours of resentment, jealousy and 'bad heart', which could often be related to suspicions of their engagement with witchcraft. Aliel Christine, a member of both 'Place of Peace' and 'Who should enrich you?', explained:

> People from the face are happy, but you don't know what's in their heart. So people do witchcraft. In Lusozi there's a lot of witchcraft.

For both Omara and Aliel Christine, concealment represents the possibility of a hidden discontent and an unknown 'heart',[61] posing a potential threat to others and to convivial livelihoods.

If someone in Lusozi is known to have accumulated sudden and significant wealth, they might be suspected of having gained money at the expense of human sacrifice, potentially even the lives of their own children and grandchildren. In these cases, a desire for money is thought to have corrupted people's hearts and overtaken care and concern for family, revealing instead the extractive potential of relationships, of concealed practices and 'bad hearts'.[62] Prioritising material gain over the lives of close relatives, particularly of children, represents the ultimate inversion of co-operative morality. On one level of many, 'witchcraft' can be understood as an explanation for pervasive wealth disparities and exploitation,[63] and the burden this imparts on an unknowable, 'giving heart'.

This highlights the fraught and complex moral role of money, as a means to both express and corrupt a 'good heart'.[64] As this monograph has sought to show, related tensions are continually managed through conviviality and 'convivial knowledge', ways of living and working together that are explicitly defined and enacted to work against economic precarity and fragmentation. Arguably, as discussed in the concluding chapter to follow, this knowledge and practice of 'togetherness' offers a moral framework with the potential to address structural inequalities and seek social justice in contextually relevant ways.[65]

Conclusion

This chapter seeks to ground co-operative moralities in various everyday interactions and public discussions.[66] The cited ethnographic examples show how goodness can be portrayed or discerned through disposition and deliberation, the display of respect for elders and the demonstration of generosity and care, as well as the public resolution of their transgression. Morality or 'ethical self-formation'[67] therefore goes beyond a normative 'script' governing behaviour or a 'pervasive and subliminal' vision of how the world could and should be;[68] it can also 'have vitality',[69] sometimes explicitly emerging through social action, exposed for ethnographic enquiry. A co-operative person is formed through displays of a 'good heart', a willingness to co-operate and show generosity and an outward acknowledgement of their social role, made visible through the manner of their approach. Perhaps my presence as a visitor encouraged these explicit definitions and depictions of goodness, or at least lent my eye and ear to them.

Conversely secrecy can conceal a 'bad heart', just as unco-operative behaviours can reveal one. As Omara and Aliel put it, 'you don't know what is in their heart'. The unknowability of other people's goodness can explain interpersonal tensions, as well as inequalities such as wealth disparities, political exploitation and an unwillingness – or inability – to share. Within this wider unco-operative economic system, financial co-operation within Lusozi and across support networks represents livelihood as well as virtue, while theft, self-interest and exploitation threaten both.

This ethnography also shows how co-operative 'moral vocabularies' can be employed either to seek dignity and compassion or to reinforce inequalities; re-establishing the authority of older men, for instance, or the socio-economic dominance of the political elite, or the colonial imposition of values. For example, the concepts of 'togetherness' and 'respect' can be employed to seek gender and social justice, to mitigate socio-economic disparities, or to serve the 'reification of the family' as a falsely standardised, hetero-normative, patriarchal entity.[70] This stresses the need for a nuanced approach to situated co-operative moralities, which recognises them to be lived and mutable, emerging through interactions and continually redefined in relation to the world. In light of the dynamic possibilities of co-operative morality, how can we seek a 'convivial middle ground' to pursue social justice? As Ugandan feminist scholar Sylvia Tamale has outlined,[71] this is arguably an effective starting point for addressing colonial capitalist inequalities and injustices based on race, gender, age, sexuality, class, geography and capital in contextually relevant ways, as discussed in the conclusion to follow. Likely many of the elders involved in this research would agree, as they seek to visibly uphold their roles and teach the younger generation about how to work together amid the many threats of the wider world.

Notes

1. Mathews and Izquierdo 2009.
2. Neveu Kringelbach 2013, 215; Nyamnjoh 2002; Nyamnjoh 2017; Tamale 2020, 204.
3. Neveu Kringelbach 2013, 215.
4. Porter 2019, 1027.
5. Curry, Mullins and Whitehouse 2019.
6. Curry, Mullins and Whitehouse 2019, 48.
7. Robbins 2013.

8. Englund 2008, 45.
9. Allen 1988.
10. Englund 2008; Lambek et al. 2015; Mattingly 2019; Robbins 2007; Zigon 2007; Jackson 1996.
11. Allen 2015; Baral 2016; Boyd 2013; Doherty 2020; Finnström 2008; Karlström et al. 2004; Kyaddondo 2008; Monteith 2018; Tamale 2020; Whyte et al. 2016.
12. Robbins 2007; Zigon 2007.
13. Mattingly 2019, 118; cf Jackson 1996, 22.
14. In analysing 'moral community in Buganda', Karlström et al. (2004) traces this sense of 'moral crisis' to the 1920s, with the zealous promotion of Christianity by British missionaries and the converted elite prompting religious civil wars and opening the way to British colonisation (Karlström et al. 2004). Later, the 'moral crisis of youth' was attributed to post-Independence political and economic insecurity and heightened by the AIDs epidemic, leading to 'the (re) making of moral community under conditions of radical transformation' (Karlström et al. 2004, 598).
15. Baral 2018.
16. Porter 2019, 1011.
17. Porter 2019, 1025.
18. Keane 2016.
19. Muehlebach 2013, 299.
20. Robbins 2007, 311; Muehlebach 2013.
21. Nguyen, Zavoretti and Tronto 2017, 206.
22. Nguyen, Zavoretti and Tronto 2017, 206.
23. Kyaddondo 2008, 29.
24. Kyaddondo 2008, 29.
25. Mbiti 1990 (1969).
26. Ugandan Bureau of Statistics 2018. 'National census main report'. Accessed 14 September 2020. https://www.ubos.org/wp-content/uploads/publications/03_20182014_National_Census_Main_Report.pdf, 19.
27. Robbins 2004, 118.
28. Robbins 2004, 129.
29. Zigon 2007, 136.
30. Robbins, 2007, 300.
31. Zigon 2007.
32. Baral 2016, 48.
33. UPPC 2009. 'The anti homosexuality bill'. Accessed 24 August 2020. https://docs.google.com/file/d/0B7pFotabJnTmYzFiMWJmY2UtYWYxMi00MDY2LWI4NWYtYTVlOWU1OTEzMzk0/edit?pli=1&hl=en.
34. Nyanzi 2013.
35. Awondo, Geschiere and Reid 2012, 149.
36. Serumaga 2023. 'Well-funded riddles: Notes on Uganda's sexual culture war'. Accessed 21 April 2022. https://africanarguments.org/2023/03/well-funded-riddles-notes-from-ugandas-sexual-culture-war/.
37. Awondo, Geschiere and Reid 2012, 154.
38. Robbins 2004, 137.
39. Boyd 2013, 713.
40. Whyte et al. 2016, 46. As discussed in Chapter 2, these otherwise spontaneous and situated rituals of forgiveness were instrumentalised after the LRA war by international agencies, which has been criticised for imposing fixity on otherwise dynamic practices, mirroring earlier colonial processes in the region (see Allen 2007).
41. Tamale 2020, 160.
42. Whyte et al. 2016, 46.
43. Tamale 2020, 160
44. Whyte et al. 2016, 46.
45. Tamale 2020, 157.
46. Baral 2018.
47. Whyte and Acio 2017, 23.
48. Whyte and Acio 2017, 23.
49. Neveu Kringelbach 2013, 213; see also Obbo 1980, 15.
50. Tamale 2020, 199.

51. Tamale 2020, 199.
52. Mamdani 1996; Mutua 2008; Mutua 2016; Tamale 2020.
53. See CPAID Centre for Public Authority and International Development, 2021 Report. https://issuu.com/lseflca/docs/centre_for_public_authority_and_international_deve, 7. Accessed 24 August 2022.
54. Wignall et al. 2019; Simone 2021. See also Bear et al. 2021.
55. Bloch and Parry 1989, 8.
56. Zelizer 2018.
57. Hart 2005.
58. Ferguson 2006, 73.
59. Bloch and Parry 1989; Hart 2005.
60. Nyamnjoh 2017, 264.
61. Geschiere 2013.
62. As Geschiere states, witchcraft can represent the 'dark side of kinship' (2013, 61) or, as Archambault observes, the 'destructive side of connectivity' (2017, 153–4). For Karlström et al. it represents the 'toxic negation' of family, generosity and 'moral community' (2004, 597).
63. Whyte has previously argued that contemporary witchcraft accusations are a 'response to modern ambiguity related to oppressive opacity in national and world systems', in which there is a 'lack of opportunity to participate' (Whyte 1997, 204).
64. Bloch and Parry 1989; Hart 2005.
65. See Tamale 2020, 11.
66. Lambek et al. 2015; Keane 2016.
67. Englund 2008.
68. Keane 2016.
69. Lambek et al. 2015, 57.
70. Nyanzi 2013; Porter 2019; Tamale 2020; Allen 1988.
71. Tamale 2020.

8
Conclusion: permanent questions

In taking the lens of the smartphone to understand experiences of ageing in Lusozi, Kampala, this ethnography presents the articulation and practice of 'togetherness in the dotcom age'. It draws from everyday concepts of co-operative morality to consider the description, impact and mitigation of profound social changes on experiences and expectations of ageing. 'Dotcom' is understood to encompass everything from the influence of ICTs, especially smartphones, to lifestyles in the city, to profound shifts in ways of knowing and relating. While the concept of 'dotcom' is familiar to many people around the world, specifically here in Lusozi, how does it manifest in relation to older people's health, their care norms, their social standing, their values and their intergenerational relationships, both political and personal? What are the situated 'social infrastructures'[1] that sustain relationships, networks and aspirations, with a view to the wider world beyond? And what can be learned both anthropologically and more broadly from the everyday reconfiguration of co-operative expectations?

Working together

In this monograph, the focus on the concept of togetherness seeks to align with an aspiration stated by many of the older participants involved in this research: to fulfil their role of advising the younger generation on how to work together, amid the many uncertainties of the dotcom era. A quote from an interview with a 60-year-old woman called Achola opens this book. Despite not having had children herself, she is a mother to many children, including her own orphaned nephews and nieces, 'they are lucky because I am here'. Outlined in Chapter 6, Achola's narration of her hopes and efforts towards their future, her own deferred aspirations and her management of these pressures expresses an intergenerational and intersubjective purpose in life. When we introduced the project to her, she said she had no questions because she felt *'the book could help my grandchildren'*, as she would not always be there to teach them. We asked what she most hoped her grandchildren would learn from the book. Achola replied that she would want them to read it and to know how to help each other as 'even if you're not from the same place, you stay together'.

Like many other older participants in Lusozi, Achola sees it as her role as an elder to educate the younger generation based on her life experience, and particularly about the importance of 'staying together', often perceived to be under threat and in decline. For example, 78-year-old Aprio Evelyn, with whom we spoke in her home village outside Gulu in the Acholi sub-region said she worries for the next generation, having seen the many problems that they face:

> *If I could give them any advice, it would be to make sure that they work together. That is how we used to live, but now I find everyone working on their own.*

The emphasis here on 'working together' relates to the Acholi farming practice of *pur aleya*, as described by Ladit, in which work parties or *awak* of 30 or more people would dig up to three gardens by hand in one day, in order to 'reduce the amount of time spent digging by an individual'. *Awak* provides a pragmatic arrangement to ensure that everyone's field is dug in 'the short time available for planting after dry season and before the rains'.[2] Individual endeavours are collectivised while both collective and individual interests are served.

This logic of pragmatic togetherness is not only located in the past, in the village or with elders, but is also continually brought to life through everyday conversation and practice in the city. As explained by Nyamnjoh, whose writing on conviviality informs this monograph:

> Interdependence is not just 'pushed aside', but continually promoted through conviviality amidst diverse worldviews.[3]

We saw this in Chapter 2, in considering what Ladit has provided for young people in Lusozi by sharing his knowledge about Acholi music and dance and adapting it for relevance to their lives in Kampala today. The weekly practice of Ladit's group provides a place for people from across the diverse community to congregate – particularly young children who also come to watch and learn. Evidently this knowledge is made dynamic and flexible, lived meaningfully in the present and across generations.[4] In this fluidity the explicit articulation and practice of values like togetherness hold the potential to enable social possibilities and imagine alternatives,[5] as shown below.

Conviviality

The concept of 'conviviality' builds on the semantics of togetherness, the Latin root of the word '*con*' (together) and '*vivo*' (to live), later combined to describe feast or celebration. 'Conviviality' has been employed as a sociological concept to describe the everyday ways people invoke, celebrate and preserve difference in diverse, multi-ethnic urban settings,[6] as in Lusozi. Phones, as platforms of communication with democratising and open-ended potential, have been theorised as 'tools for conviviality'.[7] As an analytical approach, conviviality allows for an exploration of how people create 'modes of togetherness',[8] how they envision living together and the strategies used to practise it. As a methodological tool, conviviality seeks 'holism through compassion'[9] – social knowledge through ongoing dialogue, co-production, collaboration and humility.

Nyamnjoh shows that this kind of 'convivial scholarship' is of particular significance to 'the future of anthropology in Africa' given its established role in informing colonisers about how to politically subjugate in the most contextually appropriate ways. As a discipline, anthropology has contributed directly and indirectly to the colonial reification of custom,[10] of hetero-patriarchal family and sexual norms, of fabricated borders and divisions, of global socio-economic disparities, of forced global immobility and of exclusionary academic and linguistic hierarchies.[11] Throughout this research, the older people we've worked with, the most qualified theorists of their own social reality, have suggested how this ongoing history characterises what social life should be and what it is – for example, through the disruption of elder care norms, or the declining value of older people's knowledge in line with the 'dotcom wave'.

With the weight of this past and its impact in the present, there is a critical responsibility to reflect on the ways in which knowledge is produced and reproduced through research today.[12] Nyamnjoh asks 'what role could less restrictive ways of knowing play in education and development?'[13] His proposal for a 'convivial scholarship' offers a framework for 'destabilising Eurocentric notions of validity and legitimacy' and for instead 'promoting multiple ways of knowing'.[14] In contrast with what

Sylvia Tamale describes as the 'neoliberal, White-centric/supremacist, binary/Cartesian, intellectually arrogant, depoliticising' brand of dominant Western thought,[15] convivial scholarship 'celebrates and preserves incompleteness' as a site of possibility and considers epistemological 'completeness' as delusory, futile and even harmful.[16]

Convivial research, according to Nyamnjoh, is a 'quest for knowledge in its complexity and nuance' through 'permanent questions and questioning', without any final answers.[17] This is an anthropological project that I have aspired towards – social knowledge co-produced through long-term, holistic research, conducted with rigour both personally and among people. When applying the resulting 'complexity and nuance' to social policy and practice, the aim is often to better accommodate people's everyday lived realities, and to alleviate the inequalities that can be seen to reproduce themselves perpetually and to constrain people's life chances. Convivial, cross-disciplinary collaborations with service providers and practitioners can help to contribute an understanding of how these inequalities are mitigated, in order to meet people where they are. For example, ethnography and other participatory methodologies which make existing care concepts, preferences and practices their starting point can inform the collaborative creation of more equitable, accessible care models,[18] enhancing their potential to tangibly improve people's health, wellbeing and economic situation in contextually relevant ways. In an extractive economic context, which relies on and erodes co-operative infrastructures of family, reciprocity and community care, insight into the everyday challenges and opportunities of sustaining these infrastructures can inform efforts towards needed social investment, resource redistribution and accessible service provision. In working towards this aim, this project has included collaboration with a leading digital health organisation in Uganda, sharing ethnographic insights in order to improve service accessibility in line with existing phone practices, health concepts and care-seeking approaches.[19] These efforts, too, are inevitably 'incomplete', requiring ongoing interdisciplinary, socially engaged evaluation which prioritises their relational outcomes.[20]

Imagining alternatives

In relation to ageing specifically, scholar-activist and medical anthropologist Stella Nyanzi has argued in her research with older widows in Kampala that:

> [T]he elderly must be involved in policymaking and programme design processes because their voice does not get muted with age. They understand their circumstances well and can best articulate it for themselves.[21]

As with Nyanzi's vision of a Queer African scholarship, the hope is then that exposure to knowledge generated with and by voices often 'muted',[22] such as those of people with low income levels, marginalised sexualities, ethnicities, genders or age groups, can 'infuse' and 'diffuse' knowledge and understanding.[23] As Christine Obbo earlier argued, the 'private goals, behaviours and attitudes' of women in particular have wide-reaching political implications and should therefore be taken seriously in anthropological research,[24] which ideally 'lets people speak for themselves'.[25] The assertions of both Obbo and Nyanzi imply a gradual but wide-reaching political process of knowledge distribution and incorporation.

As both Obbo and Nyanzi show in their work, anthropological research can also be applied directly to recommendations for policy and practice – such as those of Nyanzi suggesting that school fees are abolished for poor widows,[26] or that funding should be allocated to support provision for elder-headed households without access to pensions or remittances.[27] This research has informed the following recommendations, designed to prompt conversation with relevant stakeholders including delegates from the Ministries of Health and Gender and National Council for Older Persons, as well as district and village-level political leaders, civil society organisations, age-related NGOs, researchers of ageing and older participants themselves. In particular, they consider the health and social security implications for those continuing to work in the city in later life without income protection,[28] while contributing to the economy and providing 'distributed livelihoods' for their families.[29]

- In line with established 'guiding principles' of participation in current National Social Protection Policy, **older persons should be involved in the design, implementation and evaluation of interventions that impact on them.** This means reversing top-down decision-making and starting from in-depth ethnographic and collaborative methodologies.
- **Adopt a community-oriented framework for enhancing public resources and services that build on existing social infrastructures.** The ways people mitigate political inequities through self- and mutual support locate pertinent social touchpoints for policymakers and practitioners to learn from and build upon.

- In general, age categories such as 'old', 'young' and 'middle age' are found to be socially significant yet negotiable. Further, economic experiences are often shared across different age groups with, for example, structural underemployment of young people in precarious urban economies burdening the livelihoods and therefore social security of older people continuing to work in later life. **Interventions such as awareness raising, education programmes and initiatives related to employment or health should therefore be open to all people regardless of their age.** With older people in the city often advising younger people in their families and communities, enhancing their access to health information and services can have significant reach.
- **Prioritise grants and income support for older people living and working in urban areas, especially older women with dependents in single-headed households.** This will ensure they can sustain the health, education and wellbeing of their households without detriment to themselves. This also relates to recent recommendations from the Committee on Equal Opportunities to lower the age of Social Assistance Grant Empowerment (SAGE) beneficiaries from 80 to 65 years, especially for women heads of household.[30]
- As highlighted by participating health workers and older people, **further research, advocacy and investment is needed to address health system challenges for the older demographic, especially in urban areas where they are a marginalised but growing minority.** Focus areas could include: occupational health provisions in government hospitals for older people continuing to work and contribute to the economy; further training for primary health workers in age-related health conditions; more integrated service provision for older people experiencing multi-morbidity.
- Establish contributory social insurance schemes for people without formal employment. Current National Social Protection Policy including the **National Health Insurance proposals should target the inclusion of older people living in urban areas and working in self-owned businesses in the 'informal economy'.** Currently, they target people who are formally employed and therefore already have access to social security such as sick pay and pensions. They are also said to overlook community models[31] such as established cooperative health insurance and financing approaches. Targeted inclusion could involve: affordability based on income; flexibility in sign-up options and payment plans; comprehensiveness in available insurance policies, including chronic conditions, mental health and people over the age of 70; and comprehensive education programmes

to establish beneficiary trust. Evidence from previous efforts to establish community-based health insurance models, notably in Kisiizi Hospital's expansion of burial groups in south-western Uganda,[32] can also inform more inclusive approaches to public health insurance that ensures sustainable hospital financing, prevents catastrophic expenditure for households and facilitates older people's social security, especially those still in work.

Given the overlooked yet active contribution of many older people to urban economies and 'social infrastructures', re-visited in the book summary to follow, support for their inclusion and social security could have a broader impact throughout the neighbourhood, beyond the city and across generations.

Human economies

This monograph demonstrates the significance of social and domestic life to many older participants' heterogenous businesses and working routines, often based upon proximity to the household and the Lusozi neighbourhood. Like 78 per cent of the population of Kampala, the majority of older research participants run their own trade businesses in what is known as the 'informal economy', officially unregistered and unsupported by the state, but in fact intrinsic to it. The incomes of older research participants generally support many other people in their families, across generations and distances, paying school fees and sending remittances to rural areas, often for older relatives' health needs. This disrupts the stereotype of work in the capital city as a preoccupation of able-bodied youth,[33] and typical industrialised categories of age, work and personhood: childhood, education and dependence; adulthood, work and independence; older age, retirement and interdependence.[34] Age-based migration, the widely stated aspiration of returning to rural homes for rent-free rest and retirement in later life, is often delayed until school fees are paid and enough money has been saved. As shown in Chapter 3, these 'distributed livelihoods' reflect and constitute the wider socio-economic dynamics of 'the human economy'; an economy that depends on co-operative relationships and moralities, and money that is embedded within them.[35]

The pooling and distribution of resources within the Lusozi community was the focus of Chapter 4. This chapter is based on participation in the regular meetings of three community groups, including two

SACCOs (Savings and Credit Co-operative Organisations) and a Church-based NGO for single mothers. In the Togetherness is Strength organisation, a SACCO predominantly for men which Amor and I joined as members, regular savings are collected to provide a fund for people to turn to 'in times of grievance and of happiness'. As the vice chairman of the group explained:

> We thought we should come together to form an association and make light the heaviness on one person.

At their Sunday meetings, discussions often revolved around late contributions and loan repayments, and whether the group should respond 'kindly', in line with the original intention of the group and existing friendships between members, or 'constitutionally', in line with the formalised duties to participate and pay contributions. Through regular and ongoing efforts the members work through the tensions of co-operation 'formalised-from-below',[36] the everyday complexities of collectively striving for individual gain.

Participation in this group, as well as in a rotating savings group called 'Who should enrich you?' (WSEY) ('yourselves, together'),[37] showed how co-operative moralities are enacted in spite of – and in response to – a wider economy of scarcity, competition, extraction and inequality.[38] In WSEY, for example, the beneficiary members organise their party, including outfits, decorations, refreshments and attendance; this can cause competition, exposing existing disparities in incomes and putting additional financial pressures on lower-income members. However, the chairwoman of the group was glad that it had provided an incentive for the women to dress smartly and express themselves, and the weekly parties of rotating contributions and dancing were joyful occasions in the heart of Lusozi every Sunday. Other members explained how the group had allowed them to have fun, develop friendships and forget their problems at home, all while they supported their household. As Aliel, a longstanding member of the group, explained:

> *Every week in and week out, we are always very happy. Even if you leave your home with some anger, when you reach there joy starts coming out of you... WSEY is like my father, mother and sister, which brings people to associate together.*

Similarly, members of 'Place of Peace', an NGO for single mothers, said they found 'sisters, even mothers' at their regular meetings. The group provides a family-like network in their neighbourhood to offer mutual guidance and belonging, in line with the organisation's mission statement:

> Belonging to somebody else, you become free.

The successes of these women's groups in fostering self-sufficiency through belonging again mirrors Nyamnjoh's concept of convivial social action, which offers a predetermined social framework through which individuals can become self-reliant.[39]

With contributions of money raised among the family and community at a time of celebration or crisis, including costly burials at home, money as a gift or gesture can even be 'imbued with sacred qualities'.[40] This is also evident in Chapter 5 on phone use, in which care, compassion and co-operation are transmitted through mobile money transfers, especially those sent for the health needs of older relatives living at home in the village. This shows that smartphones and mobile phones are facilitating not only individualism and consumerism, as in predominant narratives, but also the expansion of long-standing relationships and intergenerational expectations.

As proposed by my colleague Patrick Awondo, who conducted research for the ASSA project in Yaoundé, Cameroon, this introduces the smartphone within AbdouMaliq Simone's idea of 'people as infrastructure', which integrates the human and technical[41] and allows for a 'reinvention of family', collective life and the transmission of cultural values. In this way, while compressing distances in unprecedented ways, 'bringing the world together' – and often thereby perceived as 'highly significant agents of change'[42] – smartphones and mobile phones also offer a platform for continuity and social reproduction. What one participant described as the 'dotcom wave' is thus domesticated in Lusozi, as around the world, the wave being an apt metaphor for the overwhelming, processual mutability of social trajectories, which phone use is both shaping of and shaped by.

Chapter 5 on phone use therefore builds on work in digital anthropology on the creative employment of ubiquitous digital tools such as phones according to specific socio-cultural preferences,[43] particularly in Africa[44] and in Uganda,[45] in turn offering insight into processes of continuity and change more broadly.[46] In particular, the ethnography offers the overlooked perspective of the 'middle generation' on the 'intergenerational implications'[47] of the phone: those neither young nor elderly, but often with care responsibilities for both. This intergenerational

CONCLUSION 187

perspective is particularly pertinent in the contemporary political context of Uganda, where discourses around the corrupting influences of 'dotcom' on the younger generation are also reflected and reinforced in policy regulations, notably the controversial social media tax imposed in 2018 at the time of the research. These regulations implicate the potential of social media both as a tool and symbol of the emancipation of young people and the disempowerment of the old.

Despite this widespread intergenerational discourse about 'dotcom' among politicians and participants alike, as well as extensive academic research about the declining experience of older people in East Africa,[48] it is perhaps surprising to see the extent to which people enact respect and care for their elders via the phone – a crucial icon of dotcom and the foremost platform for accessing social media and the internet in Uganda. This is apparent not only in the examples of 'care at a distance'[49] for older relatives in rural areas, but also in younger people's efforts to share 'dotcom' knowledge with their parents, for example by buying them phones, teaching them how to use them, keeping them connected on social media, looking up information and even sourcing music and entertainment for them. As 60-year-old Omara explained with regard to his adult sons:

> The world is changing. Everything is computerised so we need to know... Dotcom, that one came after us ... now we're trying to get at that thing from you (young) people, 'now Dotcom, what does it mean?' We learn also from them. I ask my sons, so I can be doing it myself. He can do everything for me ... my children, they respect me ... in case I need anything they can do it for me.

Omara teaches his sons to learn as much as they can about 'dotcom'. Others agree with Omara that the typical pedagogical relationship between fathers and sons is thereby both inverted and sustained in the 'dotcom era', so that dotcom knowledge among younger people does not necessarily come at the expense of respect for the older generation.[50]

Furthermore, the phone provides a 'lifeline' for relationships and resources across distances.[51] It may sometimes extend unwanted obligations, or sometimes provide an imperfect but tolerable replacement for the long and costly journeys home, for example between Kampala and Kitgum, where most participants' rural homes and older relatives are situated. When phone calls, WhatsApp groups and mobile money remittances are used for health purposes, as this research has shown to be often the case, this can be understood as an 'informal mHealth' strategy, recently found to be a 'large-scale emergent health system' in itself.[52]

Family roles, or 'ways of speaking, thinking and feeling about the family that mobilize material resources and people in ways that are considered normal and natural',[53] are thus reconfigured, despite generational shifts, digitisation, economic change and increasingly 'scattered families'.[54]

Reconfigurations of care responsibilities for older people are further detailed in Chapter 6. This includes discussions about the contested roles of the government, the hospital, health workers, relatives, especially daughters, and the older individual themselves. These discussions are particularly pertinent given the increasing numbers of older people, the devastation of the HIV/AIDS epidemic which killed many of their children,[55] limited access to formal health services and the declining accessibility of home-based intergenerational care. The latter ideal of elder care forms a benchmark against which alternatives are presented. Alternative arrangements include hired domestic care-workers, or grandchildren being sent to rural areas to help with daily chores at home while also gaining cheaper schooling. Otherwise elderly parents living at home in rural areas can be supported by care responsibilities delegated between siblings, depending on their proximity, gender and income levels, and often facilitated by remittances, family WhatsApp groups and phone calls to request financial support.

In this 'human economy' and the uncertain, entrepreneurial economic environment of Lusozi in the 'dotcom age', a strong social support system is an advantage. Mutual support within households and across the family and neighbourhood was often depicted by participants as the 'pro-social' and pragmatic mitigation of declining public provision, often characterised as neglectful, extractive, immoral and 'anti-social'.[56] As Kato, a 61-year-old former civil engineer, put it, echoing worldwide concerns about growing economic disparity:

> They get a lot of money, but they can't assist the people, that's the problem here. It's just for the people at the top.

Having lost his business due to an injury, Kato would meet with other men in Lusozi to consider the problems faced by people in the community, to seek work and play games:

> We combine knowledge and see how we can survive ... We're gambling now.

Kato said he considers their community-oriented perspective superior to that of the Ugandan government, who are seen to impose taxation without helping people. Various self-employed participants – including *boda boda* drivers and market, mobile money and street vendors – also described the significance of good relationships with suppliers, customers, neighbours and family to overcome competitive and unstable markets. Similarly work, business and job-seeking would often be referred to as 'gambling', depicting required risks and precarity, and an implicit willingness to improvise in response.[57] With the social and economic productivity of gambling and playing games, the boundary between work and play is further blurred.[58] Seldom mentioned, however, was the reliance of businesses on unpaid labour, such as domestic work from live-in maids and the care labour of women, including self-care practices which avoid medical costs and time away from work: 'the ultimate privatisation of health'.[59]

Many older participants in their forties, fifties and sixties care for their own health and finances in order to avoid 'becoming a burden' on their children's already stretched time and resources. This 'self-care' can include exercise routines, strategies to manage physical work, healthy eating habits, avoiding unprotected sex and averting stress or 'overthinking'. Self-responsibility was particularly explicit in three single grandmothers' narrations of their prayer routines to manage hypertension or 'pressure', often conceptualised as absorbed economic stress through 'over-thinking'. As shown, they would consider it their individual responsibility to 'stop over-thinking' about financial pressures and to manage and re-articulate an excess of thoughts, in order to preserve their own health, wellbeing and capacity for work. As Achola says of her worries about her children and her future old age:

> *I feel that, what am I going to be when I reach up to 70, 80 years? I will be old, I cannot dig or carry water, so what can I do? If I go to Church and pray, the thinking reduces.*

Descriptions of prayer as a way of managing uncertainty illustrate the perceived intersubjectivity between individuals, others and the wider world, and the shared meanings exposed within a shifting context.[60] As Susan Whyte showed in her earlier ethnography in eastern Uganda, this means that the dialogue, idioms and stories related to managing uncertainty 'in-the-world' are particularly useful modes of ethnographic enquiry.[61] In relation to this research, this might refer to how people expressed an understanding of their role within the family; how they would explicitly enact 'goodness' in accordance with social expectations; how they would tell stories of the past, the global or the political, to characterise the present, here and now.

In these examples, relational orientations determine individual responsibilities, with self-care serving as an act of care for others. This ethnography therefore complicates the established observation that 'ageing well' in East Africa is defined by interdependence with family, typically contrasted with aspirations to old-age independence and self-sufficiency that characterise 'successful ageing' in the Global North.[62] However, various participants did criticise the institutionalisation of older people in the care homes that they had heard about in the UK, thought to be like prisons for those without family; this depicts a 'social imagination' of elder care elsewhere,[63] against which the co-operative values underpinning home-based family care are re-established.

Some participating health workers, NGO delegates and age researchers observed that people prefer to 'abandon' older relatives rather than to institutionalise them. There were some older people in Lusozi known to have been left to rely on themselves and their neighbours. Health institutions, including the hospital in Lusozi, were often considered to fall short of expectations for the care of older people, who can feel overlooked by service provision – as stressed by various older people in Lusozi, as well as health workers and hospital administrators. Family are expected to make up the shortfall, as promoted by the hospital during community outreach programmes: 'every family must be able to take care'.

Family responsibilities and moral obligations are thus emphasised in line with the marketisation and medicalisation of health. As shown in extensive literature on health and care in medical anthropology,[64] this represents the 'broadest moral contradiction, ambivalence and hybridity of our social and political world today'.[65] In this way, broad socio-political and demographic concerns, such as population growth, de-investment in social welfare and the influence of Western care norms, are implicated in the personal and embodied experiences of health and care in later life. The hospital administrator, for example, noted the 'pressures of globalisation' responsible for turning a once more communitarian outlook inward, towards immediate family and within the household.

The people we worked with actively reflected on these paradoxes, the risks and opportunities of increased global connectivity, as encapsulated in the discourses around 'dotcom'. At this narrow intersection between the individual and others, everyday life and politics,[66] the subject of 'ageing with smartphones' can expose shifts in intergenerational expectations and their management. In the anthropology of morality, shifting moral frameworks are found to elicit active moral reflection.[67] As shown throughout the monograph and consolidated in Chapter 7, there has been an active reflection on co-operative morality or 'togetherness', perceived to be under threat by the competing influences of autonomous individualism: Pentecostalism, 'development', human rights, privatisation, consumerism, school education and 'dotcom' media. Further, many participants originated in northern Uganda, meaning that they have lived through the 20-year civil war considered to be 'the worst humanitarian crisis in human history',[68] with profound moral consequences.[69] This wider context characterises a sense of an ongoing 'moral moment' in Lusozi,[70] a time at which 'goodness' is consciously defined, discussed, displayed and made visible. A co-operative self is formed by visibly upholding respect and relatedness, for example through ways of greeting older people or of older people's respectable behaviours in public. Conversely, secrecy or an unco-operative manner can portray a 'bad heart'. This in turn may reflect threats to co-operative distribution across social networks, related to inequalities in the world and in 'human economies'.

Permanent questions

More broadly, in line with the 'ageing with smartphones' objectives, this project has shed light on the active participation of older age groups in the use of smartphones and social media. This contradicts stereotypes about ageing and the digital and has opened up extensive insights about the impact of smartphones on health, care and family life, allowing for continuities in relationships and intergenerational expectations despite wider social rupture. This contributes to the ASSA project's conceptual findings, such as the idea of the smartphone as a 'transportal home', bridging homes across distances. From the global perspective of this comparative study, we saw how the smartphone is re-configuring ageing in line with global social change, including digitisation, urbanisation and migration, often managed through the smartphone. Caregiving for older people via the phone locates a particularly intimate intersection of the moral and political,[71] offering a clear lens onto broad social trajectories and their impact on conceptions of personhood from an ethnographic consideration of everyday life and ageing.

This ethnography therefore has implications beyond Lusozi. The sense that social ideals must grapple with contemporary realities, what social life should be like versus what it actually is, forms a familiar topic of conversation around the world. Moral standards are often associated with the past, characterised as a time of purer, more authentic interconnection between people. Exposure to family norms elsewhere in the world forms a point of comparison for re-establishing or disrupting existing roles and expectations. In this vein dotcom tools are often characterised as divisive, while also employed as a platform for connection or togetherness, across distances and generations. This is particularly pertinent during ongoing COVID-19 restrictions at the time of writing. The pandemic exposed the extent to which we are all implicated in the health and care of others amid 'the vulnerability of collective life today'.[72] This necessitates further deliberations about how to build on and deploy infrastructures that enable people to sustain their lives, provide care and overcome challenges. Following the advice and actions of elders in Lusozi, it is possible to negotiate difficulty and difference with conviviality, fulfil both mutual responsibility and self-determination, revere the past and enrich the future, and uphold togetherness in the dotcom age.

Notes

1. Simone 2021.
2. Girling 2019, 71.
3. Nyamnjoh 2017, 261–2.
4. Mamdani 2012, 1996; p'Bitek 1986; Finnström 2008, 51.
5. Tamale 2020.
6. Gilroy 2009.
7. Illich 1973.
8. Nowicka and Vertovec 2014, 2.
9. Nyamnjoh 2012b, 79.
10. Mamdani, 2012,1996; p'Bitek 1986.
11. Imbo 2002; Mamdani 2012; Nyanzi 2013; Tamale 2020.
12. Ese-osa Idahosa and Bradbury 2020, 42.
13. Nyamnjoh 2012.
14. Ese-osa Idahosa and Bradbury 2020, 45.
15. Tamale 2020, 7.
16. Nyamnjoh 2017.
17. Nyamnjoh 2017.
18. Kozelka, Jenkins and Carpenter-Song 2021.
19. See Bwanika et al. 2022.
20. Bear 2015.
21. Nyanzi 2009.
22. Nyanzi 2011, 295; Nyanzi 2015, 13; Obbo 1986, 295.
23. Nyanzi 2015, 134.
24. Obbo 1980, 15.
25. Obbo 1980, 2.
26. Nyanzi 2011, 314.
27. Nyanzi 2009, 477.
28. Bukuluki and Mubiru 2014, 55.
29. Ferguson 2015, 90.
30. Parliament of Uganda 2022, 'Reduce age of SAGE beneficiaries'. Accessed 2 September 2022. https://parliament.go.ug/news/6111/'reduce-age-sage-beneficiaries'.

31. *The Economist* 2020. 'How a Ugandan hospital delivers health insurance through burial groups'. Accessed 7 July 2020. https://www.economist.com/middle-east-and-africa/2020/01/30/how-a-ugandan-hospital-delivers-health-insurance-through-burial-groups.
32. Baine, Kakama and Mugume 2018; Basaza et al. 2019.
33. Nyanzi 2009.
34. Honwana 2012, 12.
35. Bloch and Parry 1989, 8; Hart 2008; Ferguson 2015, 90; Polanyi 1957.
36. Krige 2019.
37. Real name is redacted for anonymity.
38. Otto 2013, 29.
39. Nyamnjoh 2017, 261.
40. Zelizer 2018.
41. Simone 2021.
42. Vokes 2018, 276.
43. Horst and Miller 2006; 2012.
44. de Bruijn, Nyamnjoh and Brinkman 2009; Porter et al. 2015; Pype 2017b; Archambault 2013.
45. Burrell 2010; Namatovu and Saebo 2015; Svensson and Larsson 2016; Vokes 2018.
46. de Bruijn, Nyamnjoh and Brinkman 2009; Horst and Miller 2013; Miller et al. 2016; Vokes 2018.
47. Porter et al. 2015, 38.
48. Aboderin 2004; Maharaj 2020; Maniragaba et al. 2019; Nankwanga, Neema and Phillips 2013; Nzabona, Ntozi and Rutaremwa 2016; Oppong 2006; Whyte 2017.
49. Ahlin 2018; Kamwesiga, Tham and Guidetti 2017; Pols 2012.
50. Porter et al. 2015, 44.
51. Porter et al. 2015, 41.
52. Hampshire et al. 2021, 3.
53. Coe 2014, 5.
54. Coe 2014; Sigona et al. 2015, 131.
55. Nankwanga, Neema and Phillips 2013.
56. Ferguson 2006, 74.
57. Malaby 2009, 206.
58. Malaby 2009, 206.
59. Wallman and Bantebya-Kyomuhendo 1996, 143.
60. Jackson 1998, 71: see also Finnström 2008, 52.
61. Whyte 1997, 25.
62. Lamb 2017; McIntosh 2017; Schatz and Seeley 2015; Whyte 2017.
63. Coe 2019; Coe 2020.
64. For example Han 2012; Kehr, Hansjörg and van Eeuwijk 2018; Kleinman 2015; Muehlebach 2013; Nguyen, Zavoretti and Tronto 2017.
65. Nguyen, Zavoretti and Tronto 2017, 199.
66. Jackson 1998.
67. Lambek et al. 2015; Robbins 2007; Zigon 2007.
68. Tamale 2020, 157.
69. Porter 2019.
70. See also Allen 2015; Baral 2016; Boyd 2013; Doherty 2020; Finnström 2008; Karlström et al. 2004; Kyaddondo 2008; Monteith 2018; Tamale 2020; Whyte et al. 2016.
71. Buch 2015; Black 2018.
72. Simone 2021, 1344.

Bibliography

Aboderin, I. 2004. 'Decline in material family support for older people in urban Ghana, Africa: Understanding processes and causes of change', *The Journals of Gerontology Series B: Psychological Sciences and Social Sciences* 59 (3): 128–37. https://doi.org/10.1093/geronb/59.3.S128.
Achol, I. 1987. 'Country Profile: Uganda', *African Insight* 17, 150–2.
Ahlin, Tanja. 2018. 'Only near is dear? Doing elderly care with everyday ICTs in Indian transnational families: Elderly care with ICTs in Indian families', *Medical Anthropology Quarterly* 32 (1): 85–102. https://doi.org/10.1111/maq.12404.
Akello, Grace. 2019. 'Reintegration of amnestied LRA ex-combatants and survivors' resistance acts in Acholiland, Northern Uganda', *International Journal of Transitional Justice* 13 (2): 249–67. https://doi.org/10.1093/ijtj/ijz007.
Alenda-Demoutiez, Juliette and Mügge, Daniel. 2020. 'The lure of ill-fitting unemployment statistics: How South Africa's discouraged work seekers disappeared from the unemployment rate', *New Political Economy* 25 (4): 590–606. https://doi.org/10.1080/13563467.2019.1613355.
Allen, Tim. 1988. 'Violence and moral knowledge: Observing social trauma in Sudan and Uganda', *The Cambridge Journal of Anthropology* 13 (2): 45–66.
Allen, Tim. 1991a. 'Histories and contexts: Using pasts in the present on the Sudan/Uganda border', *Bulletin of the John Rylands University Library* 73 (3): 63–92.
Allen, Tim. 1991b. 'Understanding Alice: Uganda's Holy Spirit movement in context', *Africa* 61 (03): 370–99. https://doi.org/10.2307/1160031.
Allen, Tim. 2007. 'The International Criminal Court and the invention of traditional justice in Northern Uganda', *Politique africaine* 107 (3): 147–66. https://doi.org/10.3917/polaf.107.0147.
Allen, Tim. 2015. 'Vigilantes, witches and vampires: How moral populism shapes social accountability in Northern Uganda', *International Journal on Minority and Group Rights* 22 (3): 360–86. https://doi.org/10.1163/15718115-02203004.
Allen, Tim. 2019. 'Introduction – Colonial encounters in Acholiland and Oxford: The anthropology of Frank Girling and Okot p'Bitek'. In *Lawino's People: The Acholi of Uganda*, edited by Tim Allen, Classics in African Anthropology. Zurich: Lit Verlag.
Allen, Tim, MacDonald, Anna and Radice, Henry, eds. 2018. *Humanitarianism: A Dictionary of Concepts*. Abingdon: Routledge.
Archambault, Julie Soleil. 2013. 'Cruising through uncertainty: Cell phones and the politics of display and disguise in Inhambane, Mozambique', *American Ethnologist* 40 (1): 88–101. https://doi.org/10.1111/amet.12007.
Archambault, Julie Soleil. 2017. *Mobile Secrets: Youth, intimacy, and the politics of pretense in Mozambique*. Chicago: The University of Chicago Press.
Ardener, Shirley. 1964. 'The comparative study of rotating credit associations', *The Journal of the Royal Anthropological Institute of Great Britain and Ireland* 94 (2): 201. https://doi.org/10.2307/2844382.
Ardener, Shirley and Burman, Sandra, eds. 1995. *Money-Go-Rounds: The importance of rotating savings and credit associations for women*. Cross-Cultural Perspectives on Women, vol. 15. Oxford, UK; Washington, DC: Berg.
Atkinson, R. R. 1994. *The Roots of Ethnicity: The origins of the Acholi of Uganda before 1800*. The Ethnohistory Series. Philadelphia: University of Pennsylvania Press. https://books.google.co.uk/books?id=ub6XCgAAQBAJ.

Awondo, P., Geschiere, P. and Reid, G. 2012. 'Homophobic Africa? Toward a more nuanced view', *African Studies Review* 55 (3): 145–68.

Baine, Sebastian Olikira, Kakama, Alex and Mugume, Moses. 2018. 'Development of the Kisiizi Hospital health insurance scheme: Lessons learned and implications for universal health coverage', *BMC Health Services Research* 18 (1). https://doi.org/10.1186/s12913-018-3266-8.

Baldassar, L., Wilding, R., Boccagni, P. and Merla, L. 2017. 'Aging in Place in a Mobile World: New media and older people's support networks', *Transnational Social Review* 7 (1): 2–9. https://doi.org/10.1080/21931674.2016.1277864.

Baral, Anna. 2016. 'Beyond unrest: Changing masculinities and moral becoming in an African urban market', *Etnofoor* 28 (2): 33–53.

Baral, Anna. 2018. *Bad Guys, Good Life: An ethnography of morality and change in Kisekka Market (Kampala, Uganda)*. Uppsala Studies in Cultural Anthropology, no. 58. Uppsala: Uppsala Universitet.

Basaza, Robert, Kyasiimire, Elizabeth P., Namyalo, Prossy K., Kawooya, Angela, Nnamulondo, Proscovia and Alier, Kon Paul. 2019. 'Willingness to pay for community health insurance among taxi drivers in Kampala City, Uganda: A contingent evaluation', *Risk Management and Healthcare Policy* 12 (July): 133–43. https://doi.org/10.2147/RMHP.S184872.

Batungi, N. and Rüther, H. 2008. 'Land tenure reform in Uganda. Some reflections on the formalisation of customary tenure', *Survey Review* 40 (308): 116–28. https://doi.org/10.1179/003962608X253583.

Bear, Laura. 2015. *Navigating Austerity: Currents of debt along a South Asian river*. Anthropology of Policy. Stanford, CA: Stanford University Press.

Bear, Laura, Simpson, Nikita, Bazambanza, Caroline, Bowers, Rebecca, Kamal, Atiya, Gheewala Lohiya, Anishka, Pearson, Alice, Vieira, Jordan, Watt, Connor and Wuerth, Milena (2021) *Social Infrastructures for the post-Covid Recovery in the UK*. Department of Anthropology, London School of Economics and Political Science, London, UK. https://eprints.lse.ac.uk/111011/.

Bibangambah, Jossy R. 1992. 'Macro-level constraints and the growth of the informal sector in Uganda'. In *The Rural-Urban Interface in Africa: Expansion and adaptation*, edited by J. Baker and P. Ove Pederson, 303–14. Uppsala: Nordiska Afrikainstitutet. http://www.diva-portal.org/smash/get/diva2:277421/FULLTEXT01.pdf#page=305.

Black, Steven P. 2018. 'The ethics and aesthetics of care', *Annual Review of Anthropology* 47 (1): 79–95. https://doi.org/10.1146/annurev-anthro-102317-050059.

Bloch, M. and Parry, J. 1989. 'Introduction: Money and the morality of exchange'. In *Money and the Morality of Exchange*, edited by J. Parry and M. Bloch, 1–32. Cambridge: Cambridge University Press.

Bourdieu, P. 1977. *Outline of a Theory of Practice*. Cambridge: Cambridge University Press.

Bourdieu, P. 1986. 'The forms of capital'. In *Handbook of Theory and Research for Sociology of Education*, edited by J. G. Richardson, 241–58. New York: Greenwood Press.

Boyd, Lydia. 2013. 'The problem with freedom: Homosexuality and human rights in Uganda', *Anthropological Quarterly* 86 (3): 697–724.

Buch, Elana D. 2015. 'Anthropology of aging and care', *Annual Review of Anthropology* 44 (1): 277–93. https://doi.org/10.1146/annurev-anthro-102214-014254.

Bukuluki, Paul. 2013. '"When I steal, it is for the benefit of me and you": Is collectivism engendering corruption in Uganda?', *International Letters of Social and Humanistic Sciences* 5 (September): 27–44. https://doi.org/10.18052/www.scipress.com/ILSHS.5.27.

Bukuluki, Paul and Mubiru, John-Bosco. 2014. *The Status of Social Security Systems in Uganda: Challenges and opportunities*. Kampala: Konrad Adenauer Stiftung. http://www.kas.de/wf/doc/kas_40252-544-1-30.pdf?150127125115.

Burgess, Rochelle. 2020. 'COVID-19 mental health responses neglect social realities', *Nature*, May. https://www.nature.com/articles/d41586-020-01313-9. https://doi.org/10.1038/d41586-020-01313-9.

Burgess, Rochelle and Campbell, Catherine. 2016. 'Creating social policy to support women's agency in coercive settings: A case study from Uganda', *Global Public Health* 11 (1–2): 48–64. https://doi.org/10.1080/17441692.2015.1005654.

Burrell, Jenna. 2010. 'Evaluating shared access: Social equality and the circulation of mobile phones in rural Uganda', *Journal of Computer-Mediated Communication* 15 (2): 230–50. https://doi.org/10.1111/j.1083-6101.2010.01518.x.

Bwanika, John M., Hawkins, Charlotte, Kamulegeya, Louis, Onyutta, Patricia, Musinguzi, Davis, Kusasira, Audrey, Musoke, Elizabeth K. and Kabeega, Jascintha. 2022. 'Qualitative study of mental health attribution, perceptions and care-seeking in Kampala, Uganda', *South African Journal of Psychiatry* 28 (May). https://doi.org/10.4102/sajpsychiatry.v28i0.1690.

Byaruhanga, Ivan and Debesay, Jonas. 2021. 'The impact of a social assistance program on the quality of life of older people in Uganda', *SAGE Open* 11 (1): 215824402198931. https://doi.org/10.1177/2158244021989311.

Caldwell, John C. 1976. 'Toward a restatement of demographic transition theory', *Population and Development Review* 2 (3/4): 321. https://doi.org/10.2307/1971615.

Campbell, John R. 2006. 'Who are the Luo? Oral tradition and disciplinary practices in anthropology and history', *Journal of African Cultural Studies* 18 (1): 73–87. https://doi.org/10.1080/13696850600750327.

Clifford, J. 1986. 'Introduction: Partial truths'. In *Writing Culture: The Poetics and Politics of Ethnography*, edited by J. Clifford and G. E. Marcus, 1–26. Berkeley, CA: University of California Press.

Coe, Cati. 2014. *The Scattered Family: Parenting, African migrants, and global inequality*. Chicago; London: University of Chicago Press.

Coe, Cati. 2019. 'Beyond kin care? Institutional facilities in the imaginations of older Presbyterians in Southern Ghana', *Africa Today* 65 (3): 69+.

Coe, Cati. 2020. 'Imagining institutional care, practicing domestic care: Inscriptions around aging in Southern Ghana', *Anthropology and Ageing* 39 (1): 18–32.

Coe, Cati and Alber, Erdmute. 2018. 'Age-inscriptions and social change', *Anthropology & Aging* 39 (1): 1–17. https://doi.org/10.5195/aa.2018.172.

Cole, Teju. 2017. *Known and Strange Things: Essays*, 340–9. London: Faber.

Collins, Patricia Hill. 2019. *Intersectionality as Critical Social Theory*. Durham, NC: Duke University Press. https://doi.org/10.1215/9781478007098.

Collins, Patricia Hill. 2000. 'Gender, Black feminism, and Black political economy', *The ANNALS of the American Academy of Political and Social Science* 568 (1): 41–53. https://doi.org/10.1177/000271620056800105.

Crazzolara, Joseph Pasquale. 1950. *The Lwoo*. Verona: Instituto Missioni Africane.

Curry, Oliver Scott, Mullins, Daniel Austin and Whitehouse, Harvey. 2019. 'Is it good to cooperate? Testing the theory of morality-as-cooperation in 60 societies', *Current Anthropology* 60 (1): 47–69. https://doi.org/10.1086/701478.

de Bruijn, Mirjam, ed. 2013. *SideWays: Mobile margins and the dynamics of communication in Africa*. Bamenda, Cameroon: Langaa Publishers.

de Bruijn, Mirjam. 2014. 'Connecting in mobile communities: An African case study', *Media, Culture & Society* 36 (3): 319–35. https://doi.org/10.1177/0163443714521088.

de Bruijn, M., Nyamnjoh, F. and Brinkman, I., eds. 2009. *Mobile Phones: The new talking drums of everyday Africa*. Bamenda, Cameroon: Langaa Publishers.

de Bruijn, Mirjam and van Dijk, Rijk. 2012. 'Introduction'. In *The Social Life of Connectivity in Africa*, edited by Mirjam de Bruijn and Rijk van Dijk. New York: Palgrave Macmillan. https://doi.org/10.1057/9781137278029.0005.

Dieterle, Carolin. 2022. 'Global governance meets local land tenure: International codes of conduct for responsible land investments in Uganda', *The Journal of Development Studies* 58 (3): 582–98. https://doi.org/10.1080/00220388.2021.1983165.

Doherty, Jacob. 2020. 'Motorcycle taxis, personhood, and the moral landscape of mobility', *Geoforum*, April. https://doi.org/10.1016/j.geoforum.2020.04.003.

Doom, R. and Vlassenroot, K. 1999. 'Kony's message: A new Koine? The Lord's Resistance Army in Northern Uganda', *African Affairs* 98 (390): 5–36. https://doi.org/10.1093/oxfordjournals.afraf.a008002.

Droti, B. 2014. 'Availability of health care for older persons in primary care facilities in Uganda'. https://doi.org/10.17037/PUBS.02021054.

Durham, Deborah. 2000. 'Youth and the social imagination in Africa: Introduction to parts 1 and 2', *Anthropological Quarterly* 73 (3): 113–20. https://doi.org/10.1353/anq.2000.0003.

Ekechi, F. K., Kopytoff, Igor and Falola, Toyin. 1988. 'The African frontier. The reproduction of traditional African societies', *African Studies Review* 31 (2): 170. https://doi.org/10.2307/524436.

Englund, H. 2008. 'Extreme poverty and existential obligations: Beyond morality in the anthropology of Africa?' *The International Journal of Anthropology, Social Analysis* 52 (3): 33–50.

Ese-osa Idahosa, Grace and Bradbury, Vanessa. 2020. 'Challenging the way we know the world: Overcoming paralysis and utilising discomfort through critical reflexive thought', *Acta Academica* 52 (1): 31–53. https://doi.org/10.18820/24150479/aa52i1/SP3.

Evans-Pritchard, E. E. 1967. *The Nuer*. Ann Arbor: The University of Michigan.
Fabian, Johannes (1983). *Time and the Other: How anthropology makes its object*. New York: Columbia University Press.
Fallers, M. 1960. *The Eastern Lacustrine Bantu (Ganda, Soga)*. East Central Africa: International Africa Institute.
Farmer, Paul. 2004. 'An anthropology of structural violence', *Current Anthropology* 45 (3): 305–25. https://doi.org/10.1086/382250.
Fassin, Didier. 2009. 'Another politics of life is possible', *Theory, Culture & Society* 26 (5): 44–60. https://doi.org/10.1177/0263276409106349.
Ferguson, James. 2006. *Global Shadows: Africa in the neoliberal world order*. Durham, NC: Duke University Press.
Ferguson, James. 2015. *Give a Man a Fish: Reflections on the new politics of distribution*. The Lewis Henry Morgan Lectures. Durham, NC; London: Duke University Press.
Fetterman, David M. 2010. *Ethnography: Step-by-step*. 3rd ed. Applied Social Research Methods Series 17. Los Angeles: SAGE.
Finnström, S. 2001. 'In and out of culture: Fieldwork in war-torn Uganda', *Critique of Anthropology* 21 (3): 247–58.
Finnström, Sverker. 2008. *Living with Bad Surroundings: War, history, and everyday moments in Northern Uganda*. The Cultures and Practice of Violence Series. Durham, NC: Duke University Press.
Finnström, Sverker. 2015. 'War stories and troubled peace', *Current Anthropology* 56 (12): 222–30. https://doi.org/10.1086/683270.
Fredericks, Rosalind. 2014. '"The Old Man is dead": Hip hop and the arts of citizenship of Senegalese youth', *Antipode* 46 (1): 130–48. https://doi.org/10.1111/anti.12036.
Freeman, Emily K. and Coast, Ernestina. 2014. 'Sex in older age in rural Malawi', *Ageing and Society* 34 (07): 1118–41. https://doi.org/10.1017/S0144686X12001481.
Garvey, Pauline and Miller, Daniel. 2021. *Ageing with Smartphones in Ireland: When life becomes craft*. London: UCL Press. http://public.eblib.com/choice/PublicFullRecord.aspx?p=6587062.
Geertz, Clifford. 1962. 'The rotating credit association: A "middle rung" in development', *Economic Development and Cultural Change* 10 (3): 241–63. https://doi.org/10.1086/449960.
Gertrude, Namale, Kawuma, Rachel, Nalukenge, Winifred, Kamacooko, Onesmus, Yperzeele, Laetitia, Cras, Patrick, Ddumba, Edward, Newton, Robert and Seeley, Janet. 2019. 'Caring for a stroke patient: The burden and experiences of primary caregivers in Uganda – a qualitative study', *Nursing Open* 6 (4): 1551–58. https://doi.org/10.1002/nop2.356.
Geschiere, Peter. 2013. 'Sociality and its dangers'. In *Sociality*, edited by Nicholas J. Long and Henrietta L. Moore. 1st ed., 61–82. New Directions. Oxford; New York: Berghahn Books. http://www.jstor.org/stable/j.ctt9qczjt.8.
Giddens, A. 1991. *Modernity and Self-identity: Self and society in the late modern age*. Stanford, CA: Stanford University Press.
Gilroy, Paul. 2009. *After Empire: Melancholia or convivial culture?* Repr. Abingdon: Routledge.
Girling, F. K. 2019 [1960]. *The Acholi of Uganda*. Reprinted in *Lawino's People: The Acholi of Uganda*, edited by Tim Allen. Classics in African Anthropology. Zurich: Lit Verlag. https://books.google.pt/books?id=dkWdoAEACAAJ.
Goffman, E. 1971. *Relations in Public: Microstudies of the public order*. New York: Basic Books.
Goggin, Gerard. 2012. 'Mobile phones: The new talking drums of everyday Africa and SMS uprising: mobile activism in Africa', *Ecquid Novi: African Journalism Studies* 33 (2): 100–106. https://doi.org/10.1080/02560054.2012.683802.
Golaz, Valérie, Wandera, Stephen Ojiambo and Rutaremwa, Gideon. 2017. 'Understanding the vulnerability of older adults: Extent of and breaches in support systems in Uganda', *Ageing and Society* 37 (01): 63–89. https://doi.org/10.1017/S0144686X15001051.
Goodfellow, Tom and Titeca, Kristof. 2012. 'Presidential intervention and the changing "politics of survival" in Kampala's informal economy'. *Cities* 29 (4): 264–70. https://doi.org/10.1016/j.cities.2012.02.004.
Green, Maia. 2019. 'Scripting development through formalisation: Accounting for the diffusion of village savings and loans associations in Tanzania: Scripting development through formalisation', *Journal of the Royal Anthropological Institute* 25 (1): 103–22. https://doi.org/10.1111/1467-9655.12966.
Gupta, Akhil and Ferguson, James, eds. 1997. *Anthropological Locations: Boundaries and grounds of a field science*. Berkeley, CA: University of California Press.

Guwatudde, David, Mutungi, Gerald, Wesonga, Ronald, Kajjura, Richard, Kasule, Hafisa, Muwonge, James, Ssenono, Vincent and Bahendeka, Silver K. 2015. 'The epidemiology of hypertension in Uganda: Findings from the National Non-Communicable Diseases Risk Factor Survey', edited by Yoshihiro Kokubo. *PLOS ONE* 10 (9): e0138991. https://doi.org/10.1371/journal.pone.0138991.

Hamill, Heather, Hampshire, Kate, Mariwah, Simon, Amoako-Sakyi, Daniel, Kyei, Abigail and Castelli, Michele. 2019. 'Managing uncertainty in medicine quality in Ghana: The cognitive and affective basis of trust in a high-risk, low-regulation context', *Social Science & Medicine* 234 (August): 112369. https://doi.org/10.1016/j.socscimed.2019.112369.

Hampshire, Kate, Hills, Elaine and Iqbal, Nazalie. 2005. 'Power relations in participatory research and community development: A case study from northern England', *Human Organization* 64 (4): 340–49. https://doi.org/10.17730/humo.64.4.bd9ktqj7194tyu6m.

Hampshire, Kate, Mwase-Vuma, Tawonga, Alemu, Kassahun, Abane, Albert, Munthali, Alister, Awoke, Tadesse, Mariwah, Simon et al. 2021. 'Informal mhealth at scale in Africa: Opportunities and challenges', *World Development* 140 (April): 105257. https://doi.org/10.1016/j.worlddev.2020.105257.

Hampshire, Kate, Porter, Gina, Mariwah, Simon, Munthali, Alister, Robson, Elsbeth, Owusu, Samule Asiedu, Abane, Albert and Milner, James. 2017. 'Who bears the cost of "informal mhealth"? Healthworkers' mobile phone practices and associated political-moral economies of care in Ghana and Malawi', *Health Policy and Planning* 32 (1): 34–42. https://doi.org/10.1093/heapol/czw095.

Hampshire, Kate, Porter, Gina, Owusu, Samuel Asiedu, Mariwah, Simon, Abane, Albert, Robson, Elsbeth, Munthali, Alister et al. 2015. 'Informal mhealth: How are young people using mobile phones to bridge healthcare gaps in sub-Saharan Africa?', *Social Science & Medicine* 142 (October): 90–99. https://doi.org/10.1016/j.socscimed.2015.07.033.

Hampshire, Kate and Randall, Sara. 2005. 'People are a resource'. In *Rural Resources & Local Livelihoods in Africa*, edited by Katherine Homewood, 123–36. New York: Palgrave Macmillan. https://doi.org/10.1007/978-1-137-06615-2_6.

Han, Clara. 2012. *Life in Debt*. 1st ed. Berkeley, CA: University of California Press. http://www.jstor.org/stable/10.1525/j.ctt1pncz5.

Haraway, Donna. 1988. 'Situated knowledges: The science question in feminism and the privilege of partial perspective', *Feminist Studies* 14 (3): 575. https://doi.org/10.2307/3178066.

Hart, Keith. 1973. 'Informal income opportunities and urban employment in Ghana', *The Journal of Modern African Studies* 11 (1): 61–89.

Hart, Keith. 1985. 'The informal economy', *Cambridge Anthropology* 10 (2): 54–58.

Hart, Keith. 2005. 'Money: One anthropologist's view'. In *A Handbook of Economic Anthropology* edited by James G. Carrier. Cheltenham: Edward Elgar Publishing. https://EconPapers.repec.org/RePEc:elg:eechap:2904_10.

Hart, Keith. 2008. 'The human economy', *Association of Social Anthropologists of the UK and Commonwealth*. http://www.theasa.org/publications/asaonline.html.

Harvey, Penny and Krohn-Hansen, Christian. 2018. 'Introduction. Dislocating labour: Anthropological reconfigurations', *Journal of the Royal Anthropological Institute* 24 (1): 10–28. https://doi.org/10.1111/1467-9655.12796.

Hawkins, Charlotte and Bwanika, John M. (forthcoming). 'An anthropological approach to telepsychotherapy: Providing "somewhere in-between" to go'. In *mHealth: An anthropological approach*, edited by C. Hawkins, Awondo, P. and Miller, D. London: UCL Press.

Hawkins, Charlotte, Bwanika, John M. and Ibanda, Martin. 2020. 'Socio-economic factors associated with mental health disorders in Fort Portal, Western Uganda', *South African Journal of Psychiatry* 26 (July). https://doi.org/10.4102/sajpsychiatry.v26i0.1391.

Hoffman, Jaco and Pype, Katrien, eds. 2016. *Ageing in Sub-Saharan Africa: Spaces and practices of care*. Ageing in a Global Context. Bristol; Chicago, IL: Policy Press.

Honwana, Alcinda Manuel. 2012. *The Time of Youth: Work, social change, and politics in Africa*. 1st ed. Sterling, VA: Kumarian Press Publishers.

Hopwood, Julian. 2015. 'Women's land claims in the Acholi region of Northern Uganda: What can be learned from what is contested', *International Journal on Minority and Group Rights* 22 (3): 387–409. https://doi.org/10.1163/15718115-02203005.

Horn, Vincent and Schweppe, Cornelia, eds. 2016. *Transnational Aging: Current insights and future challenges*. 1st ed. Routledge Research in Transnationalism 32. Oxford; New York: Routledge.

Horst, Heather A. and Miller, Daniel. 2006. *The Cell Phone: An anthropology of communication*. London: Bloomsbury Publishing.

Horst, Heather and Miller, Daniel, eds. 2012. *Digital Anthropology*. London: Berg.

Horst, Heather and Miller, Daniel. 2013. *Digital Anthropology*. London: Bloomsbury Academic Publishing.

Hovil, L. and Quinn, J. R. 2005. 'Peace first, justice later: Traditional justice in Northern Uganda', *The Refugee Law Project Working Papers*, no. 17. https://www.refugeelawproject.org/files/working_papers/RLP.WP17.pdf.

Illich, Ivan. 1973. *Tools for Conviviality*. Open Forum. London: Calder and Boyars.

Imbo, Samuel Oluoch. 2002. *Oral Traditions as Philosophy: Okot p'Bitek's legacy for African philosophy*. Lanham, MD: Rowman & Littlefield.

Jackson, Michael, ed. 1996. *Things as They Are: New directions in phenomenological anthropology*. Bloomington, IN: Indiana University Press.

Jackson, Michael. 1998. *Minima Ethnographica: Intersubjectivity and the anthropological project*. Chicago, IL: University of Chicago Press.

Jackson, Michael. 2002. *The Politics of Storytelling: Violence, transgression, and intersubjectivity*. Copenhagen; Portland, OR: Museum Tusculanum Press, University of Copenhagen.

Jackson, Michael. 2012. *Between One and One Another*. Berkeley, CA: University of California Press.

Kamwesiga, Julius T., Tham, Kerstin and Guidetti, Susanne. 2017. 'Experiences of using mobile phones in everyday life among persons with stroke and their families in Uganda – A qualitative study', *Disability and Rehabilitation* 39 (5): 438–49. https://doi.org/10.3109/09638288.2016.1146354.

Karlström, Mikael, Geschiere, Peter, Holtzman, Jon, Nyamnjoh, Francis B., Obbo, Christine, Whyte, Michael and Susan. 2004. 'Modernity and its aspirants: Moral community and developmental utopianism in Buganda', *Current Anthropology* 45 (5): 595–619.

Karugire, Samwiri R. 1980. *A Political History of Uganda*. Nairobi: Heinemann Educational Books.

Kasozi, Abdu B. K. 1994. *The Social Origins of Violence in Uganda, 1964–1985*. Montreal: McGill-Queen's University Press.

Keane, W. 2016. 'A reader's guide to the anthropology of ethics and morality – Part II', *Somatosphere: Science, medicine, and anthropology*. http://somatosphere.net/2016/ethics-and-morality-part-2.html/.

Kehr, J., Hansjörg, D. and van Eeuwijk, P. 2018. 'Transfigurations of health and the moral economy of medicine: Subjectivities, materialities, values', *Zeitschrift Für Ethnologie* 143: 1–20.

Kiranda, Y., Walter, M. and Mugisha, M. 2017. 'Employment, entrepreneurship and education in Uganda', Konrad Edenauer Stiftung. https://www.kas.de/c/document_library/get_file?uuid=6c7b17f7-b2d0-384b-7b63-df565c5d5450&groupId=252038.

Kleinman, Arthur. 2014. 'How we endure', *The Lancet* 383 (9912): 119–20. https://doi.org/10.1016/S0140-6736(14)60012-X.

Kleinman, Arthur. 2015. 'Care: In search of a health agenda', *The Lancet* 386 (9990): 240–41. https://doi.org/10.1016/S0140-6736(15)61271-5.

Klerk, Josien de and Moyer, Eileen. 2017. '"A body like a baby": Social self-care among older people with chronic HIV in Mombasa', *Medical Anthropology* 36 (4): 305–18. https://doi.org/10.1080/01459740.2016.1235573.

Kozelka, Ellen Elizabeth, Jenkins, Janis H. and Carpenter-Song, Elizabeth. 2021. 'Advancing health equity in digital mental health: Lessons from medical anthropology for global mental health', *JMIR Mental Health* 8 (8): e28555. https://doi.org/10.2196/28555.

Krige, Detlev. 2019. 'Debt/credit, money and social relationships in the underground credit markets of Soweto, South Africa', *Social Science Information* 58 (3): 403–29. https://doi.org/10.1177/0539018419851767.

Kusimba, Sibel, Yang Yang and Chawla, Nitesh. 2016. 'Hearthholds of mobile money in Western Kenya', *Economic Anthropology* 3 (2): 266–79. https://doi.org/10.1002/sea2.12055.

Kuteesa, Monica O., Seeley, Janet, Cumming, Robert G. and Negin, Joel. 2012. 'Older people living with HIV in Uganda: Understanding their experience and needs', *African Journal of AIDS Research* 11 (4): 295–305. https://doi.org/10.2989/16085906.2012.754829.

Kyaddondo, D. 2008. 'Respect and autonomy: Children's money in Eastern Uganda'. In *Generations in Africa: Connections and Conflicts*, edited by E. Alber, S. Geest and S. Whyte. Berlin: LIT Verlag Münster.

Lamb, Sarah, ed. 2017. *Successful Aging as a Contemporary Obsession: Global Perspectives*. New Brunswick, NJ; London: Rutgers University Press.

Lambek, Michael, Das, Veena, Fassin, Didier and Keane, Webb. 2015. *Four Lectures on Ethics: Anthropological perspectives*. Masterclass 3. Chicago, IL: HAU Books.

Larsson, Caroline Wamala and Svensson, Jakob. 2018. 'Mobile phones in the transformation of the informal economy: Stories from market women in Kampala, Uganda', *Journal of Eastern African Studies* 12 (3): 533–51. https://doi.org/10.1080/17531055.2018.1436247.

Le Polain, Maïté, Sterck, Olivier and Nyssens, Marthe. 2018. 'Interest rates in savings groups: Thrift or threat?', *World Development* 101 (January): 162–72. https://doi.org/10.1016/j.worlddev.2017.09.001.

Licoppe, Christian. 2004. '"Connected" Presence: The emergence of a new repertoire for managing social relationships in a changing communication technoscape', *Environment and Planning D: Society and Space* 22 (1): 135–56. https://doi.org/10.1068/d323t.

Linsi, Lukas and Mügge, Daniel K. 2019. 'Globalization and the growing defects of international economic statistics', *Review of International Political Economy* 26 (3): 361–83. https://doi.org/10.1080/09692290.2018.1560353.

Liu, Mei-Yan, Li, Na, Li, Wiliam A. and Khan, Hajra. 2017. 'Association between psychosocial stress and hypertension: A systematic review and meta-analysis', *Neurological Research* 39 (6): 573–80. https://doi.org/10.1080/01616412.2017.1317904.

Livingston, Julie. 2003. 'Reconfiguring old age: Elderly women and concerns over care in Southeastern Botswana', *Medical Anthropology* 22 (3): 205–31. https://doi.org/10.1080/01459740306771.

Liyong, Taban Lo. 2018. 'Indigenous African literary forms may determine the future course of world literature', *English in Africa* 45 (2): 17. https://doi.org/10.4314/eia.v45i2.2.

Lock, Margaret. 1994. 'Menopause in cultural context', *Experimental Gerontology* 29 (3–4): 307–17. https://doi.org/10.1016/0531-5565(94)90011-6.

Lunyera, Joseph, Kirenga, Bruce, Stanifer, John W., Kasozi, Samuel, van der Molen, Thys, Katagira, Wenceslaus, Kamya, Moses R. and Kalyesubula, Robert. 2018. 'Geographic differences in the prevalence of hypertension in Uganda: Results of a national epidemiological study', *PLOS ONE* 13 (8): e0201001. https://doi.org/10.1371/journal.pone.0201001.

MacNeil, Joan M. 1996. 'Use of culture care theory with Baganda women as AIDS caregivers', *Journal of Transcultural Nursing* 7 (2): 14–20. https://doi.org/10.1177/104365969600700204.

Madianou, Mirca and Miller, Daniel. 2012. *Migration and New Media: Transnational families and polymedia*. Abingdon; New York: Routledge.

Maharaj, Pranitha. 2020. *Health and Care in Old Age in Africa*. Routledge Contemporary Africa. Abingdon; New York. Routledge. http://www.vlebooks.com/vleweb/product/openreader?id=none&isbn=9780429667961.

Malaby, Thomas M. 2009. 'Anthropology and play: The contours of playful experience', *New Literary History* 40 (1): 205–18.

Mamdani, M. 1996. *Citizen and Subject: Contemporary Africa and the legacy of late colonialism*. Princeton, NJ: Princeton University Press.

Mamdani, M. 2012. *Define and Rule*. Cambridge, MA: Harvard University Press. www.jstor.org/stable/j.ctt2jbqkf.

Maniragaba, Fred, Nzabona, Abel, Asiimwe, John Bosco, Bizimungu, Emmanuel, Mushomi, John, Ntozi, James and Kwagala, Betty. 2019. 'Factors associated with older persons' physical health in rural Uganda', *PLOS ONE* 14 (1): e0209262. Edited by Maw Pin Tan. https://doi.org/10.1371/journal.pone.0209262.

Mathews, Gordon and Izquierdo, Carolina, eds. 2009. *Pursuits of Happiness: Well-being in anthropological perspective*. Oxford; New York: Berghahn Books.

Mattingly, Cheryl. 2019. 'Critical phenomenology and mental health: Moral experience under extraordinary conditions', *Ethos* 47 (1): 115–25. https://doi.org/10.1111/etho.12230.

Maurer, Bill. 2012. 'Mobile money: Communication, consumption and change in the payments space', *Journal of Development Studies* 48 (5): 589–604. https://doi.org/10.1080/00220388.2011.621944.

Mauss, Marcel and Halls, W. D. 1990. *The Gift: The form and reason for exchange in archaic societies*. London; New York: Routledge. http://public.ebookcentral.proquest.com/choice/publicfullrecord.aspx?p=169947.

Mbembe, Achille. 2002. 'African modes of self-writing', *Public Culture* 14 (1): 239–73.

Mbiti, John S. 1990. *African Religions & Philosophy*. 2nd rev. and enl. ed. Oxford; Portsmouth, NH: Heinemann.

McFarlane, Colin and Silver, Jonathan. 2017. 'Navigating the city: Dialectics of everyday urbanism', *Transactions of the Institute of British Geographers* 42 (3): 458–71. https://doi.org/10.1111/tran.12175.

McIntosh, Janet. 2010. 'Mobile phones and Mipoho's prophecy: The powers and dangers of flying language', *American Ethnologist* 37 (2): 337–53. https://doi.org/10.1111/j.1548-1425.2010.01259.x.

McIntosh, Janet 2017. 'Depreciating age, disintegrating ties: On being old in a century of declining elderhood in Kenya'. In *Successful Aging as a Contemporary Obsession: Global perspectives*, edited by S. Lamb, 185–200. New Brunswick, NJ; London: Rutgers University Press. http://www.jstor.org/stable/j.ctt1q1cqw5.17.

McQuaid, Katie, Esson, James, Gough, Katherine V. and Wignall, Ross. 2021. 'Navigating old age and the urban terrain: Geographies of ageing from Africa', *Progress in Human Geography* 45 (4): 814–33. https://doi.org/10.1177/0309132520948956.

Meier, B. 2013. '"Death does not rot": Transitional justice and local "truths" in the aftermath of the war in Northern Uganda', *Africa Spectrum* 48 (2): 25–50.

Meinert, Lotte. 2004. 'Resources for health in Uganda: Bourdieu's concepts of capital and *habitus*', *Anthropology & Medicine* 11 (1): 11–26. https://doi.org/10.1080/1364847042000204942.

Meinert, Lotte. 2009. *Hopes in Friction: Schooling, health, and everyday life in Uganda*. Charlotte, NC: Information Age Pub. http://public.ebookcentral.proquest.com/choice/publicfullrecord.aspx?p=3315061.

Meinert, Lotte and Whyte, Susan Reynolds. 2014. 'Epidemic projectification: AIDS responses in Uganda as event and process', *The Cambridge Journal of Anthropology* 32 (1). https://doi.org/10.3167/ca.2014.320107.

Meinert, Lotte and Whyte, Susan Reynolds. 2017. 'Social sensations of symptoms', *Anthropology in Action* 24 (1). https://doi.org/10.3167/aia.2017.240104.

Mendenhall, Emily, Seligman, Rebecca A., Fernandez, Alicia and Jacobs, Elizabeth A. 2010. 'Speaking through diabetes', *Medical Anthropology Quarterly* 24 (2): 220–39. https://doi.org/10.1111/j.1548-1387.2010.01098.x.

Mercer, Claire. 2006. 'Telecentres and transformations: Modernizing Tanzania through the internet', *African Affairs* 105 (419): 243–64. https://doi.org/10.1093/afraf/adi087.

Merttens et al. 2016. 'Evaluation of the Uganda Social Assistance Grants for Empowerment (SAGE) programme: Programme operations performance'. Endline final report.

Miller, Daniel et al. 2016. *How the World Changed Social Media*. London: UCL Press. https://doi.org/10.14324/111.9781910634493.

Miller, Daniel et al. 2021. *The Global Smartphone: Beyond a youth technology*. London: UCL Press. https://search.ebscohost.com/login.aspx?direct=true&scope=site&db=nlebk&db=nlabk&AN=2923617.

Monteith, William. 2018. 'Showing "heart" while making money: Negotiating proximity in a Ugandan marketplace', *Africa* 88 (1): 12–30. https://doi.org/10.1017/S0001972017001127.

Moore, Henrietta L. 1994. *A Passion for Difference: Essays in anthropology and gender*. Bloomington: Indiana University Press.

Mudege, Netsayi N. and Ezeh, Alex C. 2009. 'Gender, aging, poverty and health: Survival strategies of older men and women in Nairobi slums', *Journal of Aging Studies* 23 (4): 245–57. https://doi.org/10.1016/j.jaging.2007.12.021.

Muehlebach, Andrea. 2013. 'On precariousness and the ethical imagination: The year 2012 in sociocultural anthropology: year in review', *American Anthropologist* 115 (2): 297–311. https://doi.org/10.1111/aman.12011.

Mulumba, Moses, Nantaba, Juliana, Brolan, Claire E., Ruano, Ana Lorena, Brooker, Katie and Hammonds, Rachel. 2014. 'Perceptions and experiences of access to public healthcare by people with disabilities and older people in Uganda', *International Journal for Equity in Health* 13 (1): 76. https://doi.org/10.1186/s12939-014-0076-4.

Musinguzi, Geofrey and Nuwaha, Fred. 2013. 'Prevalence, awareness and control of hypertension in Uganda', *PLOS ONE* 8 (4): e62236. Edited by Nick Ashton. https://doi.org/10.1371/journal.pone.0062236.

Mutua, Makau. 2008. *Human Rights: A political and cultural critique*. Pennsylvania Studies in Human Rights. Philadelphia, PA: University of Pennsylvania Press.

Mutua, Makau. 2016. *Human Rights Standards: Hegemony, law, and politics*. Suny series, James N. Rosenau series in Global Politics. Albany, NY: State University of New York Press.

Nahemow, Nina. 1979. 'Residence, kinship and social isolation among the aged Baganda', *Journal of Marriage and the Family* 41 (1): 171. https://doi.org/10.2307/351741.

Najjumba-Mulindwa, I. 2003. 'Chronic poverty among the elderly in Uganda: Perceptions, experiences and policy issues'. Kampala: Institute of Statistics and Applied Economics, Makerere University. https://assets.publishing.service.gov.uk/media/57a08cdde5274a31e00014dc/Najjumba-Mulindwa.pdf.

Nakirya, Joan Wakida and State, Andrew Ellias. 2013. '"*Nigiina*"s as coping mechanisms of peri-urban low-income mothers in Kampala, Uganda', *Eastern Africa Social Science Research Review* 29 (1): 31–57. https://doi.org/10.1353/eas.2013.0000.

Namasinga Selnes, Florence and Orgeret, Kristin Skare. 2020. 'Social media in Uganda: Revitalising news journalism?' *Media, Culture & Society* 42 (3): 380–97. https://doi.org/10.1177/0163443719900353.

Namatovu, Esther and Saebo, Oystein. 2015. 'Motivation and consequences of internet and mobile phone usage among the urban poor in Kampala, Uganda'. In *2015 48th Hawaii International Conference on System Sciences (HICSS)*, 4335–44, IEEE. Kauai, HI, 5 January to 8 January 2015. https://doi.org/10.1109/HICSS.2015.519.

Nankindu, Prosperous, Kirunda, Rebecca F. and Ogavu, Titus. 2015. 'Language in education in Uganda: The policy, the actors and the practices', *Indian Journal of Research* 4 (5): 190–93.

Nankwanga, Annet, Neema, Stella and Phillips, Julie. 2013. 'The impact of HIV/AIDS on older persons in Uganda'. In *Aging and Health in Africa*, edited by Pranitha Maharaj, 139–55. Boston, MA: Springer US. https://doi.org/10.1007/978-1-4419-8357-2_7.

Nankwanga, Annet and Neema, Stella. 2020. 'Access to health and healthcare among older persons in Uganda'. In *Health and Care in Old Age in Africa*, edited by Pranitha Maharaj, 78–93. Routledge. https://www.taylorfrancis.com/books/9780429667961.

Neveu Kringelbach, Hélène. 2007. '"Cool play": Emotionality in dance as a resource in Senegalese urban women's associations'. In *The Emotions: A Cultural Reader*, edited by Helena Wulff. Oxford: Berg.

Neveu Kringelbach, Hélène. 2013. *Dance Circles: Movement, morality and self-fashioning in urban Senegal*. 1st ed. Oxford; New York: Berghahn Books. http://www.jstor.org/stable/j.ctt9qcw06.14.

Ngũgĩ wa Thiong'o. 2005. *Decolonising the Mind: The politics of language in African literature*. Reprint. Studies in African Literature. Oxford: Currey.

Nguyen, Minh T. N., Zavoretti, Roberta and Tronto, Joan. 2017. 'Beyond the global care chain: Boundaries, institutions and ethics of care', *Ethics and Social Welfare* 11 (3): 199–212. https://doi.org/10.1080/17496535.2017.1300308.

Nguyen, Vinh-Kim. 2016. *Anthropology and Global Health*. Oxford: Routledge.

Nowicka, Magdalena and Vertovec, Steven. 2014. 'Comparing convivialities: Dreams and realities of living-with-difference', *European Journal of Cultural Studies* 17 (4): 341–56. https://doi.org/10.1177/1367549413510414.

Nshakira-Rukundo, Emmanuel, Mussa, Essa Chanie, Nshakira, Nathan, Gerber, Nicolas and von Braun, Joachim. 2019. 'Determinants of enrolment and renewing of community-based health insurance in households with under-5 children in rural South-Western Uganda', *International Journal of Health Policy and Management* 8 (10): 593–606. https://doi.org/10.15171/ijhpm.2019.49.

Nussbaum, Martha C. 2000. *Women and Human Development: The capabilities approach*. Cambridge: Cambridge University Press.

Nyamnjoh, Francis. 2002. 'A child is one person's only in the womb: Domestication, agency and subjectivity in the Cameroonian grassfields'. In *Postcolonial Subjectivities in Africa*, edited by Richard Werbner. London: Zed Books.

Nyamnjoh, Francis. 2005. *Africa's Media, Democracy, and the Politics of Belonging*. London; New York: Zed Books.

Nyamnjoh, Francis. 2012a. '"Potted plants in greenhouses": A critical reflection on the resilience of colonial education in Africa', *Journal of Asian and African Studies* 47 (2): 129–54. https://doi.org/10.1177/0021909611417240.

Nyamnjoh, Francis. 2012b. 'Blinded by sight: Divining the future of anthropology in Africa', *Africa Spectrum* 47 (2–3): 63–92.

Nyamnjoh, Francis. 2012c. 'Fiction and reality of mobility in Africa'. Standard Form for African Studies. https://www.nyamnjoh.com/2012/11/francis-nyamnjoh-fiction-and-reality-of-mobility-in-africa.html.

Nyamnjoh, Francis. 2013. 'From quibbles to substance: A response to responses', *Africa Spectrum* 48 (2): 127–39.

Nyamnjoh, Francis. 2017. 'Incompleteness: Frontier Africa and the currency of conviviality', *Journal of Asian and African Studies* 52 (3): 253–70. https://doi.org/10.1177/0021909615580867.

Nyanzi, Stella. 2009. 'Widowed mama-grannies buffering HIV/AIDS-affected households in a city slum of Kampala, Uganda', *Gender & Development* 17 (3): 467–79. https://doi.org/10.1080/13552070903298485.

Nyanzi, Stella. 2011. 'Ambivalence surrounding elderly widows' sexuality in urban Uganda', *Ageing International* 36 (3): 378–400. https://doi.org/10.1007/s12126-011-9115-2.

Nyanzi, Stella. 2013. 'Dismantling reified African culture through localised homosexualities in Uganda', *Culture, Health & Sexuality* 15 (8): 952–67. https://doi.org/10.1080/13691058.2013.798684.

Nyanzi, Stella. 2015. 'Knowledge is requisite power: Making a case for queer African scholarship'. In *Boldly Queer: African perspectives on same-sex sexuality and gender diversity*, edited by T. Sandfort, F. Simenel, K. Mwachiro and V. Reddy, 125–35. The Hague: Hivos. https://knowledge.hivos.org/sites/default/files/15._knowledge_is_requisite_power_by_stella_nyanzi.pdf.

Nzabona, Abel and Ntozi, James. 2017. 'Does education influence the value of older persons? Assessing socio-demographic determinants of older persons' value in Uganda', *African Population Studies* 31 (2). https://doi.org/10.11564/31-2-1042.

Nzabona, Abel, Ntozi, James and Rutaremwa, Gideon. 2016. 'Loneliness among older persons in Uganda: Examining social, economic and demographic risk factors', *Ageing and Society* 36 (4): 860–88. https://doi.org/10.1017/S0144686X15000112.

Obbo, C. 1980. *African Women: Their struggle for economic independence*. Hutchinson University Library for Africa. London: Zed Press.

Obbo, C. 1986. 'Some East African widows'. In *Widows in African Societies: Choices and constraints*, edited by B. Potash, 84–106. Stanford, CA: Stanford University Press.

Ogot, Bethwell. 1967. *History of the Southern Luo, Volume 1: Migration and Settlement*. Nairobi: East African Publishing House. https://hdl.handle.net/2027/heb.02656.

Onyango-Ku-Odongo, J. M. and Webster, J. B. 1976. *The Central Lwo During the Aconya*. Nairobi: East African Literature Bureau. https://books.google.co.uk/books?id=FIy4AAAAIAAJ.

Onyango-Ouma, W. 2006. 'School knowledge and its relevance to everyday life in rural Western Kenya', *Nordic Journal of African Studies* 15 (3).

Oppong, Christine. 2006. 'Familial roles and social transformations: Older men and women in sub-Saharan Africa', *Research on Aging* 28 (6): 654–68. https://doi.org/10.1177/0164027506291744.

Otto, Opira. 2013. *Trust, Identity and Beer: Institutional arrangements for agricultural labour in Isunga village in Kiryandongo District, Midwestern Uganda*. Uppsala: Dept. of Urban and Rural Development, Swedish University of Agricultural Sciences. http://urn.kb.se/resolve?urn=urn:nbn:se:slu:epsilon-e-1715.

Oudshoorn, Nelly. 2011. *Telecare Technologies and the Transformation of Healthcare*. Health, Technology and Society. Basingstoke; New York: Palgrave Macmillan.

p'Bitek, Okot. 1970. *African Religions in Western Scholarship*. Nairobi: East African Literature Bureau. https://books.google.co.uk/books?id=bKXXAAAAMAAJ.

p'Bitek, Okot. 1971. *Religion of the Central Luo*. Nairobi: East African Literature Bureau. https://books.google.co.uk/books?id=EZPXAAAAMAAJ.

p'Bitek, Okot. 1986. *Artist, the Ruler: Essays on art, culture, and values, including extracts from Song of Soldier and White Teeth Make People Laugh on Earth*. Studies in African Literature. Nairobi: Heinemann Kenya. https://books.google.co.uk/books?id=bWugVZ1CaJsC.

p'Bitek, Okot and Girling, F. K. 2019. *Lawino's People: The Acholi of Uganda*, edited by Tim Allen. Classics in African Anthropology. Zurich: Lit Verlag. https://books.google.pt/books?id=dkWdoAEACAAJ.

Park, Sung-Joon and Akello, Grace. 2017. 'The Oughtness of Care: Fear, stress, and caregiving during the 2000–2001 Ebola outbreak in Gulu, Uganda', *Social Science & Medicine* 194 (December): 60–6. https://doi.org/10.1016/j.socscimed.2017.10.010.

Parkin, D. J. 1969. *Neighbours And Nationals In An African City Ward*. London: Routledge & Kegan Paul. https://books.google.co.uk/books?id=-IwkL3tSuMkC.

Polanyi, Karl. 1957 (1944). *The Great Transformation: The political and economic origins of our time*. Beacon Paperback edition. Boston, MA: Beacon Press.

Pols, J. 2012. *Care at a Distance: On the closeness of technology*. Care & Welfare. Amsterdam: Amsterdam University Press.

Porter, Gina, Hampshire, Kate, Abane, Albert, Munthali, Alister, Robson, Elsbeth, Bango, Andisiwe, de Lannoy, Ariane et al. 2015. 'Intergenerational relations and the power of the cell phone: Perspectives on young people's phone usage in sub-Saharan Africa', *Geoforum* 64 (August): 37–46. https://doi.org/10.1016/j.geoforum.2015.06.002.

Porter, Gina, Hampshire, Kate, Abane, Albert, Munthali, Alister, Robson, Elsbeth, de Lannoy, Ariane, Tanle, Augustine and Owusu, Samuel. 2020. 'Mobile phones, gender, and female empowerment in sub-Saharan Africa: Studies with African youth', *Information Technology for Development* 26 (1): 180–93. https://doi.org/10.1080/02681102.2019.1622500.

Porter, Gina, Hampshire, Kate, Abane, Albert, Munthali, Alister, Robson, Elsbeth and Mashiri, Mac. 2017. 'Introduction: Children, young people and the "Mobilities Turn" in sub-Saharan Africa'. In *Young People's Daily Mobilities in Sub-Saharan Africa*, edited by Gina Porter, Kate Hampshire, Albert Abane, Alister Munthali, Elsbeth Robson and Mac Mashiri, 1–22. New York: Palgrave Macmillan US. https://doi.org/10.1057/978-1-137-45431-7_1.

Porter, Holly. 2019. 'Moral spaces and sexual transgression: Understanding rape in war and post conflict', *Development and Change*, March, dech.12499. https://doi.org/10.1111/dech.12499.

Pringle, Yolana. 2019. *Psychiatry and Decolonisation in Uganda*. 1st ed. 2019. Mental Health in Historical Perspective. London: Palgrave Macmillan UK. https://doi.org/10.1057/978-1-137-60095-0.

Pype, Katrien. 2016. 'Brokers of belonging; elders & intermediaries in Kinshasa's mobile phone culture'. In *Everyday Media Culture in Africa: Audiences and Users*, edited by Wendy Willems and Winston Mano, Chapter 10. Routledge Advances in Internationalizing Media Studies 18. New York and London: Routledge.

Pype, K. 2017a. 'Smartness from below: Variations on technology and creativity in contemporary Kinshasa'. In *What Do Science, Technology and Innovation Mean from Africa?*, edited by Clapperton Chakanetsa Mavhunga, 97–117. Cambridge, MA: MIT Press.

Pype, Katrien. 2017b. 'Dancing to the rhythm of Léopoldville: Nostalgia, urban critique and generational difference in Kinshasa's TV music shows', *Journal of African Cultural Studies* 29 (2): 158–76. https://doi.org/10.1080/13696815.2016.1189816.

Qureshi, Ayaz. 2022. 'Valuing care: Community workers and bureaucratic violence in global health', *Anthropology in Action* 29 (2): 35–43. https://doi.org/10.3167/aia.2022.290204.

Randall, Sara and Coast, Ernestina. 2016. 'The quality of demographic data on older Africans', *Demographic Research* 34 (January): 143–74. https://doi.org/10.4054/DemRes.2016.34.5.

Reubi, David, Herrick, Clare and Brown, Tim. 2016. 'The politics of non-communicable diseases in the Global South', *Health & Place* 39 (May): 179–87. https://doi.org/10.1016/j.healthplace.2015.09.001.

Robbins, Joel. 2004. 'The globalization of Pentecostal and charismatic Christianity', *Annual Review of Anthropology* 33 (1): 117–43. https://doi.org/10.1146/annurev.anthro.32.061002.093421.

Robbins, Joel. 2007. 'Between reproduction and freedom: Morality, value, and radical cultural change', *Ethnos* 72 (3): 293–314. https://doi.org/10.1080/00141840701576919.

Robbins, Joel. 2013. 'Beyond the suffering subject: Toward an anthropology of the good', *Journal of the Royal Anthropological Institute* 19 (3): 447–62.

Roth, Claudia. 2010. 'Les relations intergénérationnelles sous pression au Burkina Faso', *Autrepart* 53 (1): 95. https://doi.org/10.3917/autr.053.0095.

Schatz, Enid and Seeley, Janet. 2015. 'Gender, ageing and carework in East and Southern Africa: A review', *Global Public Health* 10 (10): 1185–1200. https://doi.org/10.1080/17441692.2015.1035664.

Schatz, E., Seeley, J., Negin, J. and Mugisha, J. 2018. '"They "don't cure old age": Older Ugandans' delays to health-care access', *Ageing and Society* 38 (11): 2197–2217. https://doi.org/10.1017/S0144686X17000502.

Seeberg, Jens and Meinert, Lotte. 2020. 'Can epidemics be noncommunicable?', *Medicine Anthropology Theory* 2 (2): 54–71. https://doi.org/10.17157/mat.2.2.171.

Shambare, Richard. 2014. 'The adoption of WhatsApp: Breaking the vicious cycle of technological poverty in South Africa', *Journal of Economics and Behavioral Studies* 6 (7): 542–50. https://doi.org/10.22610/jebs.v6i7.515.

Sigona, Nando, Gamlen, Alan John, Liberatore, Giulia and Neveu Kringelbach, Hélène, eds. 2015. *Diasporas Reimagined: Spaces, practices and belonging.* Oxford: Oxford Diasporas Programme.

Simone, AbdouMaliq. 2021. 'Ritornello: "People as infrastructure"', *Urban Geography* 42 (9): 1341–48. https://doi.org/10.1080/02723638.2021.1894397.

Singer, Merrill, Bulled, Nicola, Ostrach, Bayla and Ginzburg, Shir Lerman. 2021. 'Syndemics: A cross-disciplinary approach to complex epidemic events like COVID-19', *Annual Review of Anthropology* 50 (1): 41–58. https://doi.org/10.1146/annurev-anthro-100919-121009.

Singer, Merrill, Bulled, Nicola, Ostrach, Bayla and Mendenhall, Emily. 2017. 'Syndemics and the biosocial conception of health', *The Lancet* 389 (10072): 941–50. https://doi.org/10.1016/S0140-6736(17)30003-X.

Singh, Aneesha, Gibbs, Jo, Estcourt, Claudia, Sonnenberg, Pam and Blandford, Ann. 2017. 'Are HIV smartphone apps and online interventions fit for purpose?' In DH '17: Proceedings of the 2017 International Conference on Digital Health', 6–15. New York: ACM Press. https://doi.org/10.1145/3079452.3079469.

Sokolovsky, Jay, ed. 2020. *The Cultural Context of Ageing.* Santa Barbara, CA: Praeger.

Southall, A. W., Gutkind, P. C. W. and Sempa, A. Kalule. 1957. *Townsmen in the Making: Kampala and its suburbs.* Vol. 2. East African Studies 9. Kampala, Uganda: East African Institute of Social Research.

Spruill, Tanya M. 2010. 'Chronic psychosocial stress and hypertension', *Current Hypertension Reports* 12 (1): 10–16. https://doi.org/10.1007/s11906-009-0084-8.

Ssengonzi, Robert. 2007. 'The plight of older persons as caregivers to people infected/affected by HIV/AIDS: Evidence from Uganda', *Journal of Cross-Cultural Gerontology* 22 (4): 339–53. https://doi.org/10.1007/s10823-007-9043-5.

Sutton, Theodora. 2020. 'Digital harm and addiction: An anthropological view', *Anthropology Today* 36 (1): 17–22. https://doi.org/10.1111/1467-8322.12553.

Svensson, Jakob and Larsson, Caroline Wamala. 2016. 'Situated empowerment: Mobile phones practices among market women in Kampala', *Mobile Media & Communication* 4 (2): 205–20. https://doi.org/10.1177/2050157915619212.

Tamale, Sylvia. 2020. *Decolonization and Afro-Feminism.* Ottawa: Daraja Press.

Thieme, Tatiana Adeline. 2018. 'The hustle economy: Informality, uncertainty and the geographies of getting by', *Progress in Human Geography* 42 (4): 529–48. https://doi.org/10.1177/0309132517690039.

Ukah, Asonzeh. 2018. '"Everything is plastic": The faith of unity movement and the making of a post-Catholic religion in Uganda', *Journal for the Study of Religion* 31 (2): 138–60. https://doi.org/10.17159/2413-3027/2018/v31n2a6.

Van der Geest, Sjaak. 1997a. 'Money and respect: The changing value of old age in rural Ghana', *Africa: Journal of the International African Institute*, 67(4): 534–59.

Van der Geest, Sjaak. 1997b. 'Between respect and reciprocity: Managing old age in rural Ghana', *Southern African Journal of Gerontology* 6 (2): 20–5. https://doi.org/10.21504/sajg.v6i2.116.

Van der Geest, Sjaak. 2011. 'Loneliness and distress in old age: A note from Ghana'. In *Roads and Boundaries: Travels in Search of (Re)Connection*, edited by Marian Tankink and Marianne Vysma, 67–74. Diemen: AMB Publications.

Velkoff, Victoria A. and Kowal, Paul R. 2007. 'Population aging in sub-Saharan Africa: Demographic dimensions', *U.S. Census Bureau, Current Population Reports.* https://www.census.gov/prod/2007pubs/p95-07-1.pdf.

Vokes, Richard. 2018. 'Before the call: Mobile phones, exchange relations, and social change in South-Western Uganda', *Ethnos* 83 (2): 274–90. https://doi.org/10.1080/00141844.2015.1133689.

Vokes, Richard and Mills, David. 2015. '"Time for school"? School fees, savings clubs and social reciprocity in Uganda', *Journal of Eastern African Studies* 9 (2): 326–42. https://doi.org/10.1080/17531055.2015.1042627.

Vokes, Richard and Pype, Katrien. 2018. 'Chronotopes of media in sub-Saharan Africa', *Ethnos* 83 (2): 207–17. https://doi.org/10.1080/00141844.2016.1168467.

Wallman, Sandra and Baker, Maia. 1996. 'Which resources pay for treatment? A model for estimating the informal economy of health', *Social Science & Medicine* 42 (5): 671–79. https://doi.org/10.1016/0277-9536(95)00412-2.

Wallman, Sandra and Bantebya-Kyomuhendo, Grace. 1996. *Kampala Women Getting by: Wellbeing in the time of AIDS*. Eastern African Studies. London; Kampala; Athens, OH: James Currey; Fountain Publishers; Ohio University Press.

Wandera, Stephen Ojiambo, Kwagala, Betty and Ntozi, James. 2015. 'Prevalence and risk factors for self-reported non-communicable diseases among older Ugandans: A cross-sectional study', *Global Health Action* 8 (1): 27923. https://doi.org/10.3402/gha.v8.27923.

Wandera, Stephen Ojiambo, Ddumba, Isaac, Akenyemi, Joshua Odunayo, Adedini, Sunday A. and Odimegwu, Clifford. 2017. 'Living alone among older persons in Uganda: Prevalence and associated factors', *Ageing International* 42 (4): 429–46. https://doi.org/10.1007/s12126-017-9305-7.

Wang, Xinyuan and Happio-Kirk, Laura. 2021. 'Emotion work via digital visual communication: A comparative study between China and Japan', *Global Media and China*, April, 205943642110080. https://doi.org/10.1177/20594364211008044.

Wanume, P., Nduhura, A., Mugerwa, B., Bagambe, H., Ninsiima, J. 2019. 'The dangerous boda boda transport mode: Mitigating an impending war on the roads in a transforming city? Case of Kampala City', *Journal of Logistics Management* 8 (1): 1–13.

Whyte, Susan Reynolds. 1997. *Questioning Misfortune: The pragmatics of uncertainty in Eastern Uganda*. Cambridge Studies in Medical Anthropology 4. Cambridge; New York: Cambridge University Press.

Whyte, Susan Reynolds. 2014. 'The publics of the new public health: Life conditions and "lifestyle diseases" in Uganda'. In *Making and Unmaking Public Health in Africa: Ethnographic and historical perspectives*, edited by R. J. Prince and R. Marsland, 187–207. Athens: Ohio University Press.

Whyte, Susan Reynolds. 2016. 'Knowing hypertension and diabetes: Conditions of treatability in Uganda', *Health & Place* 39 (May): 219–25. https://doi.org/10.1016/j.healthplace.2015.07.002.

Whyte, Susan Reynolds. 2017. 'Epilogue: Successful ageing and desired interdependence'. In *Successful Aging as a Contemporary Obsession: Global perspectives*, edited by Sarah Lamb, 243–8. New Brunswick, NJ; London: Rutgers University Press. http://www.jstor.org/stable/j.ctt1q1cqw5.21.

Whyte, Susan Reynolds and Acio, Esther. 2017. 'Generations and access to land in postconflict Northern Uganda: "Youth Have No Voice in Land Matters"', *African Studies Review* 60 (3): 17–36. https://doi.org/10.1017/asr.2017.120.

Whyte, Susan Reynolds, Meinert, L., Obika, J. and Parkin, D. 2016. 'Untying wrongs in Northern Uganda'. In *Evil in Africa*, edited by William C. Olsen and Walter E. A. Van Beek, 43–60. Encounters with the Everyday. Bloomington, IN: Indiana University Press. http://www.jstor.org/stable/j.ctt17t75bk.7.

Whyte, Susan R. and Whyte, Michael A. 2004. 'Children's children: Time and relatedness in Eastern Uganda', *Africa: Journal of the International African Institute* 74 (1): 76–94. https://doi.org/10.2307/3556745.

Wiegratz, Jörg. 2010. 'Fake capitalism? The dynamics of neoliberal moral restructuring and pseudo-development: The case of Uganda', *Review of African Political Economy* 37 (124): 123–37. https://doi.org/10.1080/03056244.2010.484525.

Wignall, Ross, McQuaid, Katie, Gough, Katherine V. and Esson, James. 2019. '"We built this city": Mobilities, urban livelihoods and social infrastructure in the lives of elderly Ghanaians', *Geoforum* 103 (July): 75–84. https://doi.org/10.1016/j.geoforum.2019.03.022.

Zavoretti, Roberta. 2017. 'Get yourself an insurance! Negotiating family and intergenerational care in post-Mao urban China', *Ethics and Social Welfare* 11 (3): 248–60. https://doi.org/10.1080/17496535.2017.1300306.

Zelizer, Viviana A. Rotman. 2018. *Morals and Markets: The development of life insurance in the United States*. New York: Columbia University Press. https://doi.org/10.7312/zeli18334.

Zigon, Jarrett. 2007. 'Moral breakdown and the ethical demand: A theoretical framework for an anthropology of moralities', *Anthropological Theory* 7 (2): 131–50. https://doi.org/10.1177/1463499607077295.

Web resources

- Centre for Public Authority and International Development (CPAID). 2021. 'Report'. Accessed 7 November 2022. https://issuu.com/lseflca/docs/centre_for_public_authority_and_international_deve.
- Clifford, K. 2020. 'The causes and consequences of mobile money taxation: An examination of mobile money transaction taxes in sub-Saharan Africa', *GSMA Mobile Money*. Accessed 18 November 2019. https://www.gsma.com/mobilefordevelopment/wp-content/uploads/2020/06/GSMA_The-causes-and-consequences-of-mobile-money-taxation.pdf.
- Deloitte. 2017. 'Deloitte's mobile consumer survey: The Africa cut 2015/16'. Accessed 29 November 2018. https://www2.deloitte.com/content/dam/Deloitte/za/Documents/technology-media-telecommunications/ZA_Deloitte-Mobile-consumer-survey-Africa-300816.pdf, 4.
- GEM Consortium. 2014. 'Economy profiles: Uganda'. Accessed 18 November 2019. https://www.gemconsortium.org/economy-profiles/uganda.
- GEM Consortium. 2014. 'Entrepreneurial behaviour and attitudes: Uganda profile'. Accessed 18 November 2019. https://www.gemconsortium.org/economy-profiles/uganda.
- GSMA. 2020. 'The mobile gender gap report'. Accessed 14 January 2021. https://www.gsma.com/mobilefordevelopment/wp-content/uploads/2020/05/GSMA-The-Mobile-Gender-Gap-Report-2020.pdf.
- LivingGoods. 2019. 'Health for all: Uganda's cabinet approves the National Health Insurance Scheme Bill 2019'. Accessed 7 July 2020. https://livinggoods.org/media/health-for-all-ugandas-cabinet-approves/#.
- Mwebaza, E. 'A historical perspective of the land problem in Uganda', HRAPF Uganda. Accessed 23 May 2022. https://hrapf.org/images/researchpapers/a_historical_perspective_of_the_land_problem_in_uganda.pdf.
- National Labour Force Survey (NLFS). 2018. Accessed 18 November 2019. https://www.ubos.org/wp-content/uploads/publications/10_2018Report_national_labour_force_survey_2016_17.pdf.
- NITA Uganda. 2018. 'National information technology survey, 2017/18 report'. Accessed 31 July 2019. https://www.nita.go.ug/sites/default/files/publications/National%20IT%20Survey%20April%2010th.pdf.
- Obaikol, E. 2014. 'Draft final report of the implementation of the land governance assessment framework in Uganda'. Accessed 23 May 2022. Washington, DC: World Bank Group. http://documents.worldbank.org/curated/en/611841504873425190/Draft-final-report-of-the-implementation-of-the-land-governance-assessment-framework-in-Uganda.
- Parliament of Uganda. 2022. 'Reduce age of SAGE beneficiaries'. Accessed 2 September 2022. https://parliament.go.ug/news/6111/'reduce-age-sage-beneficiaries'.
- Serumaga, K. 2023. 'Well-funded riddles: Notes on Uganda's sexual culture war'. Accessed 21 April 2022. https://africanarguments.org/2023/03/well-funded-riddles-notes-from-ugandas-sexual-culture-war/.
- *The Economist*. 2020. 'How a Ugandan hospital delivers health insurance through burial groups'. Accessed 7 July 2020. https://www.economist.com/middle-east-and-africa/2020/01/30/how-a-ugandan-hospital-delivers-health-insurance-through-burial-groups.
- The Refugee Law Project Working Paper. 2005. 'Peace first, justice later: Traditional justice in Northern Uganda'. Accessed 10 March 2021. https://www.refugeelawproject.org/files/workingpapers/RLP.WP17.pdf, 3.
- Uganda Bureau of Statistics (UBOS). 2014. 'Uganda national census main report'. Accessed 8 June 2021. https://www.ubos.org/wp-content/uploads/publications/03_20182014_National_Census_Main_Report.pdf.
- Uganda Bureau of Statistics (UBOS) 2017. 'Education: A means for population transformation. Based on the National Population and Housing Census 2014', 50. Accessed 1 April 2020. https://www.ubos.org/wp-content/uploads/publications/03_2018Education_Monograph_Report_Final08-12-2017.pdf.
- Uganda Bureau of Statistics (UBOS). 2017. 'National labour force survey 2016'. Accessed 18 November 2019. https://www.ubos.org/wp-content/uploads/publications/10_2018Report_national_labour_force_survey_2016_17.pdf, xiv.

- Uganda Bureau of Statistics (UBOS). 2018. 'Uganda manpower survey report'. Accessed 19 November 2019. https://www.ubos.org/wp-content/uploads/publications/08_20182018_Uganda_Manpower_Survey_Report.pdf.
- Ugandan Bureau of Statistics (UBOS). 2018. 'Uganda national census main report'. Accessed 14 September 2020. https://www.ubos.org/wp-content/uploads/publications/03_20182014_National_Census_Main_Report.pdf.
- Uganda Bureau of Statistics (UBOS). 2020. 'Uganda national survey report 2019/2020'. Accessed 15 June 2022. https://www.ubos.org/wp-content/uploads/publications/09_2021Uganda-National-Survey-Report-2019-2020.pdf, 14.
- Uganda Communications Commission (UCC) 2016. 'Facts and figures'. Accessed 27 November 2017. http://www.ucc.co.ug/data/qmenu/3/Facts-and-Figures.html.
- Uganda Communications Commission (UCC). 2018. 'UCC sector report'. Accessed 31 July 2019. https://www.ucc.co.ug/wp-content/uploads/2017/09/UCC-Sector-Report-December-2018_260719.pdf, 30.
- Uganda Communications Commission (UCC). 2020. 'Market performance Q1 2020'. Accessed 23 September 2020. https://www.ucc.co.ug/wp-content/uploads/2020/08/UCC-Market-Performance-1Q20-Report-FINAL.pdf, 4.
- United Nations. 2019. 'New measures of population ageing'. Accessed 23 May 2022. https://www.un.org/en/development/desa/population/events/pdf/expert/29/session1/EGM_25Feb2019_S1_SergeiScherbov.pdf, 6.
- United Nations, Department of Economic and Social Affairs, Population Division. 2015. 'World population ageing 2015'. Accessed 9 February 2021. https://www.un.org/en/development/desa/population/publications/pdf/ageing/WPA2015_Report.pdf, 144.
- United Nations, Department of Economic and Social Affairs, Population Division. 2019. 'World population ageing 2019'. Accessed 22 October 2019. https://www.un.org/en/development/desa/population/publications/pdf/ageing/WPA2015_Highlights.pdf.
- UPPC. 2009. 'The anti homosexuality bill'. Accessed 24 August 2020. https://docs.google.com/file/d/0B7pFotabJnTmYzFiMWJmY2UtYWYxMi00MDY2LWI4NWYtYTVlOWU1OTEzMzk0/edit?pli=1&hl=en.
- Wine, Bobi. 2018. 'Museveni is as good as his word'. Accessed 4 April 2019. https://w.soundcloud.com/player/?url=https%3A//api.soundcloud.com/tracks/342295943&color=%23ff5500&auto_play=false&hide_related=false&show_comments=true&show_user=true&show_reposts=false&visual=true.
- World Bank. 2017. 'Data for Uganda'. Accessed 26 May 2017. http://data.worldbank.org/?locations=UG-XM.
- World Bank. 2016. 'Uganda poverty assessment report'. Accessed 2 July 2017. http://pubdocs.worldbank.org/en/381951474255092375/pdf/Uganda-Poverty-Assessment-Report-2016.pdf.
- World Bank. 2017. 'From regulators to enablers: The role of city governments in economic development of Greater Kampala'. Accessed 18 November 2019. https://development-data-hub-s3-public.s3.amazonaws.com/ddhfiles/143567/119806-revised-public-the-wb-book-2017-report-web-individual-page-layout_0.pdf.
- World Bank. 2019. 'Population ages 65 and above (% of total population)'. Accessed 8 June 2021. https://data.worldbank.org/indicator/SP.POP.65UP.TO.ZS?name_desc=false.
- World Bank. 2019. 'Population growth (annual %): Uganda'. Accessed 8 June 2021. https://data.worldbank.org/indicator/SP.POP.GROW?locations=UG.
- World Health Organization (WHO). 2005. 'Health and mortality survey among internally displaced persons in Gulu, Kitgum and Pader districts, northern Uganda'. Accessed 28 April 2020. https://reliefweb.int/report/uganda/health-and-mortality-survey-among-internally-displaced-persons-gulu-kitgum-and-pader.
- World Population Review. 2021. 'Uganda population 2021'. Accessed 8 June 2021. https://worldpopulationreview.com/countries/uganda-population.

Index

Figures are denoted by the use of *italic* page numbers and notes by 'n'.

abandonment, elder 145–6, 157, 160n50, 191
Achola
   on development 18
   on old age 190
   on role of older generation 1, 153–6, 179–80
Acholiland (Acholi sub-region) 12–14, 33, 105n1
addiction, to smartphones 120
advice 40–1, 48–9
   following 34, 46, 50, 193
   going against 168
   health 136, 140, 148
   seeking 4, 22, 43, 67, 104, 164, 170, 184
   value of 52n13, 180
age categories 184
'age inscription' 28n29, 78n59
'age-set system' 52n31
Aged Family Uganda (TAFU) 37
Ahlin, Tanja 126
Ahmed (Lusozi Muslim) 39–40
Aida ('pressure' sufferer) 152
Akello, Grace 158–9, 159n23
Al-Quds, East Jerusalem 83
Alber, Erdmute 28n29
alcohol and drugs 73, 153, 168, 170–1
Allen, Tim 27n5
alternatives, imagining 182–5
Alur people 9, 29n37
Amor
   family 11, 12, 20, 67–8, 87, 116, 173
   on gambling 63
   linguist 9
   loses smartphone 169
   'our book' 1, 22
   respect for elders 38, 148
'Anthropology of Smartphones and Smart Ageing' (ASSA) study 1, 3–4, 36, 55, 83, 136, 147, 192
anti-homosexuality bill 167
antiretroviral treatment (ART) 99, 144, 148
apps 62, 69, *90*, 113, 115
Archambault, Julie Soleil 118, 178n62
Ardener, Shirley 83, 106n9
Awondo, Patrick 187

Baganda people 9, 10, 114, 119, 146, 167–8
bananas, selling 65–6, *69*, 70

Bantebya-Kyomuhendo, Grace 59, 148
bayaayes (young people in the city) 171
beeped calls 113
Black, Steven P. 161n109
boda boda (motorbike taxi) 7, 61, 68–70, 87, 89, 152
   film 69, *69*
Botswana 53n46, 53n48
burial and death
   excess 14
   home burials 15–16, 84
   support networks and 103–4

Cameroon 83, 187
care and health
   approaches to health system 136, 184
   care choices 140–1
   care homes 136, 146, 191
   care roles 142–4
   chronic conditions 141
   context 137–41
   healthy living 149
   HIV treatment 99, 144
   information through WhatsApp 127–8
   'oughtness of care' 159n23
   paid carers 136, 191
   physiotherapists 74
   self-care 147–50, 156, 157, 158, 190
   who is responsible? 135–59
   working to keep fit 72
caring responsibilities 4, 55, 66–7, 70, 71, 135–59, 189
   at a distance 6, 28n29, 63, 109, 110, 114–15, 117, 121–2, 129, 145–7
Chile 57
China 137, 142, 147
cholera outbreak, Lusozi (2018) 127
co-operative morality 163–76
Coast, Ernestina 160n42
Coe, Cati 28n29, 78n59, 146
colonisation, British 165
Community Based Health Insurance (CBHI) schemes 74
complex ecologies 124
computers 111
'convivial scholarship' 2, 20–3
conviviality 6–7, 49, 84, 126, 156, 180, 181–2
COVID-19 132n16, 193, 1151

211

Cuan, Ireland 136–7
'customary' (definition) 51n4

dance and music 5, 22, 34, 45–7, *45*, *47*, 49–51, 180–1
  on phones 118–19, 132n31
day-to-day life 7–9, 60–1
death and burial
  excess 14
  home burials 15–16, 84
  support networks and 103–4
development 18–20, 31n97
diabetes 149, 150–1
diets 148–50
digital capital 20, 110, 115, 130
digital health 3–4, 25, 105
displacement 2–3, 11, 14, 15, 30n74
dotcom (definition) 179
dotcom generation 117–20, 171–2
  elders of 2–7, 49
dotcom wave 109–31, 187
drugs and alcohol 73, 153, 168, 170–1
Dublin 83

Ebola outbreak, Gulu (2000) 159, 159n23
economy
  formal 60, 65
  informal 11, 56, 58–60, 65, 74, 185
education 19–20
  graduates 153
  homework *116*
  Place of Peace 98–103, *101*
  primary *10*
  'We as elders have a duty' film *45*
  See also school fees
elder leadership (definition) 37–8
elders (definition) 36–8
elders, in the city 33–51
Englund, H. 164
Evans-Pritchard, E. E. 52n31
'Everyday life' film 68, *68*
exercise 72, *99*, 100, 147

Facebook 45, 50, 113, 118, 125, 127, 129
family repertoires 28n29
family responsibilities 98, 101–3, 141–2
farming
  awak (work parties) 5, 81, 96, 104, 105n1, 180
  subsistence agriculture 59
  'working together' practices 5, 81, 105n1, 180
Fassin, Didier 160n50
Finnström, Sverker 21, 28n25, 33, 44–5
formal economy 60, 65

'gambling' 55, 56, 60–3, 76, 189–90
Geertz, Clifford 106n9
Geschiere, Peter 178n62
Ghana 28n29, 52n13, 146, 147
Gipir and Gifol story 29n37
Girling, F. K. 105n1, 146
global caring 146, 158, 165
Global Entrepreneurship Monitor (GEM) 11, 59
'goodness', moral 163–76

Haapio-Kirk, Laura 57
Hart, Keith 59, 91, 106n6
health and care
  approaches to health system 136, 184
  care choices 140–1
  care homes 136, 146, 191
  care roles 142–4
  chronic conditions 141
  context 137–41
  healthy living 149
  HIV treatment 99, 144
  information through WhatsApp 127–8
  'oughtness of care' 159n23
  paid carers 136, 191
  physiotherapists 74
  self-care 147–50, 156, 157, 158, 190
  who is responsible? 135–59
  working to keep fit 72
Hill-Collins, Patricia 31n118
HIV/AIDs
  antiretroviral treatment (ART) 99, 144, 148
  deaths related to 4, 35, 50
  funding for treatment 150
  respect for patients 5
  single mothers with 82, 99–100
'home' (definition) 12
housing 7, 12, 17–18, *17–18*, 19
'human economies' 83, 91, 144, 185–92
human economies 189
hypertension ('pressure') 6, 71, 136, 143, 150–2, 155–6, 158, 190

Illich, Ivan 126
incompleteness 6, 23, 26, 109, 182
India 146
inequalities 11, 19, 26, 49, 115, 143, 176, 182
informal economy 11, 56, 58–60, 65, 74, 185
informal mHealth 124, 188
intergenerational relationships 34–42, 43, 52n13, 52n23, 109–31, 142–4
  TIS and 91
  via the phone 53n40
Internally Displaced People (IDP) 14, 30n74
International Monetary Fund 11
intersectional gender analysis 22, 31n118
'intersubjectivity' 28n25, 165, 180, 190
Ireland 136–7
isolation 52n13, 76, 100, 146, 147, 157
Italy 57

Jackson, Michael 28n25
Japan 57, 147
justice, community 33, 42, 44, 52n10, 175, 176

Kampala City Council Authority (KCCA) 67, 68, 92
Karlström, Mikael 177n14, 178n62
Kasolo (bicycle deliveries) 72–3, 76
Keane, W. 161n109
Kenya 118
Kevin (on land protection) 16
Kilongeni (Amor's dad) 115–16
  Amor and smartphone 169–70
  being respected 39, 48
  convenience of phones 117, 120
  family 20, 67

212 INDEX

on healthy living 149
Ladit and 34
regulating use of phones 119–20
on sickness 144
Kisiizi Hospital 74
Kitgum District 12, *15*, 146
Kleinman, Arthur 158
Kochi, Japan 57
Kony, Joseph 13–14
Kusimba, Sibel 118
Kyaddondo, David 166
Kyoto, Japan 57

Ladit (Acholi elder) 42–7, 49–51
on healthy living 149
on 'home' 57
music and dance 34, *47*, 180–1
respected 170
storytelling 48
TIS and 82, 84, 87, 88
on togetherness 81
Lamb, Sarah 146
land 14–18
claims/disputes 16, 44
ownership 14–15, *15*, 40, 51n4
languages 9, 11, 20, 27n5, 87, 94, 138
livelihoods 12, 55–76
Livingston, Julie 53n46, 53n48
Liyong, Taban Lo 150
loneliness 52n13, 146, 147, 157
Lord's Resistance Army (LRA) 13–14, 15, 34
Luo people 27n5, 28n29, 29n37, 150
Lusozi Hospital 74, 136, 137–40
staff 139–40, *140*
Lusozi, Kampala 7–12, *8*

maids 70–1
Mamdani, M. 29n61, 51n4
market, the 65–71
vendors 7, 59, 65, 129
marriage 16, 41, 50, 171
mato oput ('drinking the bitter herb') 44–5, 169–70, 177n40
Matthew, Ocen 90
Maurer, Bill 124
Mauss, Marcel 106n6, 106n27
Mbiti, John 10
'the Medical Concierge Group' (TMCG) 4
medicines 71, 98, 122, 137, 148
self-medication 71, 148
Meinert, Lotte 148
methodology 22, 23–6
microfinance model 106n9
'middle generation' 4, 35, 116, 187
migration 11, 28n29, 57, 121, 126, 185
Milan, Italy 57
Miller, Daniel 136–7
mobile money 63–5, 121–4
for elder care 12, 105, 109, 129, 172, 187
film *64*, 121
taxation 126
use in Kenya 118
vendors 112, 119
mobile phones 187

mobile phones ('buttons') 111–13, *111*, 116–17, *116*, 119
definition 110
money, and morality 174–5
morality 28n25, 191–2
caregiving and 158–9, 161n109
co-operative 44, 163–76
money and 174–5
moral crises 177n14
moral moment 165–7
'rights' and 44, 171–2
Mozambique 118
Muehlebach, Andrea 165
Museveni, Yoweri 35, 124
music and dance 5, 22, 34, 45–7, *45*, *47*, 49–51, 180–1
on phones 118–19, 132n31
mutual support 75–6, 91, 106n6, 142, 144, 173, 189

Nahemow, Nina 146
Nankwanga, Annet 139
National Health Insurance Scheme 74, 184–5
National Information Technology Authority Uganda (NITA-U) 111
National Labour Force Survey (NLFS) 11, 59, 77n16
Neema, Stella 139
Nguyen, Minh T. N. 158, 165
non-communicable diseases (ncds) 31n97, 150–1
Non-Governmental Organisations (NGOs) 24, 58
Nyamnjoh, Francis
'convivial scholarship' 2, 22, 126, 181, 182
convivial sociality 126, 130, 187
conviviality 6–7, 84, 106n20, 142, 180
critical approaches 21–2
on English language 20
on 'intimacy and distance' 174
Nyanzi, Stella 57, 58, 77n20, 167, 182–3

Obbo, Christine 16, 183
older persons (definitions) 4
olugambo (gossip) 124–7, 130
Omara
care choices 140–1
on disagreements between neighbours 174
'dotcom' and 188
on respect 170–1, 172–3
smartphone user 118, 119, 120–1
Otaegui, Alfonso 57
Otto, Opira 105n1
'oughtness of care' 159n23
over-thinking 152, 155, 190
Owiny (Local Councillor) 123–4

Palabek, Kitgum 12, 67, 94, 117, 149
Park, Sung-Joon 158–9, 159n23
Parkin, D. J. 28n29
'Parliament' 60–2, 65, 76
p'Bitek, Okot 2, 12, 29n37, 33, 38, 46
pensions 56, 58, 184
Pentecostal Christianity 165, 166, 167
permanent questions 179–93
phone sharing 113–17

INDEX   **213**

physiotherapists 138, 139, 159n24
'Place of Peace' (single mother support) 82–3, 98–104
   education 98–103, *101*
   exercise group *99*, 100
   family responsibilities 101–4
   formed 24
   mission statement 98
   school fees 98–100
   success of 186–7
population 2–3, 4, 6
Porter, Holly 30n74, 51n4, 53n40, 118, 131
poverty 60, 159n24
practices, values and 43–7
'pressure' (hypertension) 6, 71, 136, 143, 150–2, 155–6, 158, 190
proverbs 40
public authority 40, 123, 164, 169
Pype, Katrien 21, 51n4, 132n31

questions, permanent 179–93

Randall, Sara 160n42
recommendations from research 183–5
religion 9–10, 164–5, 171
   British missionaries 177n14
   importance of 70, 86
   mosques *18*
   Pentecostal Christianity 165, 166, 167–8
   prayer 88, 93, 95, 97, 117, 136, 154–6, 190
   signs *10*
respect, and respectability 4, 38–42, 48, 52n31, 148, 164, 169, 170–3
restitutive ceremonies 44–5, 169–70, 177n40
'rights', moral language of 44, 171–2
Robbins, Joel 166, 167

Santiago, Chile 57
Savings and Cooperative Credit Organisations (SACCOs) 24, 59, 82–98, 104–5, *105*, 106n9, 173, 186
school fees 66–8, 152–5
   abolishing 183
   gambling 63
   mobile money 64, 122
   paying 19, 47, 70, 117, 173, 185
   Place of Peace 98–100
self-care 147–50, 156, 157, 158, 190
self-employment 59, 64, 74, 75
Senegal 52n23
Shanghai, China 137
sick pay 74, 184
Simone, AbdouMaliq 187
single mothers 24, 31n118, 94–5, 154
   See also 'Place of Peace' (single mother support)
'smart-from-below' approach 105, 124
smartphones 111–13, 115–16, 117, 187
   definition 110
'Social Assistance Grants for Empowerment' (SAGE) 58, 74, 184
social infrastructures
   digital platforms and 70
   Facebook and 129
   importance of 76, 91, 118, 173, 182

   online 172
   phones and 135
   public provision and 60, 183
   reality and 192
   role played by elders 52n13, 56
social insurance 56, 58, 73–5, 184
   children as 141, 142
social media
   influence 109
   OTT tax 36, 124–7
   platforms 45, 118
   use 127–30
social protection/security 55, 58, 59, 74, 183, 184
Soda Bar meetings, Lusozi 82, 85, 86, *86*, 91, 92, 96
songs and stories 1–2, 28n25, 45–7, 48
spirituality 11, 40, 53n48, 136, 166, 167
Ssebowa (on respect) 38, 48
strokes 126, 151, 155

Tamale, Sylvia 42, 44, 51n4, 176, 182
taxation 61, 68, 126
   OTT (social media tax) 36, 124–7
technology, introduction of 43–4
Thiong'o, Ngũgĩ wa 20
togetherness is strength concept 5, 6, 22, 81–105, 179, 180
'Togetherness is Strength' organisation (TIS) 42–3, 84–91, 104–5
   constitution 24, 88, 89, 186
   Lottery 90
   meetings *86*
   music and dance 46
'tribe' (definition) 29n61

Uganda 10–11, 12
   ageing in 35–6
   British colonisation 10–11, 12, 44
   civil war 2, 11, 13, 30n74, 34, 165, 192
   crops 12, 13, 50
   housing 12
   industry 13
   land 14–18
   sub-regions *13*
Uganda Bureau of Statistics (UBOS) *13*, 59, 77n16
Uganda National Household Survey (UNHS) 145
ulcers, stomach 151, 152
under-employment 77n16, 153, 184
unemployment 77n16, 153
Urapmin people, Papua New Guinea 166

values and practices 43–7
van der Geest, Sjaak 52n13, 147

Wade, Abdoulaye 52n23
Wallman, Sandra 59, 148
Walton, Shireen 57
Wandera, Stephen Ojiambo 145
Wang, Xinyuan 137
'We as elders have a duty' film *45*
wellbeing, health and 94, 137
WhatsApp 50, 109, 113, 118, 125, 172
   groups 95, *95*, 115, 123, 127–30

whiteness 21, 31n97, 31n118, 39, 182
'Who should enrich you?' (WSEY) 92–8
  beneficiary/'*mugoole*' (bride) 24, 92–5, 186
  chairwoman 82, 92–3, 95–7, 127, 164, 174, 186
  dances 93–4, *93*
  meetings 91, *93*
  members 83, 86
  WhatsApp group 127
Whyte, Susan 28n25, 137, 147, 152, 158, 177n40, 178n62, 190
Wine, Bobi 35, 36, 125, 126
witchcraft 167, 174, 175, 178n62–3
women
  as carers 22, 38–44, 56, 59–60, 65–7, 70–2, 75–6, 135, 148, 153–7
  dancing and 46, 50, 93–4, *93*
  dressing up 93, *93*, *95*, 96–7, *97*
  elderly 40, 53n48
  family responsibility 141–3
  intersectional gender analysis 22, 31n118
  land claims and 16
  market vendors 60, 71–2
  mutual support 67
  phone ownership 112, 118
  poverty and 66
  self-care 148, 156, 190
  sole carers of children 16, 168
  support for 184
  under-employment 77n16
  women's leader 65–6
  See also 'Place of Peace' (single mother support); 'Who should enrich you?' (WSEY)
work, age and 55–76
World Bank 11, 60

Yaoundé, Cameroon 83, 187
youth-centricity 2, 35, 48
YouTube 45, 115

Zigon, Jarrett 167

Milton Keynes UK
Ingram Content Group UK Ltd.
UKHW051343230524
443174UK00025B/399